HISTORY OF CRIME AND CRIMINAL JUSTICE
David R. Johnson and Jeffrey S. Adler, Series Editors

Gender and Petty Violence in London, 1680–1720

Jennine Hurl-Eamon

The Ohio State University Press
Columbus

Library of Congress Cataloging-in-Publication Data

Hurl-Eamon, Jennine.
Gender and petty violence in London, 1680–1720 / Jennine Hurl-Eamon.
p. cm.—(History of crime and criminal justice)
Includes bibliographical references and index.
ISBN 0–8142–0987–4 (cloth : alk. paper)—ISBN 0–8142–9061–2 (CD-ROM) 1. Assault and battery—England—London—History—17th century. 2. Assault and battery—England—London—History—18th century. 3. Trials (Assault and battery)—England—London—History—17th century. 4. Trials (Assault and battery)—England—London—History—18th century. 5. Women—Violence against—England—London—History—17th century. 6. Women—Violence against—England—London—History—18th century. 7. Female offenders—England—London—History—17th century. 8. Female offenders—England—London—History—18th century. I. Title. II. History of crime and criminal justice series.
HV6618.H87 2005
364.15'55'08209421—dc22
2005000182

Paper (ISBN: 978-0-8142-5729-6)

Cover design by Dan O'Dair.
Type set in Adobe Garamond.

CONTENTS

Illustrations

Figures

Tables

Textual Notes

All dates are in the old style, but the years are interpreted as if they begin on January 1. The spelling of primary source quotations has been maintained as in the original. The following abbreviated forms have been used:

- *OBP* The various titles of the *Old Bailey Proceedings*
- *OED* *Oxford English Dictionary*
- R Recognizance, used in the footnotes following the archival reference to the Middlesex or Westminster Sessions Rolls (MJ/SR)

Acknowledgments

I have incurred many debts in researching and writing this book. Since its inception as a doctoral dissertation at York University, it has traveled with me through two continents and three universities. In the production of the dissertation, I am very grateful to my supervisory committee for their generous assistance. My supervisor, Nicholas Rogers, made microfilms of primary sources available to me and gave me references from his own research. Douglas Hay also gave me some primary source material, offered many hours of his time in helping me to understand more of the legal aspects of my work, and provided me with a wealth of unpublished secondary sources. Ian Gentles was also active at the production stage of the dissertation and was very kind and positive about the results. I am additionally grateful to Professor Elizabeth Cohen and to my fellow York graduate students, especially James Muir, Robin Ganev, and Todd Webb. I also appreciate my colleagues at both Carleton and Trent universities for providing nurturing environments in which to work. For the former, special thanks to Sonya Lipsett-Rivera, Roderick Phillips, Barry Wright, and Bruce Elliott.

Margaret Hunt, John Beattie, Louis Knafla, and Robert Shoemaker read my dissertation and offered suggestions on how it could be revised into a book. I take full responsibility for stubbornly refusing to follow some recommendations, but my sincerest thanks for the many improvements they have helped to facilitate. Robert Shoemaker also very kindly helped me to navigate through the Consistory Court records at the London Metropolitan Archives, and for this and many other acts of generosity I consider him a true mentor. Norma Landau patiently responded to e-mails with detailed questions about the Latin component of the recognizances and agreed to let me read her work prior to its publication. Peter Lefevre, John Black, Matthew Szromba, and Alexandra Shepard generously shared their findings from their own research areas. The staff of the London Metropolitan Archives, especially Bridgett Howlett and Harriet Jones, assisted with palaeography and translation problems. Louise Falcini deserves special mention for having long conversations with me, on her own time, about quarter sessions procedure and alerting me to conferences in London during my sojourn there. The same research trip brought another gift: the beginning of a wonderful friendship with fellow researcher Kathy Callahan.

Robert Shoemaker, John Beattie, Sonya Lipsett-Rivera, Sharon Howard, and Karen Pearlston very charitably allowed me to view their writing before its publication. Ideas in chapter 4 have already appeared in J. Hurl-Eamon, "'She being bigg with child is likely to miscarry': Pregnant Women Prosecuting Assault in London, 1685–1720," *London Journal* 24, no. 2 (1999): 18–23, and idem, "Domestic Violence Prosecuted: Women Binding over Their Husbands for Assault at Westminster Quarter Sessions, 1685–1720," *Journal of Family History* 26, no. 4 (2001), 435–54. I have also been fortunate enough to receive the generous funding from the Rotary Foundation, the Social Sciences and Humanities Research Council of Canada, the Ontario Government, and York and Carleton universities. I am additionally indebted to the editorial board for the History of Crime and Criminal Justice Series and the staff of The Ohio State University Press for dealing so kindly with a first-time book author.

My family—John and Sheri Hurl, and Nadine, Mark, and Allison Simpson—have been very loving and encouraging throughout, and I am extremely grateful to them. My grandma, war bride Muriel Hurl (née Windebank), instilled in me a love of all things British, virtually from the cradle. Finally, my husband, Michael Eamon, is owed my deepest thanks, for being my closest confidante from the beginning and sharing all of my joys and stresses with unfailing patience and insight.

1

Introduction

On April 23, 1692, Thomas Taylor came before Justice Lawrence to report that Elizabeth Woosey had assaulted him with a pitchfork.[1] Taylor decided against prosecuting Woosey by indictment because of the expense, but he wanted her to be punished in some small way, and, hopefully, dissuaded from attacking him again. An indictment could lead to a trial and a court-ordered fine or imprisonment for Woosey, but it meant a likely cost of several pounds for Taylor—more than a week's wages for many Londoners—so Taylor asked only that Woosey be bound over.[2] She would not be tried, but she would at least be inconvenienced. Had Woosey committed a felony against him, Taylor would have been legally required to prosecute her by indictment, but since assault was only a misdemeanor, Taylor was free to choose how to prosecute Woosey, and indeed whether to prosecute her at all.[3]

Deciding that Taylor's story was sufficiently plausible to take action, Lawrence had Elizabeth Woosey brought before him and told her to find two respected members of the community willing to enter into bonds of at least £20 to guarantee her appearance before the magistrates at the next Quarter Sessions, to be held at Westminster Hall June 23. Having found sufficient sureties to satisfy Lawrence, Woosey entered into a recognizance, which bound her to "appear and answer" Thomas Taylor for assaulting and beating him and which described her using a pitchfork against him as Taylor had recounted. After her name was called at Quarter Sessions, Elizabeth Woosey presented herself to the clerk, paid the two-shilling fee for the clerk and fourpence for the town crier, and walked away a free woman.[4]

The incident of Woosey attacking Taylor with a pitchfork does not seem to be recorded anywhere but in the recognizance taken by Justice Andrew Lawrence. This small slip of parchment, tucked away in the London Metropolitan Archives, is a window to petty violence in Augustan London.

Aside from homicides, the courts were not particularly interested in violence, and most Londoners, like Thomas Taylor, were reluctant to spend large sums of money on prosecutions unless they had lost valuable property. More than seven thousand assault prosecutors at the Westminster Quarter Sessions asked JPs to bind their assailants to appear, and the vast majority of these incidents of petty violence are recorded nowhere else. Until now, there has been little historical interest in these recognizances, but this book uses them extensively for both qualitative and quantitative analyses of petty violence, gender, and the courts in London from 1680 to 1720.

At the outset, I must define what I mean by *petty violence.* I have used the term to refer to acts of aggression—physical or verbal—that were viewed by their contemporaries as relatively minor, but nonetheless unacceptable. As the following chapters will demonstrate, even attacks that caused their victims serious physical injury were considered petty by prosecutors and the courts, worthy only of magisterial censure, rather than an expensive trial and court-ordered punishment.[5] Although petty, the acts studied in this book were simultaneously seen as "violence"—as unacceptable physical behavior, worthy at least of a complaint before a magistrate. In the early modern world of state-sanctioned executions and whippings, and regular physical correction of children, wives, and servants in many households, objectionable violence was much more narrowly construed than in our modern parlance. Nevertheless, *Gender and Petty Violence in London* will show that a surprisingly wide range of petty violence was perpetrated, deemed unacceptable, and prosecuted between 1680 and 1720.

This book is based primarily on recognizances for assault. As a misdemeanor, assault comprised a significant portion of the business of the lower court. Legally defined, *assault* could be as minor as aggressive *talk,* where violence was only threatened by words and gestures and no injury was visible.[6] As an initial attempt to harm, "assault" was the basic charge for other, more serious attacks, defined under the law as "battery," "bloodshed," and "maihem."[7] As one JP's manual succinctly stated, "[E]very battery includes an assault," making it an ideal category for the study of early modern violence.[8] The Westminster recognizances show the variety of violence that fell under the assault rubric, and JPs enjoyed great latitude in describing such acts and classifying them as assaults.[9] The recognizances in *Gender and Petty Violence in London* were chosen on the basis of their use of the word *assault* and represent a virtually comprehensive set of all such recognizances brought before the Westminster Quarter Sessions for 1685 to 1720.[10] All of the 7,129 recognizances binding offenders (rather than prosecutors) had the general purpose of requiring assailants to appear at Quarter Sessions to answer the charges against them.[11]

This chapter will outline the contextual framework for the book, first with an overview of the various chapters within their relevant historiographical debates. The subsequent section explains why London is the ideal setting in which to explore early modern violence and describes the structure of London's criminal law courts.

Gender and Petty Violence in London is divided into two main parts. Part One focuses upon the *prosecution* of petty violence, Part Two upon its perpetration. As prosecutors, the book argues, assault victims were empowered. Chapters 2, 3, and 4 explore the prosecution of assault from rape to wife beating, arguing that victims should be viewed as assertive, savvy litigants. Part Two explores the types of violence described in these prosecutions. Gender was not often a factor in petty violence; many types of assault were as much feminine forms of misbehavior as they were masculine. However, chapters 5, 6, and 7 depict certain types of petty violence that *were* gendered, and we see that early modern women could become very assertive and aggressive in particular instances. Men were more prominent in attacks on the state, however, while feminine violence was generally a result of more immediate neighborhood tensions.

Until this study, petty violence had largely been ignored by historians of early modern England.[12] As John Beattie has argued, nonfatal attacks were considered insignificant for the early modern courts. The bench "did not think the public interest seriously engaged" by the control of petty violence and tended to regard it as a private and rather trivial matter.[13] England's criminal courts were far more concerned with homicides, and historians have shared this focus. Lawrence Stone, James Sharpe, Susan Amussen, J. S. Cockburn, Malcolm Gaskill, and Robert Shoemaker studied early modern violence only in its most serious forms.[14] Although Susan Amussen admitted that women were probably much more violent than the records suggest, she felt that any real knowledge of such acts was impossible. "Since women . . . rarely carried weapons that caused death," Amussen argued, "their brawls, though frequent, were rarely recorded."[15]

Many of these incidents *were,* in fact, recorded, however, as well as many similar nonfatal attacks by men. In order to find the incidents, we must shift the focus from homicide (or its attempt) to assault. We must also accept the fact that assault was of little interest to the courts and was not likely to go to trial and generate rich depositions that would give the attack more historical prominence. Instead, the assaults that occurred in early modern England can be found mainly in very small slips of parchment, numbered, tied, and wrapped within the court rolls of Quarter Sessions. These slips, otherwise known as recognizances, have been used very little by historians, yet they were extremely popular among prosecutors in eighteenth-century London.

We should not exaggerate this study's uniqueness, however. Several other historians have used recognizances to explore tensions in early modern society.[16] Steve Hindle used the recognizances from early-seventeenth-century Cheshire to reveal the existence of "a gradually emerging sense of abhorrence . . . of deeds and words" that had formerly been considered fairly "commonplace."[17] Garthine Walker's recently published book-length study of seventeenth-century Cheshire also made significant use of recognizances. Although she devotes as much space to homicide and theft as she does to assault, and our ideas developed entirely independently, Walker's approach to violence is markedly similar to my own.[18] Hindle's work has influenced my book in its emphasis upon the need to focus upon "plaintiff's priorities," rather than "magistrate's strategies," and Walker's perceptive study also underscores the power of prosecutors.[19]

Indeed, prosecutors' agency is very significant in illuminating popular attitudes toward petty violence. If the courts were as apathetic toward assault as Beattie ascertained, then the assault victims he acknowledges who "did insist on pressing charges" must reveal an extralegal concern over petty violence.[20] In chapter 2, we will see that Londoners of all walks of life interacted confidently with JPs and actively sought to bind over their attackers. Rather than focusing only upon the acts themselves, *Gender and Petty Violence in London* argues that the prosecution of violence—particularly by recognizance—was a significant force in the definition of what constituted unwelcome aggression in early modern society.

Gender played an interesting role in this definition and had an impact upon both the perpetrator and his or her prosecutor. Chapter 3 shows that male sexual and youth violence was hampered to various degrees by formal prosecution and informal shifts in public opinion. This chapter adds to recent works on masculinity in early modern England, reflecting their contention that men, like women, faced gender restraints, though to a lesser degree.[21] Chapter 2 reveals a lesser-studied aspect of early modern masculinity: men's eagerness to accept the role of victimhood when it strengthened their position as prosecutors. Chapter 6 reinforces more traditional perceptions of early modern males by arguing that men engaged in violence against the state much more frequently than did women.[22]

The book's insights on early modern femininity are perhaps even more significant than its contribution to the history of masculinity. Chapter 4 focuses specifically upon women as prosecutors of assault. Most studies of female victimization have ignored their role as prosecutors.[23] *Gender and Petty Violence in London* offers the possibility that many of these women were empowered by actively attempting to gain satisfaction in the courts for the crimes against them. Chapters 5 and 7 depict women as perpetrators of violence, in contrast to much of the historiography on the criminality of women, which tends to concentrate upon crimes such as theft and defamation.[24]

In many cases, of course, the reluctance to focus upon women's violent activity in its own right was especially important. Though there have been several investigations of infanticide, for example, historians have been understandably disinclined to use them as an illustration of the violent tendencies of femininity.[25] Several historians have investigated popular pamphlet and broadsheet depictions of female murderers and other feminine transgressions, revealing an image of women as powerful—though the fears evoked by such literature may have paradoxically resulted in women's further suppression.[26] In examining female defendants in lower-court cases of assault, then, this book returns the emphasis to the misbehavior itself. Chapters 5 and 7 underscore women's role in petty violence to show that, in many ways, their gender did not prevent them from resorting to physical aggression in many situations.

I should note here that my emphasis upon women being empowered as assault prosecutors also needs to be set against the backdrop of scholarship that recognizes women's lower position in early modern society. We must acknowledge that female prosecutors' likelihood of being believed and vindicated was in no way assured. Indeed, their prosecutions of rape and husbandly violence faced overwhelming obstacles, launched as they were in a society where sexual double standards and ideas of the appropriateness of physical chastisement of wives existed in varying degrees. In fact, feminist historiography has recognized the importance of female resistance to patriarchal aggression—in the words of one scholar, "without such activity by women, complex mechanisms of male control over women would be superfluous."[27] It is not surprising, then, that more studies have been done on the areas where these complex gendered values have *dis*empowered women. Nevertheless, the simple fact that women prosecuted petty violence at all means that eighteenth-century law and society must have held *some* incentives for women as victims, and the chapters that follow explore this issue further.

These women benefited from a surprisingly accessible magistracy. As chapter 2 shows, women interacted very assertively with JPs, and Robert Shoemaker's work on the Middlesex Quarter Sessions records revealed the substantial numbers of women who came before these courts to prosecute by recognizance.[28] *Gender and Petty Violence in London* adds to the image he has created of the accessibility of the English courts at this level, and it echoes his contention that recognizances were a valuable tool for misdemeanor prosecutors. Other rich social histories have been written on popular involvement in litigation, but they have relied primarily upon church court records.[29] Margaret Hunt's investigation of family life for the middling sort also used court records and noted that "middling people . . . resorted frequently to the courts to resolve business disputes, to combat crimes against their property, to extricate themselves from bad marriages, and to adjudicate problems having to do with inheritance, marriage settlements, guardianship, and debt."[30] Timothy Stretton has written on women's involvement in the Elizabethan civil law courts, most appropriately titled *Women Waging Law*.[31] This book supplements their work, showing the ways in which men and women were empowered in their prosecution of crime in the capital—most especially the nonfelonious crime of assault.

From a broader historical perspective, *Gender and Petty Violence in London* contributes to the historiography of private prosecution in the eighteenth-century English courts. In the late 1970s, E. P. Thompson and his students depicted the courts as a tool for upper-class interests, concentrating upon the legislation ending customary rights and perquisites, and especially the laws against poaching.[32] Unlike Sir Leon Radzinowicz's celebration of the development of the criminal courts into an instrument of rational, fair justice, the Thompson group argued that the law worked as a tool of the propertied classes to curb the freedom of the poor.[33] Douglas Hay theorized that the belief in the law as "the guardian of all Englishmen . . . gave the ideology of justice an integrity which no self-conscious manipulation could alone sustain," and he exposed the way in which the courts used a mixture of mercy, majesty, and terror to mask its true concern, which was "upholding a radical division of property."[34] John Beattie subsequently brightened this dark image slightly by underscoring the courts' movement away from capital sentences in favor of transportation, and the occasional opportunities for common people to find redress under the law.[35] The end result of the work of scholars such as Thompson, Hay, and Beattie was an overall picture of an English legal system motivated by anxieties around property and maintenance of the social order, yet simultaneously concerned with having an appearance of fairness, legitimacy, and accessibility. This book will focus upon the latter.

As we shall see, thousands of Londoners forced Quarter Sessions magistrates to police petty violence at a time when the rest of England's courts' concern over violence extended only to homicide or its attempt.

London is by far the best location in which to examine petty violence in early-eighteenth-century England.[36] More than anywhere else in the nation, this bustling metropolis had the necessary conditions for petty violence to appear in the historical record. London's high geographic mobility meant that many people interacted as relative strangers. When arguments heated to violence, the informal measures that might have worked in smaller, more stable communities were discarded in favor of formal legal action. In addition, London's crowded conditions ensured that tensions often ran higher and provoked more aggressive outbursts.

One of the most prominent features of London in this period was its burgeoning population. Wrigley estimated that the metropolis had grown "from about 200,000 in 1600, to perhaps 400,000 in 1650, 575,000 by the end of the century, 675,000 in 1750 and 900,000 in 1800."[37] By 1700, the population of greater London was 10 percent of the population of England and Wales as a whole.[38] These figures are even more significant when it is considered that the population was fundamentally fueled from without, rather than within, by huge waves of migration—London's high mortality rate, combined with the substantial exodus of disenchanted Londoners, had to be exceeded by a high rate of migration into the city.[39] Many people walking around London's streets would thus have been relatively new to the city, frightened perhaps, and therefore more defensive—and aggressive—than they would have been in the towns and villages of their birth.

Similarly, Londoners did not have the informal controls that existed in the closed social hierarchies of rural England. This is most visible among those who were usually the most subordinate. London's women, for example, were much more autonomous than their rural counterparts. John Beattie found women more likely to be accused of assault or theft in the city because they were freed from the strong "community pressures and . . . restraints" of the country, where "the figures of authority—the parson, and especially the magistrate were more immediate."[40] When they became part of London's vast, anonymous populace, men and women of all social stations acted more aggressively.

Freedom from the more informal restraints of rural life also ensured that these city dwellers turned more frequently to the courts to resolve disputes, generating thousands of records of offenses that would have been lost to historians had they occurred in the countryside. After comparing legal records of rural and urban parishes in Middlesex, Robert Shoemaker concluded that, in the former, many quarrels were settled informally by JPs' mediation, often leaving no record of the offense.[41] In the countryside the disputants often knew one another and could rely on the vigilance of friends and neighbors to ensure that the conditions of an informal agreement were met. In contrast, whether they knew one another or not, urban adversaries preferred to have the courts formally involved so that law officials could enforce resolution.

Londoners' reliance on the legal system simultaneously ensured its effectiveness. The metropolitan law clerks, unique among their counterparts in the rest of England, could make a tidy profit from Quarter Sessions business, as Norma Landau has shown in her detailed study of the Middlesex court. Acting in their own interest, these clerks worked with great efficiency in dispatching court orders. Defendants who did not fulfill the terms of their recognizance, for example, were arduously pursued, located, and forced to pay the penalty, and Landau has emphasized the way that this clerical efficiency virtually guaranteed appearance at Quarter Sessions and thus encouraged the use of recognizances as a prosecutorial tool in much greater proportions to the rest of England.[42]

Londoners were also conveniently located in the administrative center of the nation—and the heart of its criminal justice system. Whereas the counties in the rest of England had Quarter Sessions for minor crimes (which usually met four times a year) and assizes for more serious crimes (which were presided over by traveling circuit judges and met twice a year), Middlesex County had many more courts.[43] The metropolis had three separate commissions of the peace conducting Quarter Sessions. The city of Westminster held four Quarter Sessions per year at Westminster Hall, and the City of London and the rest of the county each held eight Quarter Sessions per year, with the Middlesex Quarter Sessions meeting at Hick's Hall in Clerkenwell and the City Quarter Sessions at the Guildhall.[44] The metropolis also housed King's Bench, the highest criminal court, which enjoyed unlimited jurisdiction by this period.[45] It was, ironically, the presence of King's Bench that released Middlesex Quarter Sessions from having four sessions a year, only to double its workload because "King's Bench tried so few criminal cases."[46] The higher court did allow for a potential check on the lower courts, however, and defendants before Quarter Sessions could choose to have their case removed to King's Bench.[47] Living in the capital, Londoners had much easier access to all levels of the criminal justice system.

The Old Bailey was to the Westminster, City, and Middlesex Quarter Sessions what the assizes were to the counties' Quarter Sessions in the rest of England. Those accused of felonies and imprisoned by the magistrates were sent from the various county prisons to Newgate jail, which was adjacent to the Old Bailey, at the time of each session.[48] Like the assizes, the Old Bailey had the power to hold the sessions of oyer and terminer and to enforce jail delivery for "all charges involving the taking of property (as well as violent offences that could result in a sentence of death, and occasional matters involving particular interest or difficulties)."[49] Unlike the rural assizes however, the Old Bailey met eight times per year. The City of London was a county by its charter, and from 1327 its Lord Mayor, Recorder, and Aldermen had the right to preside over the Old Bailey Sessions, along with the judges of the high courts.[50] This was actually a point of contention for the magistrates of the other commissions of the peace in the county, for JPs from Westminster and Middlesex were excluded.[51] Aside from the officials presiding being from the City, however, the cross section of people at the Old Bailey—defendants, plaintiffs, constables, etc.—represented the entire metropolis.

The metropolis housed, collectively, the borders of two counties, Middlesex and Surrey, along with the cities of Westminster and London, the borough of Southwark, and numerous out parishes. I will focus upon the records of one jurisdiction in particular: the City of Westminster. Quarter Sessions magistrates received the majority of assault prosecutions, and Westminster was one of the three sites of these courts. I have chosen to use the Westminster Quarter Sessions records because it is the only one of the three that met four, rather than eight, times a year. The lesser number of annual meetings allows a full and complete collection of recognizance data, while the voluminous records of the Middlesex or City Quarter Sessions would instead require a sampling technique. The book is thus able to offer stronger conclusions about less numerous phenomena, such as the eighty-seven pregnant assault victims analyzed in chapter 4. In a broader sampling, we would inevitably miss this and other fascinating insights.

Most often, the JPs in the commission of the peace for Middlesex also served in the commission of the peace for Westminster, lending further commonality between Westminster and greater London.[52] The 7,129 recognizances for assault from the Westminster Quarter Sessions offer a wealth of evidence of petty violence in early modern London as a whole. Although Westminster was as unique as any of London's other complex jurisdictions, the majority of the metropolis—Westminster included—bore many common characteristics of urban life. More specifically, most of the thousands of assaults that were described in the Westminster recognizances are virtually indistinguishable from those that occurred anywhere else in the metropolis, and thus can be seen as evidence of violence in greater London.

The metropolitan municipal governing system was described by Roy Porter as "a fragmented historical relic, divided between hundreds of bodies, mutually distrustful and antagonistic," and the various territories suffered frequent jurisdictional disputes.[53] Westminster was no exception.[54] This is particularly relevant to my purposes because arguments over jurisdictional authority sparked violence in several cases. Chapter 6 shows how Londoners could become angry when they felt officials were acting outside their territorial boundaries. Westminster residents came into particular conflict with the Courts of the Verge, which held jurisdiction over a twelve-mile radius of the royal palace, inevitably overlapping that of other Westminster courts.

Westminster was emerging as a fashionable suburb during this period. The Restoration saw an upsurge in the numbers of the landed elite requiring residences in the capital, which coincided with the growing duties of courtiers and parliamentarians, and a need among the newly emerging mercantile class to house themselves in the same areas as the gentry, and all gravitated toward the West End.[55] In contrast to Westminster's more elite residential profile, the East End was more industrial, characterized by the distilling, sugar-refining, and brewing industries; and even the City housed potters, glassblowers, blacksmiths, gunsmiths, and dyers, among other trades.[56] It might seem that Westminster Quarter Sessions records would mainly involve elite prosecutors compared to the Quarter Sessions of the more industrial areas, but in fact Westminster housed many people of fairly moderate income levels. In addition to the retainers and servants of the gentry, Nicholas Rogers has noted the presence of "artisans, inn-keepers, and traders of a burgeoning luxury-economy, even a few unskilled labourers who had established semi-permanent dwellings in [Westminster's] poorer courts and alley-ways."[57]

Many middling men and women found recognizances a very affordable method of prosecuting assault. The warrant usually required to begin the binding-over process could cost 2s, which could be a prohibitive amount for a laborer (who might have earned 20d per day in 1700[58]), but this cost was well within reason for the middling shopkeepers and tradesmen who populated the West End. In fact, the Westminster assault recognizances include all levels of London society. Because complainants' occupations are rarely recorded on recognizances, we can only estimate, but it seems likely that at least one hundred laborers came before the Westminster Quarter Sessions during the years of this study.[59]

We must, however, acknowledge a few areas where the violence in Westminster was distinct from that in other regions of the metropolis. Several of the more tumultuous events of this period appear to have had little impact upon Westminster. The Spitalfields weavers or their supporters, who attacked and threw ink upon women wearing Indian calico in the riot of 1719, are absent from the Westminster Sessions records. Instead, offenders were undoubtedly brought before the Middlesex Quarter Sessions because Spitalfields fell within its jurisdiction. Less understandable, however, is the lack of any evidence of the Sacheverell riots in the Westminster recognizances. The popular High Church Tory Rev. Sacheverell was tried in Westminster Hall in 1710, and the coach carrying him from the Temple to the courtroom was followed by a large procession. On February 28, the day after his trial began, Sacheverell's sympathizers rioted, attacking nonconformist meetinghouses.[60] None of the assaults in the Westminster recognizances from 1710 bear any description to link them with the Sacheverell riots, and indeed almost none of the recognizances for the entire period offer evidence of religiously motivated violence. The Westminster records do, however, provide valuable evidence of Jacobitism. The recognizances bear echoes of episodes of violence relating to William of Orange's challenge to James II in 1688, the Coronation riots in 1714, and the Jacobite rioting of 1715, which allow us to explore politically motivated violence in more detail. Chapter 7 makes use of these records to focus on female Jacobite violence.

Despite their limitations, the Westminster Quarter Sessions records offer a fairly representative image of the metropolis as a whole in a digestible quantity. To broaden the analysis as much as possible, I have used supplementary material from courts that served *all* of London. Some records of violence, such as sexual assault or violent robberies, were brought to the Old Bailey, and I have used the descriptions of assault and rape in extant copies of the *Old Bailey Proceedings* (*OBP*) to present a picture of violence in greater London. Similarly, Londoners, particularly women, also brought their conflicts to the Bishop of London's Consistory Court. This ecclesiastical court served the entire metropolis on the north side of the Thames, as well as Southwark and parts of Essex, Surrey, Kent, and Hertfordshire.[61] The records from this court most relevant for my purposes are the depositions for defamation, because defamation suits often stemmed from quarrels similar to those in the assault cases heard by the secular courts. The rules governing the records of the Old Bailey and the Bishop of London's Consistory Court, along with recognizances, are explained in more detail in the appendices.

⁂

The chapters that follow will explore the constructions of gender in the records of assault from Westminster Quarter Sessions recognizances, the Bishop of London's Consistory Court depositions, the *Old Bailey Proceedings*, and a host of other popular and legal publications. This chapter has shown the significance of focusing upon petty violence, rather than murder or attempted murder, in arriving at a clearer image of early modern men's and women's perception and experience of violence. We have also been reminded of London's cultural and legal uniqueness, which alone allows for the rich accounts of petty violence that follow.

The period between 1685 and 1720 is an ideal one in which to study petty violence through assault recognizances. Prior to 1685, the Westminster recognizances have not survived in reliable numbers. After 1685, these small slips of parchment have been preserved virtually in their entirety within the Westminster Sessions rolls. The year 1720 is a good termination point for my study, however, because, as the eighteenth century wore on and Quarter Sessions business grew to unprecedented proportions, clerks began to use preprinted recognizance forms.[62] Unlike the recognizances in our period, these preprinted forms left only small spaces for names and for a word or two recounting the misconduct. In the interests of speed, the descriptions of the offenses in recognizances became much briefer and more formulaic. Thus, by the second half of the eighteenth century, these evocative accounts of assault are again lost to history.

More than 7,000 assaults were reported to Westminster JPs between 1685 and 1720. As a misdemeanor, assault was a relatively minor act, and one could consider oneself assaulted by having only the threat of a fist raised in anger some distance away. We will never know the so-called dark figure of unreported assaults that occurred during this period. We cannot even know how many assault reports were laughed at by JPs for their implausibility and never entered into the record. All we know is the thousands of assaults that were brought to a prosecution—and only one type of prosecution (though the most common on record). Recognizances were by far the most popular way for the courts to deal with assault in this period, and the following pages offer a detailed look at gender and the prosecution and perpetration of petty violence in the capital at the beginning of the eighteenth century.

This account of petty violence is peopled by a cast of many characters from the grassroots of London society. We will see knowledgeable prosecutors, with conscious and subconscious strategies for gaining satisfaction for the attacks against them. We will explore the ways in which members of some of the most powerful categories of early modern society—men, gentry, patriarchs—were exposed to censure for their violence. A variety of perceptions of women are offered as well: assertive prosecutor, protective mother, valiant rescuer, and eager rioter, among many. We will view violence as a language, intended, in some cases, to humiliate as much as wound, or hold special significance depending upon the space in which it was perpetrated, or the gender of the assailant. At the same time, however, throughout this book I will underscore the banality of violence in early modern London and the likelihood of many Londoners to resort to assault, regardless of gender.

Part One
Prosecutors

2

A Litigating Society:
Victimhood and the Prosecutors of Assault

Unlike today, many early-eighteenth-century assault victims had a great deal of agency as prosecutors.[1] Victims chose whether or not they would prosecute. They could decide to prosecute an assault by indictment, which could result in a trial, or by bringing their complaint to a JP, which would usually generate a recognizance against their attacker. The majority chose the latter.[2] They had to convince a local JP of the legitimacy of their complaint in order to prosecute by recognizance. If the JP was convinced, he issued a warrant, and, if a constable was not present, the victims themselves might have to take the warrant to the constable and ask him to serve it.[3] The victims established the identity of their attacker, if at all possible, and the victims, rather than the police, investigated the crime and accumulated evidence against him or her.[4]

These victims' agency was, of course, heavily circumscribed by their means. If assault victims could not pay for a prosecution, or if they could not spend the time developing a strong case against their attacker, or if they were grievously injured and lacked friends and family to prosecute on their behalf, their assailant would never be brought to justice. In many cases prosecutors were also limited to choosing the binding-over method of prosecution because it was all they could afford. Conversely, people with sufficient means and motive could take advantage of this prosecutorial agency, inventing false prosecutions and aggressively promoting their passage through the courts.[5] Nevertheless, as one of the most affordable methods of prosecution, recognizances bear the echoes of hundreds of active prosecutors, bringing stories of real or imagined violence. This chapter will highlight prosecutors' agency in documenting the petty violence against them and gaining satisfaction from their assailants. I have coined the word *victimhood* to describe the source of these assault victims' power. The term *victimization* is insufficient, for it implies an action, something done *to* the victim in addition to the assault. *Victimhood,* instead, should be understood as a status taken on by the victim after he or she decided to go to the courts. *Victimization* implies powerlessness; *victimhood,* as I shall argue, allows for empowerment.

This was not necessarily a conscious strategy on the part of eighteenth-century prosecutors. Indeed, it probably often happened at an instinctive level. Nevertheless, it is best understood as "self-fashioning," a practice that literary scholars have discerned in the writing of Renaissance England. From this era on, they argue, "there appears to be an increased self-consciousness about the fashioning of human identity as a manipulable, artful process."[6] The assault prosecutions studied here are thus also an exercise in self-fashioning, where litigants artfully establish their identity as injured victims in order to strengthen their case.

Because recognizances reveal little of what transpired after a prosecution began, we can focus only upon prosecutorial initiative. It may seem incomplete to address the issue of prosecutorial power without looking at the eventual success of a suit, but as many records of nonfelonious prosecutions in the courts of Augustan London end before a trial ever took place, we must assume that trial verdicts were not the prosecutorial goal when minor offenses were involved. The brunt of the punishment of the binding-over method of prosecution was most likely in the infamy of having to appear before Quarter Sessions. By using the courts, prosecutors could bring an attack to the attention of their community. They frequently resorted to this formal channel to resolve fairly minor interpersonal disputes.

We should not be surprised that Londoners made use of the courts in their disagreements, because men and women of all classes were expected to participate in the administration of the law. They responded to cries of "stop thief" and "bear witness." They apprehended suspected offenders and appeared before the secular and church courts as witnesses for a variety of matters. Many Londoners could receive an education in the criminal justice system through the course of daily life.

In addition, JPs were fairly accessible in the early eighteenth century. They heard complaints, issued warrants, examined defendants, and often personally arbitrated disputes, helping the parties in conflict find resolution. In assault cases, JPs listened carefully to victims' accounts of the attack upon them and their injuries, and often prosecutors' own descriptions affected the wording of the recognizances. Thus, prosecutors could use particular tactics to strengthen their case in assault recognizances. In some instances, of course, the JP or his clerk may have prompted them, but in other cases, as we shall see, the victims' own vehemence as prosecutors probably influenced the record and strengthened their prosecutions. One of the most obvious strategies for assault victims was to stress their weakness and the severity of their injuries. Men did so as much as women, showing that masculinity and victimhood were not mutually exclusive.

The final section explores the agency of a particular group of victims. A significant number of recognizances were counterprosecutions—an individual binding over a defendant who had also had him or her bound for a similar offense. These counterprosecutions were often labeled *vexatious* prosecutions, but—as we shall see—they are more appropriately understood as a competition for victimhood.

Almost any early-eighteenth-century Londoner could become a savvy prosecutor in the lower courts. It would have been difficult to move about on London's streets without receiving some sort of informal education on the workings of the criminal justice system. When Shorland Adams heard a watchman call, "'stop theife,'" he gave chase to a fleeing culprit and helped to bring him before the authorities.[7] James Mortimer, a Middlesex "Cowkeeper," spotted a man whom (for various reasons) he suspected "to be a Horsestealer."[8] He immediately marshaled some nearby haymakers "to assist him in apprehending" the man, who was later indeed formally charged with horsetheft.[9] When a man tore Hester Pepper's pocket and ran away with it, she followed him, grabbing hold of him and tearing his sleeve. Though he eluded her twice, she kept the torn cuff and cried, "'stop theif,'" and other Londoners came to her aid. As with the capture generated by James Mortimer, Hester Pepper's tenacity resulted in the accused thief being "taken and carry'd before a Justice, where the Cuff was produc'd and agreed with his coat."[10]

Unlike modern cities, where, rather than getting actively involved, people are generally advised to call the police when they witness a violent crime, early modern Londoners were expected to help.[11] When Job Famworth, John Presley, and Richard Page "heard a woman calling out for help, or else her husband would bee murdered," they went "hastily" in the direction of her cries and tackled the pistol-wielding aggressor, apprehending him and bringing him to the proper authorities.[12] Elizabeth Webster deposed that when she was attacked while walking down a London street, she "cryed out murder murder," and because she was just outside her home, her father and mother rushed into the fray.[13] We are safe in assuming that Webster might not have been helped so readily if she had not been so near to her home, and that not everyone was as brave as Famworth, Presley, and Page. However, the summoning potential in the scream "murder!" was nevertheless very well known. Assailants tried to prevent their victims from crying "murder," realizing that most people who heard would respond.[14]

Although it was generally male Londoners who answered calls of "stop thief" and "murder," women could also be called upon to assist victims of crime, and both women and men used the courts in their interpersonal disputes. The rich depositions for defamation cases heard at the Bishop of London's Consistory court reveal that many women played an important role as witnesses, and it is clear that both men and women understood the workings of London's justice system. Mary Hall had a very heated verbal exchange with her former employer Phillip Ruggsby in 1695, and when he "called the sayd Mary Damme theevish whore," Hall immediately "bid" the women around her to "bear witness."[15] Beth Clarke also warned witnesses to take note of Jane Barnes's insulting words because she would need their testimony in a defamation suit. In fact, witness Catherine Hartill claimed that she remembered Barnes's insulting words specifically because of Clarke's "calling out to Beare witness."[16] These female prosecutors and their female witnesses knew that the courts could intervene in these matters. By telling bystanders to "bear witness," both Hall and Clarke reveal their knowledge of the laws against defamation and their need to have reliable supporting testimony. Their witnesses, in turn, knew that they must make careful note of the insults in question.

Though there are no depositions to indicate what happened in similar disputes brought to the Westminster Quarter Sessions, Londoners made even more frequent use of these courts to resolve minor conflicts. When Richard Beale, a carpenter, got into an argument with widow Mary Pearson in her shop, he shouted at her and her customers and vowed "not to stir from thence until forced by Law."[17] We know about this incident only because Mary Pearson did go to the law. She wound up asking Justice Crake that Beale be bound to appear and answer for assaulting her. Though Pearson was the prosecutor, this record suggests that Richard Beale was just as insistent upon involving the law in their dispute. The recognizances for assault show many different tensions between Londoners.[18] Sarah Glover prosecuted John Williams for assault; on the same day, he prosecuted her for assaulting his wife.[19] John Allen, a butcher, complained that Ann Mcgrath had assaulted him "when he came to demand mony due to him for Butchers meat," yet four days before, Mcgrath had identified herself as the victim, binding Allen "for assaulting her in her house."[20] More often than their rural counterparts, Londoners brought their disagreements into the courts and launched formal prosecutions.[21]

Londoners' knowledge of the mechanics of the law was further aided by the comparative accessibility of Justices of the Peace. The Consistory Court depositions again offer a window into the secular courts—specifically, into the potential for very personal interaction between Londoners and their JPs. Mary Clift charged Justice of the Peace Narcissus Lutrell in 1720 with defamation over an insult he gave her during petty sessions. The testimony reveals the intimate contact that was possible at these sessions. With her second husband, Peter, Mary Clift (formerly Mary Regatty) had gone to Fulham to renew her alehouse license at a petty sessions held at the Upper King's Arms. The JPs sat at a table in the tavern, and when Peter Clift approached, Justice Lutrell reportedly said, "[D]id you marry that common whore Mrs Regatty, to wch the sd Peter reply'd" in the affirmative, and Lutrell "then added . . . she is a whore & has had sevll bastards & putt the Parish to an hundred pounds charge."[22] Mary Clift immediately went "up to the table where they were sitting at, & desired in handsome terms, that his worship would let her know her accusers."[23] Justice Lutrell was of a much higher station than Mary Clift. He was a wealthy and prominent member of the Chelsea community, involved in national as well as local affairs, and the familiarity of his interaction with Clift (and hers with him) reveals much about the relationship between Londoners and their JPs.[24]

Though he moved in elite circles, Lutrell knew Mary Clift. If his allegations were true, he would have come into contact with her in an earlier petty session where she petitioned for poor relief as a bastard bearer. He recognized her and expressed his sympathy to her husband, another man well below his station, and Clift herself was not so intimidated by Lutrell's status to avoid approaching him directly and demanding to know why he had insulted her. The personal hostility between Lutrell and Clift could exist only in a context that allowed a certain amount of familiarity between Londoners and JPs. Petty Sessions occurred between the Quarter Sessions' sittings and generally involved a gathering of two or more JPs, who mainly ruled upon matters of parish administration, including licensing. Though the Westminster Quarter Sessions were held in the formal surroundings of Westminster Hall, petty sessions could be held in taverns and inns.[25] Most significantly for our purposes, JPs could take recognizances in their homes.[26] Though such informality was decreasing by 1720, it is not entirely unthinkable that a Justice of the Peace—even one of the elite stature of Narcissus Lutrell—could interest himself in the sexual proclivities of a woman who was no longer a cost to the

Table 2.1
Individuals Appearing More than Once as Complainants in Assault Recognizances

Time*	Repeat Complainants	Total Complainants	%
Apr 1685–Jul 1690	289	858	33.7
Jan 1701–Oct 1705	216	763	28.3
Jan 1716–Oct 1720	648	1772	36.6

Note: Recognizances to prosecute assault have not been included.
*This column is broken down into three periods of exactly twenty sessions each, with each roughly corresponding with a five-year period. Note that rather than four there are only two extant sessions for 1689 (27 Jun and 2 Oct).

parish and could deny a license brought to him by her husband.[27] The people of the metropolis had relatively easy access to the JPs and the courts, knew their avenues for prosecution, and made use of them with assurance.

The thousands of prosecutors who asked Westminster JPs to bind over their assailants reveal this confidence. A substantial proportion of complainants returned more than once to prosecute new assaults, which suggests that they were satisfied with the outcome of their original case and had decided to use the same method again rather than trying one of the alternative forms of prosecution available to them.[28] Aside from wartime, more than one-third of all the prosecutors in a sample of three five-year periods between 1685 and 1720 appeared more than once as complainants in assault recognizances (table 2.1).[29] In every period, the proportion of repeat prosecutors is higher than the number of assailants who were bound over multiple times by recognizance (table 2.2). Though these numbers may be skewed slightly by cases where a complainant has been named in several recognizances because he or she charged multiple defendants for one assault, it nevertheless seems safe to say that prosecutors were not dissatisfied with the outcome of their case, and they often returned, resorting to similar channels to resolve subsequent conflicts.[30]

Edward Vaughan complained about Robert Dickenson in August of 1717 and turned again to Westminster Quarter Sessions in June of 1718, before a different justice to have Ann Keel and Mary and Edward Hubbard bound over for assaulting him.[31] Two years later he went to a third justice to have three gentlemen bound for an alleged attack upon him.[32] Daniel Allen was bound for assaulting Mary Dunkey, who, three years later, had John Brabin bound before a different JP for assaulting her.[33] Clearly, this procedure was deemed worth-

Table 2.2
Individuals Appearing More than Once as Defendants in Assault Recognizances

Time*	Repeat Defendants	Total Defendants	%
Apr 1685–Jul 1690	112	869	12.9
Jan 1701–Oct 1705	114	779	14.6
Jan 1716–Oct 1720	510	1849	27.6

Note: Recognizances to prosecute assault have not been included.
*This column is broken down into three periods of exactly twenty sessions each, with each roughly corresponding with a five-year period. Note that rather than four there are only two extant sessions for 1689 (27 Jun and 2 Oct).

while for Vaughan and Dunkey, and though Vaughan seems to have met with a fair amount of petty violence over the years, he was not plagued by attacks from the same individuals after he prosecuted them. Because complainants returned to Quarter Sessions more often than defendants, we can see that they considered recognizances to be an effective form of prosecution.

Indeed, we can consider early-eighteenth-century assault prosecutors as consumers, making particular choices by balancing the relative cost and efficacy of a particular avenue of prosecution. This is most visible when victims sought assault recognizances for goals more commonly associated with civil suits. One handbook warned JPs to be wary of savvy prosecutors who tried to use the cheaper criminal courts to redress primarily civil grievances. According to this author, these prosecutors could disguise their civil case "under the Colour of Felonies, Force, or Assault."[34] Norma Landau has discerned a similar sort of practice in assault indictments, but the descriptions in several assault recognizances suggest that prosecutors sometimes resorted to this even cheaper avenue.[35]

We will never know for sure, but it seems likely that certain prosecutors who had defendants bound over for assault actually wanted to extract money from the defendant for economic losses suffered in the attack. Several recognizances recount financial damage that is at least as substantial as the physical. Market vendor Joan Griffith complained that a man and two women had "throw[n] about her goods . . . and Stamp[ed] them under their Feet," and William Hopkins complained that a man had spoiled his bread, in the course of two separate assaults at the Covent Garden Market.[36] According to the information on their recognizances, neither Griffith nor Hopkins pursued the matter to an indictment, so they must have found sufficient satisfaction in binding their antagonists to appear.[37] Presumably, they used the recognizance to show their seriousness as prosecutors—perhaps they threatened further action—forcing their attackers to compensate them for the goods they had damaged. There are many other examples that suggest a similar strategy, and the financial losses range from shopkeepers' goods to the loss of an apprentice's labor.[38] These recognizances reveal wily complainants, constrained by a slim purse, who prosecuted assaults in order to involve the courts in their economic disputes.

Having established that Londoners were familiar with their courts, benefited from relatively easy access to JPs, and made effective use of recognizances in prosecuting assaults, we can now examine assault victims' strategies more closely. Many prosecutors stressed their personal vulnerability and weakness in order to gain power before the law. Elizabeth White's petition to the Westminster JPs in 1705 offers some insight:

> The Humble Petition of Elizabeth White wife of Barnett White Marriner on board the [torn] Eagle: Every night . . . Mary Tully sent one of her Fellows to abuse your Poor Petitioner as she stood at her own door Calling her Bitch and threatning to kick her & the said Mary Tully did likewise throw two pails of clean water upon your poor Petitioner & young Infant as sucking at her Breast & did likewise barbarously beat her sister who is blind & not being satisfied therewith she falsely swore a Robbery of Burglary & Felony agt your Poor Petitioner. Therefore . . .what is sworn agt yr Poor Petitioner by the sd Mary Tully is nothing but spight for having amongst other neighbours informed the Worship Justis Dyer of the Disorderly hous kept by sd Mary Tully.[39]

Though she is trying to reverse a robbery charge against her by alleging plaintiff Tully's malicious motivations, White's overall stress is upon her own defenselessness to Tully's abuse. She begins by presenting herself as the wife of an absent mariner, and her claims of injury go on to state nightly visits from people who, in fact, do no serious physical damage to her personally. The effectiveness of her allegations lay in her self-depiction as suckling an infant and the mention of a blind sister, which implicitly provided an image of a female head of household, laden with helpless dependents.[40] In the construction of pardon tales for sixteenth-century France, Natalie Zemon Davis notes that a common tactic was to "fatten the preamble with other facts which made the supplicant appear more pitiful," for example, "poor disabled widow," "burdened with five children," and the like.[41] Even if she was genuinely guilty of the felony against Tully, White's petition provides insight into the ways in which London's prosecutors paradoxically strengthened their position by emphasizing their own weakness.

There is substantial evidence to suggest that JPs cooperated with assault complainants in deciding the wording of recognizances.[42] Whereas indictments were governed by stringent rules, making the account of the offense conform to very specific criteria, recognizances bore no such restrictions. Indeed, JPs frequently advocated colorful descriptions of assaults that visibly departed from any legal formula. It seems highly likely that they were informed by the victim's account of the attack. When the JP issued a warrant to summon the accused, with sureties, before him, one manual strongly recommended that he "read" the proposed text of the warrant "to the Complainant, that if any Mistake has been made, . . . it may be rectified."[43] In other words, should an individual feel that the JP missed a significant factor in describing his or her complaint, he or she could actively solicit an addition. Though we will never know for certain, it seems likely that warrants—because they were formed at the initiation of a prosecution—would be helpful in the subsequent stage, when the JP's clerk drew up the recognizance.[44]

Also, when a recognizance had been drawn up, the JP was expected to "read the condition to the Parties bound," asking them to "acknowledge to owe unto our Sovereign Lord the King" the full amount of the bond, if the condition was not met.[45] Possibly, when plaintiffs were also present at this time, wording on the condition may have been changed slightly, and such additions are visible in some of the Westminster recognizances.[46] Such evidence is very rare, however, and the interaction between plaintiffs and recording officials probably occurred more often during the drawing up of the warrant. Nevertheless, because of these interactions between prosecutors and JPs with the binding-over method of prosecution, the former enjoyed a fair amount of agency in defining the attack upon them.

The assault recognizances make clear that JPs (and the clerks who actually wrote the recognizance) were swayed by tales of dramatic injury. Charles Brent came in his wife's place, presumably because she was too ill from the attack to prosecute it herself, and his claim that George Martiner had assaulted her "in so violent a manner that she vomitted handfulls of blood" found its way into the record, and strengthened the Brents' case against Martiner.[47] Similarly, Grace Tongue successfully convinced the JP that her husband's attacker should be bound, and the justice accepted her account that the assault had left him "bruiz'd in his side" and unable to leave his bed.[48] One recorder deemed it necessary to underscore the fact that an assault on

Elizabeth Albon caused "*A Rupture* in her belly," presumably because Albon's account had been so dramatic.[49] Mary Andrews's claim of the severity of a cut to her hand caused the JP to indicate in the record against her attacker "that it is believed that she will loose the use of [it]." [50] Prosecutors' claims of vulnerability found their way into the record in a significant number of cases, and the added descriptions attest to the influence complainants might have over the charges leveled at defendants. These prosecutions are clearly an opportunity for victims' self-fashioning.

Although the majority of these cases depict female victims, the mantle of victimhood was just as easily a masculine fashion in the early eighteenth century. Male prosecutors also needed to stress their weakness in order to strengthen their assault charges, and they did so with apparent success. James Lewis convinced a JP that Diana Laughlin should be charged with "threatening to Kill him with a knife she then had in her hand, unless he was Lewd with her," and many other men represented themselves as victims of female seduction.[51] The thousands of male assault victims were not afraid of losing their masculinity by describing their injuries from an attack. JPs readily included this testimony in the recognizances binding their attackers. Laborer Rober Eddows said that he had been assaulted "in a most barbarous and cruell manner" by a glazier, who attacked him first with a large ring of church keys, and then with a "steel shod shovel," which caused him to lose so much blood "that he swounded away twice."[52] John Storman's wounds were carefully listed as "six . . . wounds on his face, arms and finger," and Henry Bateman was said to be "in danger of loosing one of his eyes" and was heavily bruised after being assaulted "in a violent manner."[53] William Ogleby claimed to have been knocked down, bruised, and wounded by Gilbert Norwell, and Ogleby swore an oath that he was so afraid of Norwell that "he dare not go about his business for fear of" him.[54] Like women, male assault victims stressed their weakness and injury in order to strengthen the case against their attacker.

The legal definition of assault included "fearfull speech," which allowed prosecutors to target people who had not actually laid a hand upon them. We have seen that bruised or bleeding prosecutors aroused JPs' sympathies, but complainants who were only emotionally harmed would have had a more difficult task. They needed to wax eloquent before their JPs in order to carefully recount how their antagonist's behavior had caused them emotional harm. Of the total of 7,129 recognizances to answer assaults, 129 attested to the complainant's "fear" for his or her life or bodily harm, and many more express complainants' opinions about the danger they were in or about future damage they anticipated from the assailant. Some of these were undoubtedly part of a legal formula, as victims who wished to bind people over to keep the peace or ensure good behavior toward them had to swear, as part of the process, that they were in fear of their lives.[55] However, we should not presume this to remove all real meaning from the words. For example, when Constable Thomas Shepheard claimed to fear for his life after being beaten with "a red hott poker and tongs," the fear was certainly no less real for its having been part of a legal formula.[56] Even without bruises, complainants may have told a convincing tale of psychological terror and thereby convinced the JP to issue the recognizance primarily on this basis. Jane McKensey's complaint of an assault resulted in a recognizance professing "that she believes and has good Reason to think her life to be in Danger," and another record depicts assault victim Edward Reynolds as giving "his corporall Oath . . . that he goes in danger of his life by [his assailant] or by her procurem[en]t."[57] Victims recounted their fright in order to strengthen their prosecution.

In addition to fashioning themselves as weak and vulnerable, assault complainants sometimes convinced JPs that the attacks upon them were entirely unprovoked. Justicing handbooks allowed "any private man to beat, stricke, or wound another, in defence and safegard of his own person, from killing, wounding or beating."[58] In addition, the eighteenth-century courts allowed a fair amount of behavior to be characterized as provoking, giving manslaughter verdicts to cases that today would be considered murders.[59] Carleton Allen has dubbed the eighteenth-century individual found guilty of manslaughter as "the phlegmatic Englishman"—a man who draws his sword to deal a death blow at the slightest sign of physical aggression.[60] The *Old Bailey Proceedings* recount many cases where provocation was a central issue.[61] Given the law's capacity for more lenience in assaults that involved provocation, prosecutors would have been eager to establish its absence in their complaints.

This is very clear in some of the recognizances. Thomas Hatch and Thomas Jones had two men bound to appear at the same sessions "for assaulting them without any provocation."[62] Interestingly, this idea that provoked assaults were more acceptable applied to female assailants as well as male. Elizabeth Wright had Mary Wright bound for "assaulting her without any provocation" with a blow that had knocked her down, and Sarah Boddy had to appear to answer Steven Davdale "for violently assaulting [him] . . . without any provocation."[63] The complainant and Justice of the Peace also did not balk at binding "gentleman" Thomas Probatt "for assaulting beating and abusing . . . in the street in the night without any provocation."[64] Though it is possible that court officials influenced the record by prompting the complainant to attest to the lack of provocation, it is equally likely that Londoners knew that only certain forms of petty violence were justified. Several prosecutors testified to the fact that the violence was unprovoked in order to help their case.

Prosecutors' agency in fashioning themselves as victims is most visible in a very particular category of assault recognizances. Many recognizances are scattered among the Westminster Quarter Sessions rolls between 1685 and 1720 in which X charged Y with assault, and Y turned around and prosecuted X (or his/her spouse) for the same or a similar offense. Sharon Howard has also discerned a significant number of reciprocating recognizances in Wales over the same period, and Ruth Paley noticed a similar phenomenon when editing Henry Norris's justicing notebook for eighteenth-century Hackney.[65] Paley dubbed these counteraccusations "vexatious actions," noting that "such examples could be multiplied virtually *ad infinitum.*"[66] However, Paley found only *one* actual malicious prosecution "in the strict legal sense of the word," where the complainant had pursued his suit "in the full knowledge that the accusations [were] without foundation."[67] In that single prosecution Justice Norris refused to accept the charges because he discerned the complainant's pernicious motives. Nevertheless, complainants frequently got away with the lesser "vexatious actions," where each had some grounds for—and perhaps genuinely believed—their own victimhood.

Most recognizances could be taken only if the complainant was successful in convincing the JP that his or her suit was not malicious.[68] However, in these "vexatious action"–based recognizances, the victim actually had more agency than the justice, according to Michael Dalton's justicing handbook. According to Dalton, if a JP had reason to doubt a prosecutor's motives, he "shall doe well (as I think) not to be too forward in granting" the recognizance.[69] Dalton instead advised the justice "to perswade" the prosecutor of the danger of such a prosecution. However, if the prosecutor "will not be perswaded, but will take his oath that he is in fear (where indeed he neither doth fear, nor hath cause to fear) this oath shall discharge the Justice, and the fault shall remain upon such complainant."[70] In other words, if a defendant bound by recognizance insisted on counterprosecuting the complainant, a JP could allow this seemingly malicious prosecution by asking the victim to take full responsibility for it. These types of recognizances would thus occur in an instance when both complainants were extraordinarily vehement in attesting to their own victimization. Thus, rather than simply labeling them "vexatious actions"—lesser versions of malicious prosecutions—as Paley does, it is more illuminating to investigate them as competing claims to victimhood.

Given the greed of the "trading justices"—infamous London JPs reputed to be interested in their office only to line their own pockets—we might instead argue that the JPs were the real motivating factor. It is possible, we might think, that they *encouraged,* not merely permitted, so many apparently vexatious prosecutions.[71] If this were the case, however, the recognizances themselves would indicate that the parties had come to an agreement well before Quarter Sessions, and the defendant would have been released from his or her obligation to appear.[72] None of the assault recognizances studied below indicate that such a process had occurred, and very few of them appear to have come from JPs fitting the profile of a trading justice.[73] In fact, this type of prosecution would probably be an area that such JPs would try to avoid, having been warned extensively in their handbooks about the dangers of promoting malicious prosecutions.[74] Thus, although JPs certainly bore a role in creating these records, we can safely examine them as evidence of early-eighteenth-century prosecutors' strength and initiative in assault litigation. These types of recognizances represent roughly 4 to 10 percent of the total number of assault recognizances in a given year, showing that, when Londoners competed for victimhood before a Justice of the Peace, the JP often gave both of their claims legitimacy.[75]

When these Westminster JPs were presented with contradictory suits for very *different* offenses brought by the same parties against one another, the resulting recognizances reveal the justices' personal views of the allegations. They also reveal the relative success of one prosecutor over the other, in convincing the JP of his or her greater claim to victimhood. Throughout the period there are recognizances binding X for assaulting Y, and separate recognizances binding Y to keep the peace or be of good behavior toward X.[76] On the same day that Anne Lewis was bound for "assaulting . . . and causing a Ryot about" Hannah Rumbold, Justice Hawke issued a recognizance binding Rumbold "to be of good behaviour toward Anne Lewis," and many other justices took similar actions for other complainants.[77] Did one recognizance have more impact than the other? Historians are uncertain of the impact of binding over to keep the peace or be of good behavior, and Norma Landau argues that neither was enforceable with any effectiveness.[78] Londoners were legally entitled to swear the peace against someone for any breach of the peace and to bind to good behavior anyone believed guilty of "stealing, being common disturbers of the peace, idleness, frequenting bawdy . . . or gaming houses, and begetting bastard children."[79] We simply cannot know for certain whether JPs had more sympathy for the victims of assault or for those who required the peace or good behavior of their opponents. Nevertheless, both of the conflicting demands for a recognizance were granted.

The relative strengths of competing claims to victimhood are more apparent in other recognizances. The JP who agreed to bind Richmond Brewer "for violently Assaulting" John Palmer "without any Provocation given" probably felt considerably less sympathy for Brewer than for Palmer, whom he bound only for "assaulting" and "beating" Brewer and his companion.[80] After hearing Richard Ward's complaint, Justice Saintlo bound George and Andrew Ward for "assaulting" Richard Ward "in a violent manner."[81] In contrast, Richard's recognizance "for assaulting" George and Andrew Ward specified that the offense occurred "in a *very* violent manner," and additionally it labeled Richard "a very dangerous person."[82] Abigall Cole was only bound for "assaulting" Thomas Cavanaugh on May 18, while he was accused of putting her "in dainger of her life" by raising the mob on her—an illegal act he was said to have performed "severall times."[83] These recognizances seem to show JPs valuing the claims of one complainant over the other. Both men and women brought counterclaims of victimhood, and the hundreds of conflicting recognizances suggest that both male and female victims could garner more judicial sympathy, depending upon the circumstances.

In other recognizances with two different claims of full and rich description, both victims apparently convinced their justice that two entirely different scenarios could have taken place.[84] Richard Dermeth was bound for assaulting Mary Taylor, but she was in turn bound the same day to "answere . . . Richard Dermeth upon suspicion of having feloniously taken from him several padlocks and keys."[85] It is certainly plausible that Dermeth could have assaulted Taylor *and* she could have stolen from him, but it is fascinating that they both attested so vehemently to their victimization, and the JP accepted both claims. Sharlott Bragg probably did assault Margery Rant and threw "Durt on her," and Rant may have assaulted Bragg "in a Riotous manner" and struck her, as the recognizances, taken by Justice William Stone on the same day, read.[86] These actions sound like a fight, but rather than charging them both with disturbing the peace, Justice Stone allowed each to represent herself as a victim in her own right—which attests to their own assertiveness in their audience with him. Similarly, two "brokers" of the "Church Court St. Martins"—Elizabeth Moye, who thought that Joseph Sketchley had assaulted her, and Sketchley, who instead accused Moye of "disturbing his servants at their work"—may both have had valid claims.[87] JPs heard conflicting interpretations of these people's victimhood and accorded each complainant the possibility of being genuine. For prosecutors, male and female, the more evidence one could marshal to fashion oneself as weak and injured, the stronger one could appear.

Many recognizances were taken by Westminster Quarter Sessions officials between 1685 and 1720 which record opposite accounts of virtually the same type of offense. The recognizances effectively mirror one another, in other words. Presumably, complainants were giving two different versions of the same incident, with each presenting a tale where he or she was the victim. By granting a recognizance to both complainants, JPs accorded equal credibility to both parties. Margaret Budden brought a complaint accusing Rebecca Mall for "assaulting & beating" her, and on the same day Mall had Budden bound for "assaulting and beating" her.[88] Similarly, Mary Symcock and Elizabeth Roberts stood before Justice Knollys on the same day, each accusing the other of "assaulting and beating" her.[89] Not all of the mirroring recognizances used such formulaic language, either. On August, 28, 1717, Justice Alex Hardine took two recognizances against female fruiterers. Mary Brown was accused of giving Elizabeth Hutchinson "reproachfull scandalous Language, saying she and her husband had the Pox . . . creating a Riot, and putting her in fear of her life."[90] Hutchinson, on the other hand, was also said to have used "reproachfull language" against Brown, "calling her husband cuckhold, creating a Riot and being a common disturber."[91] Both Francis Mills and Joseph Leach, coachmen, were accused of "assaulting" each other, and both William Hopkins and Luke Pemberton were bound on the same day "for violently assaulting" each other.[92]

Recording officials thus seemed to have no problem utilizing *exactly* the same language in many of the counter-recognizances. Ann Haies was bound by Elizabeth Robinson "who chargeth her upon oath for assaulting & beating her," yet Robinson was simultaneously "chargeth . . . upon oath for assaulting and beating" Haies.[93] Robert Clayton and Mary Thornerly both had "sworne" that they went "in danger of [their] life" by the other, and Humphrey Walbosse and John Bushnell both brought complaints of each "assaulting and strikeing" the other "in the streete in the night," and both claimed to have lost their hats as a result.[94] In two recognizances involving the same four people, Elizabeth Axton and Ann Smith were separately bound for "assaulting and beating" each other, as were Mary Smith and George Hand, though Ann Smith's husband Thomas was also named in the assault on Hand and Axton.[95] Thomas Spratley and Thomas Sabin each went before the same JP on the same day to be bound at the complaint of the other for "raising a mob and tumult about" the other's house.[96] Margaret Murfield was both plainant and defendant opposite Edith Williams, who had accused her of "calling her common Whore & Bitch, . . . being a common Disturber, . . . assaulting . . . & threatning" Williams, and Murfield in turn accused her of "calling her whore to a bargeman . . . daily disturb[ing] her peace, & assaulting her."[97] Many more recognizances exist where parties have brought a complaint and been bound on the same day for virtually the same offense. Certainly, in some instances, these charges must have resulted from a pitched battle where blows fell almost simultaneously, and choosing a single aggressor would be impossible. In other cases one party or both parties may have trumped up a suit in anticipation of their rival's litigation. Nevertheless, the virtually duplicate language chosen to describe the offenses in the recognizances indicates that the Justice of the Peace was faced with two contradictory claims of victimhood and was forced to give them equal relevance. In the above examples both men and women approached the Westminster Quarter Sessions with the dual identity of victim and aggressor and were sufficiently credible on both counts to appear in the record. They were able to fashion their own victimhood.

It may seem counterintuitive to look for empowerment beneath the tales of blood, fear, and suffering told by the Westminster assault recognizances. Nevertheless, the records themselves stand as evidence that a prosecution had occurred and that an individual had actively sought satisfaction for the act against himself or herself. Those people associated with the beatings and bruising described in the final two sections of this chapter are no different from the "savvy litigants" recounted in the previous sections. Londoners knew enough about the power of the justice system to call out "stop thief" or "bear witness." They knew their potential power as prosecutors. Whether consciously or subconsciously, they relied on the status of victimhood, paradoxically stressing their weakness in order to strengthen their case.

Although there was no legal pressure upon early-eighteenth-century Londoners to prosecute assault, they came out in substantial numbers to bind over their attackers. In some cases their stories of victimhood may have been imagined or invented. Whether genuine or malicious, the thousands of assault recognizances show that Londoners were knowledgeable prosecutors who frequently made use of the Westminster Quarter Sessions to resolve even minor disputes. Because the public played a significant role in the administration of criminal justice, Londoners of all walks of life could get a rudimentary education on the workings of the law by simply being out in the street. Both men and women donned the mantle of victimhood, with the cooperation of their JPs, and stressed their weakness or used assault recognizances as a cheaper way to gain civil damages. Some disputes continued long after Westminster Quarter Sessions had become involved, and when Londoners were especially vehement, they could launch counterprosecutions in a drawn-out competition for victimhood. By focusing on prosecutorial initiative, rather than the outcome of suits, we can see London litigants released from passivity and, to a certain extent, empowered by their own profession of victimhood. The assault recognizances, therefore, represent an exercise in self-fashioning not dissimilar from that observed by scholars of early modern literature.

3

Curbing Masculine Petty Violence: *The Victims of Sexual Assault and the Mohock Scare*

Two-thirds of all Londoners who came before the Westminster Quarter Sessions brought complaints about male attackers. Though—as chapter 5 will argue—feminine violence was not insignificant and came in many forms, we cannot deny that masculine violence was far more prevalent. Male aggression was not allowed to flourish unhindered, however, and we will explore some examples of prosecutions directed specifically at men. This chapter takes up a common theme in the book: that the dichotomies of weak female and powerful male so prominent on the surface of early modern life often become blurred when we take a closer look.

The first two sections of the chapter are concerned with male sexual violence. Sexual violence was (and is) overwhelmingly masculine. Both men and women prosecuted sexual assaults, but the targets of such prosecutions were almost always men. The laws against sexual violence were made to constrain male behavior, and the successful prosecution of sexual violence delineated appropriate forms of masculine sexuality. The first section underscores the fact that within the legal system victims of attempted rape received more satisfaction than victims of rape. It seems likely that sexual assault victims were aware of this and may have even reduced their charges to increase the likelihood of obtaining satisfaction through the courts.

However, even the *un*successful prosecution of sexual violence had an impact on men. We can see all of the sexual assault prosecutions as attempts to curb male sexual aggression, and this is another area where the sexual double standard was less prominent.[1] To discuss rape in the context of "petty" violence may seem to trivialize a horrible crime. However, the English courts' acquittal of 80 percent of all men charged with rape shows that, in practice, this capital crime was not taken very seriously.[2] It is difficult to argue that eighteenth-century women were empowered by rape prosecution, but we will at least see that men were somewhat disempowered as defendants in such cases. The evidence of the policing of male heterosexuality adds to the scholarship on the ways that cultural norms circumscribed male heterosexual behavior.[3]

The Mohock scare is a more self-contained example of prosecutors' power in curbing male violence. The Mohocks, as we will see, were a group of elite male rakes who terrorized Londoners at night in 1712. The popular press depicted these young men as slitting open people's noses and lifting women's dresses in the streets, but the magnitude of their assaults was hugely exaggerated. Nevertheless, the fictitious male youth violence of the Mohocks provoked a very real retaliation among the London public in subsequent years. Previous historians have been unable to statistically analyze the impact of the Mohocks, but we will see that a markedly greater number of gentlemen were prosecuted for assaults after 1712 than before. The anxiety over Mohock violence caused a sort of moral panic in the metropolis, and its victims united to curb this form of male aggression.

One of the largest obstacles faced by female rape prosecutors was the early modern perception of mendacity and sexual insatiability as distinctly feminine traits. Victims invariably battled hostile questioning and presentation of evidence about their credibility and moral character. Men on trial for rape frequently claimed that their prosecutor had falsely accused them, expecting them to pay her to drop the suit. This pattern was so common—and so successful—a defense strategy in rape cases that legal historians have since dubbed it "the blackmail myth."[4] It is not surprising, therefore, that rape prosecutions were at their most powerful in their earliest stage. Immediately after the crime had occurred, rape victims bore the visible marks of male sexual violence. In 1718, a woman came to a JP's clerk for a warrant to arrest her rapist. The clerk saw her "sobbing and crying so that she could not for some time speak and tell him what she came about . . . [and] when she came her Clothes were much rumpled, her Arms bruised, and, as she said, was hurt in other Parts, which he did not inquire into."[5] At this stage of the criminal process, the victim's silence over the details of the attack worked against the man accused. His only tools of self-advocacy were verbal denials, which were much less powerful in comparison to the silent, physical attestations of the woman's bruising, torn clothing, and sobbing. What was left unsaid communicated much more than explicit detail would have at this stage. The eventual trial, held long after the prosecutor's bruises had healed, brought verbal description back to the fore and allowed the defendant to marshal witnesses to question the victim's "character" and credibility to secure his victory.[6] At this stage feminine modesty gave the jury an excuse for acquittal: if the woman did not describe the details of rape, it left open the possibility that the rape had not occurred at all. The initiation of prosecution, in contrast, was much more in the woman's favor. Here, feminine reticence effectively silenced the man accused of raping her, because, aside from the charge of rape, there were no concrete details to deny.

A similar advantage might be gained by women who chose to bind a sexual assailant over in a recognizance. Such prosecutions usually described an attempted rape, but it seems likely that some women could have chosen to characterize a much more serious attack in this way in order to avoid prosecuting through the higher courts. They faced a more hostile audience in the latter and had a lesser likelihood of receiving satisfaction than they did before a JP. Many more men were bound for the misdemeanor of attempted rape at Westminster Quarter Sessions than were convicted of the felony of rape at the Old Bailey. Dorothy Pooley convinced Justice Thomas Railton to bind James Pawlet to appear "for endeavouring to debauch" her.[7] Elinor Punt had barber Patrick Smith bound over "for Endeavouring & using all the forceable ways and means he could to Ravish" her.[8] Justices frequently showed their willingness to bind over putative rapists.

Though recognizances might simply refer vaguely to the "undeasent manner" of the assault, they could just as often portray quite explicitly the sexual aspects which had been deemed unacceptable.[9] Elizabeth Meers said that Henry Chamberlayne, a gentleman, put "his Members into her hand" in the street and frightened her, and Hester Coe asked that yeoman Andrew Montiere be bound for "taking up her cotes and pulling oute his private parts attempting thereby to Ravish her."[10] Male sexual transgression might include invasion of territory beyond the body, as in the case of Richard Tabor, specifically charged with having "forced himself into" Rebecca Marther's chamber.[11] Tabor "very rudely" abused Marther "by thrusting his hands into the bed where she was naked."[12] Elizabeth Nicholly claimed that George Watson had assaulted her "in her own Lodging" and had tried "to comitt a rape on her body," and she convinced the JP to bind him over for it.[13] Judicial vigilance is also very strong in the recognizance brought against Richard Backwell "for incessantly haunting" Jane Ball, "notwithstanding his being forbid her company," or that against Richard Price for "his *second* attempt to Debauch" Eleanor Priffins."[14] Rather than turning a blind eye to male sexual proclivities, Westminster magistrates granted credibility to women's complaints and condemned many sexual encounters as assault.

One of the few remaining justicing notebooks sheds some light upon what might occur when a woman approached a JP to complain about male sexual violence. Wiltshire Justice William Hunt kept a notebook to record the many settlements he had orchestrated informally as part of his official magistrate duties. On June, 28, 1745, Hunt "granted a warrant against John Newman . . . for . . . assaulting [Jane Biggs] with intent to have carnal knowledge of her body," and Hunt found that "the fact was so clearly proved upon him, . . . that I adjudged him to pay unto [Bigg's husband] for damages 5 guineas, and at the same time [Newman] entered into a bond penalty £100 never to molest John Biggs or his wife any more."[15] When Anne Heath accused Samuel Perrat of "assaulting her with intention to lie with her," Hunt forced him to pay her eight shillings in compensation, and Edward Coles had to pay "three guineas" for attempting "to ravish" a fellow townswoman, "besides entering into a bond of £50 penalty never to molest" her and her husband in the future.[16] Hunt found Rebecca Phillpot's charge that John Holmes had tried to rape her sufficiently convincing to issue a warrant for his arrest. Holmes was so frightened by the warrant that he "absconded."[17] Antony Simpson recognized the advantage, though slight, accorded "the unknown number of rape victims who were forced to settle for a public apology and perhaps a small sum of money in a magistrate's court" over those who pursued their charge to a trial.[18] At this lower level of the court system, female victims were more likely to be believed, and male sexual violence was acknowledged and punished.

The parish had a vested interest in punishing lewd attacks by men. John Broe had to "find sufficient securitys to indemnify the parrish" after he had assaulted Mary Spiny "by throwing her downe in a stable laying with her and giving her the Foul disease whereby she is chargable to the parish."[19] One wonders if Broe would have been punished at all if Spiny had not caught the venereal disease that made her a parish charge, but their case nevertheless stands as another example of a curb on male sexual violence. Similarly, Mary Fuller testified to the Westminster Bastardy Examiner that "Thomas, one of Mr. Neal's carters" was father of her unborn baby and that he had "made her drink so much strong Drink . . . [that] she was overcome with the said Drink & . . . was persuaded to goe & Lye with him."[20] John and Thomas were censured only indirectly for assaulting these women, but Mary Spiny and Mary

Fuller used the self-interest of the parish to document the violence against them and see their attackers punished in some way.

Elizabeth Sample was another victim of male sexual aggression who was somewhat empowered. She was a married woman but was picked up by Constable William Lovelace and bound for "makeing a great noyse in a tavern in Company with fower men (whome she did not know) one of which pickt her up in the streete and receiveing from each of them halfe a Crowne to show them postures."[21] The imagery of a woman willing to go to a tavern with strange men she met on the street was no doubt purposely included in the recognizance to allow officials a full sense of her questionable morality. Nevertheless, the JP allowed Elizabeth Sample to log a complaint giving her own version of the night's events. A recognizance was drawn up on the same day as Constable Lovelace's, which bound John Hasting and Terrell Cooke, gentlemen, along with watchmaker John Sutton and vintner Henry Turner—the four men Sample was found with in the tavern—to appear to answer Sample. In her version, the men were "assaulting beateing and bruising her taring her clothes and causeing her thereby to loose her EareRings."[22] Thus, Sample ensured that the charges alleging her lewdness were, if not eradicated, at least balanced by her counterclaim of having instead been nonconsenting and victimized. By convincing the Justice of the Peace to issue a recognizance, Sample capitalized on the court's tacit disapproval of male libertinism in her description of the actions of Hasting, Cooke, Sutton, and Turner.

Men were also occasionally the victims of male sexual violence, and the courts found this form of attack particularly repugnant.[23] Westminster JPs carefully recorded prosecutions of London men for this "sinful" act, often in great detail. Francis Hollis charged John Jeffries with "Picking him up in the Parke & kissing him, . . . putting his hand in his codpiece & feeling his members [and] . . . also telling him that every one had their way & that was his: with several other obscene expressions."[24] Similarly, Humphrey Bowen claimed that "gentleman" William Gage had "used all the Inticeing Actions hee could to draw . . . Bowen . . . to commit with him . . . the abominable and detestable sin of Buggery And after they were out of the house and in the streets Mr Gage drew his yard privately and put it into . . . Bowen's . . . hand."[25] Although Randolph Trumbach has argued that "the most daringly masculine men had . . . sexual relations with both women and adolescent males" during this period, it is clear that the majority of London society—including its courts—abhorred sodomy.[26] The idea of one man trying to force another to commit buggery was especially objectionable, and homosexual male violence was probably treated more seriously than most heterosexual rapes.[27]

Both men and women came before the Westminster JPs to prosecute male sexual violence, and the latter, especially, found this lower level of the justice system much more satisfactory than a full trial at the Old Bailey. Those who described more minor sexual assaults and sought a recognizance would not find their credibility questioned to as great a degree—nor would they be exposed to as much general hostility—as those who sought to prosecute a felonious sexual assault in London's higher court. As we have seen, these victims also often saw more remedy with a lesser charge. They weighed the greater likelihood of their attackers receiving a fine before a magistrate against a probable acquittal before an Old Bailey jury, and chose accordingly.

It is thus more difficult to see how most of the men tried for rape at the Old Bailey experienced much discomfort. Given the low rate of success of women's rape prosecutions, we might understandably conclude that they failed to curb male sexual violence. This is true for the most part, but—in very small subtle ways—male sexual violence was at least *problematized* by rape prosecutions. This line of argument may seem dangerously counterintuitive because it goes against the obvious fact that the prosecution of rape generally victimized women a second time. However, without denying the fact that eighteenth-century rape trials were less humane toward the female victims of rape than to the men they charged, it is still possible to glimpse a slight constraint upon male violence in the law against rape.

In the early modern concept of heterosexual sex, "normal" intercourse was commonly conceived as an aggressive male overpowering a reluctant female. Early modern women who had sex were "used" by their partners—in their own minds as well as those of the men who "used" them.[28] The construction of the "normal" heterosexual encounter as one of a voracious man preying upon a reluctant woman is illustrated by Henry Hurt's trial at the Old Bailey in 1717. Hurt, accused of raping "one Mary Lye, a Virgin of 13 years of age," claimed instead that consensual sex had occurred. Hurt defended himself by "saying that he indeed was eager and she *not very unwilling*," showing that, even in licit sex, a man's role was highly aggressive in contrast to the submissiveness of his partner.[29] The jury echoed this perception, acquitting Hurt because "it appeared that the Unwillingness was at least a willing one."[30] However, the fact that many heterosexual encounters, popularly conceived as "normal," could at least be *prosecuted* as rape may indicate that men could not enjoy complete sexual freedom. Had the legal definition of rape as "the carnal knowledge of a woman . . . against her will" been totally without wider social foundation, women would not have even thought about initiating prosecutions.[31] Mary Lye's charges against Hurt had sufficient merit to win an indictment before a grand jury. Notwithstanding their low rate of ultimate success, the prosecutions that did occur represent an alternative concept of appropriate sex. Rape's existence in the law books negates the idea that a man overpowering his female partner in order to penetrate her constituted a "natural" sex act.

Society sometimes agreed with the female victims of rape, even when the courts did not. Sibyl May, an elderly woman, claimed to have been raped in the course of a robbery. May's rapist was acquitted by the jury, but the report of her trial in the *OBP* told Londoners that she had indeed been raped and that the defendant was acquitted only because he had blindfolded her so that she could not positively identify him.[32] Dorothy Palmer, "a Girl about 11 years of age," accused Samuel Smith of raping her in 1681.[33] Smith had actually confessed to the crime before a magistrate, but he was acquitted on "some nice point in Law," the very vagueness of the characterization attesting to its lack of credence with the nonlegal public.[34] We can only guess at the reception these men would have had when they were freed. The infamous Colonel Charteris, convicted of rape in 1730 and pardoned, may offer some insight. Popularly dubbed "Rape-Master General of Great Britain," Charteris elicited great hatred among Londoners. The crowds so disagreed with his pardon that the *Daily Post* recounts how they "fell upon him and beat him in a barbarous manner" when they spotted him in a Hackney Coach near Chelsea, "for no other Reason than that there were two Women with him in the Coach."[35] At his funeral two years later, Pope described how "the populace . . . rais'd a great riot, almost tore the body out of the coffin, and cast dead dogs &c. into the grave along with it."[36] Although Charteris's high social position certainly added to the popular sentiment against him, people were also outraged at the fact that a known rapist was allowed to walk free.

Certainly, when the courts upheld the fact that male sexual violence had occurred, the guilty men were held in great contempt. William Harding was convicted of raping Sara Bentley, "a Girl of about 7 or 8 years of age," in 1680, and his perversions were widely broadcast.[37] One report described him as "a very debauched fellow, for . . . he was wont to act carnally with his own mother, threatning when she refused to permit his incestuous desires, to fire the house about her Ears."[38] John Price, a.k.a. Ketch, hanged in 1718 for murdering Elizabeth White in the course of a rape, was described as beating her "so cruelly that streams of blood issued from her eyes and mouth . . . forced one of her eyes from the socket, and otherwise so ill treated her, that the language of decency cannot describe it."[39] When eighteenth-century society acknowledged male sexual violence, they regarded it with the highest contempt.

Judging from a randomly selected five-year period of the *Old Bailey Proceedings*, more than half of the rapes prosecuted were brought by young girls.[40] Although almost none of their rapists were convicted, the high proportion of child rape that was prosecuted has great significance. The age of consent at this time was ten for women and fourteen for men, yet only three of the eight cases involving young victims in all of the rapes between 1714 and 1719 were below age ten; the rest were between ten and fourteen.[41] Clearly, the added burden of proving nonconsent did not deter these girls and their families from prosecuting. Victims had to be cold and calculating; rape was not worth prosecuting unless they felt they had a strong case. The high proportion of young girls among rape prosecutors suggests that social attitudes were more sympathetic to these victims.[42] The courts were not: all of the defendants accused of raping children below ten were acquitted, and convictions for the rest were as low as those for rapes of women over fourteen. Nevertheless, society despised men who had sex with girls of tender years, and these sentiments ensured that more victims from this group came forward to prosecute. Again, social attitudes placed subtle curbs on male sexuality even though the law did not.

The rape acquittals themselves originated more from the harsh penalty that came with a guilty verdict than from a jury's sense of the defendant's true innocence. Rape was a serious felony in the law books, and the hangman's rope loomed as a possibility—no matter how distant—over every charge brought to trial. The doctor who examined Elizabeth Banks after her rape warned her that swearing a rape against a man "would take away his Life."[43] The doctor then "endeavoured to make up the Matter between them."[44] Many surgeons, midwives, or even JPs, often among the first to hear rape allegations, would have tried to steer women away from a capital prosecution, but nevertheless would have acknowledged the woman's right to some satisfaction for the wrong done to her. Once a woman went to court, rape's capital penalty would act against her. Laurie Edelstein described the way in which judges "often emphasized" the severity of the penalty during the trial, to remind juries of the fate awaiting any man found guilty.[45] The fact that women such as Elizabeth Banks persisted in a trial suggests that their motive was as much to publicize the great wrong done to them as to see their attacker hanged. Regardless of the probability of a hostile jury, women clearly had their own reasons for publicly fighting back against their rapists. As Clare Brant has suggested, "[A]n idea of justice can survive its failings in practice," an idea also echoed by Garthine Walker.[46] The tenacity of such rape prosecutors added to the terror of those accused, even though capital sentences were rarely given. Men faced the possibility that their conquest might be viewed by the public as sexual violence, if not so viewed by the courts.

As the most serious form of male sexual violence under the law, rape paradoxically freed and constrained men. The death penalty awaiting any man convicted of rape meant that few men were actually ever convicted, but this did not stop women from bringing prosecutions. In a world where "normal" heterosexual sex demanded male aggression, however, it is significant that any men were even accused of rape. In the context of this crime, male sexual violence was more *socially* defined than legally defined, often meaning the act of a man overpowering a child.

Elite youth violence received particular attention in our period because of the notorious activities of the Mohocks. The Mohocks were a group of aristocratic rakes who "terrorized" the city of London over a period of several months in 1712. The most recent works on the subject have concluded, after thorough research, that the Mohock stories were largely fabrications.[47] These violent youths did not really exist, but the terror they caused among Londoners was very real. In a footnote comment, Daniel Statt recognized the potential to view the Mohocks as a moral panic.[48] Though peripheral to Statt's argument, it is central to mine, and I will describe the ways in which society's fear and sense of victimization led to a very real curb upon upper-class youths.

It is not surprising that Londoners believed the Mohocks' violence to be real. Queen Anne issued a proclamation, which appeared in a broadside of 17 March, 1711/2. Asking for vigilance and offering a £100 reward to anyone who notified JPs of possible Mohocks, the proclamation alluded to "great and Unusual Riots and Barbarities, which have lately been committed in the night time in the open streets."[49] Another pamphlet offered *A True List of Names of the Mohocks . . . who were Apprehended and Taken on Monday Night, Tuesday and this morning,* with more than seventy names—many of titled gentry.[50] The Mohocks were, apparently, real people. They were young men with sufficient resources to be idle—and idle young men had long been a source of disorder in London.[51]

When even the Queen acknowledged the existence of this mysterious band of rakes, one would imagine that their violence must have escalated to a very serious level indeed. In fact, there is little real evidence of an increase in assaults in 1712. A draft report by legal officials on "the assaults and injuries on Citizens by the Mohocks" recounted several beatings, a riot on a constable, and an additional fifteen victims whose assailants had not been found.[52] These are not extraordinary numbers in light of the hundreds of assaults by men every year (see table 5.1 in chapter 5). In addition, constables' searches of their wards for Mohocks or their victims were largely fruitless. Asked to "make diligent inquiry . . . of any . . . persons that have been assaulted beaten wounded bruised maimed or evill intreated by any . . . persons called mohawks, or suspected to be such . . . since the first day of Feb last," the constables of the various wards filed reports, twenty-two of which are available among the Middlesex Sessions papers.[53] Rather than the seventy arrests and the rash of slashings and riots alluded to in the popular press, nine of the twenty-two ward reports listed no violence of any kind, such as David Edwards, constable of St. James Market ward, who said that "everything was Quiet with his Ward."[54] The ones that do list violence mainly depict run-of-the-mill incidents: a military officer wounded in a sword fight with another officer, a man and his wife "beaten & bruised" in the early evening, and a vague reference to "one person . . . wounded several places in the Back."[55]

Awareness of the lack of an unusual expansion in real violence on the streets did percolate into the press. One pamphlet, picking up on the rumors that the Mohocks were part of a Whig plot, referred skeptically to "the mischeif *said* to be done . . . *if true*" by the Mohocks.[56] John Gay satirized the press inventions about the Mohocks, promising that his broadside on the connection between the Mohocks and "the Gog and Magog mention'd in the Revelations" would prove "not only the things that are, but also the things that are not."[57] Even in the eighteenth century, contemporaries expressed misgivings over the tendency of the press to sensationalize or deliberately concoct a story to attract readers. According to one of the pamphleteers, the stories surrounding the Mohocks were written by a "Grub Street Half-penny scribler . . . set at work by an empty Pocket and sharp Stomack."[58] A poem on the Mohocks recognized that, even if they had been captured, their "growing fame" would "stand untouched."[59] Jonathan Swift recognized that, though "Grubstreet Papers about them fly like Lightning," the list printed of those arrested was "all a Lye; and I begin to think there is no Truth or very little in the whole Story."[60] Historians have since reinforced such conclusions, asserting that the Mohock scare was far more a literary creation than a historical reality.[61] The Mohocks' contemporaries were skeptical of their real existence, and discussions of the rakes coincided with awareness of the power of the popular press to manufacture stories.

In light of this popular skepticism, the commonly expressed fear of the Mohocks becomes even more interesting. Swift had voiced strong doubts about their existence, but he nevertheless continued to "forbear walking late. . . . for fear of the Mohocks," and subsequent entries in his journal mentioned curbing his routine to avoid a Mohock attack, declaring, at the same time, "tho I believe nothing of it."[62] Daniel Defoe, arguably the most likely to doubt the rumors about the Mohocks—being himself painted as their co-conspirator—still treated their danger as genuine and recommended the "Protestant Flail" as the best weapon of defense against them.[63] By April of 1712, Budgell admitted in *The Spectator* "that very many begin to doubt whether there were ever any such Society of Men" as the Mohocks, but he still confessed to a persistent belief in the truth of the "great Alarm the whole City has been in."[64] Conspiracy theories abounded, linking the Mohocks with both pro- and antigovernment factions, which served simultaneously to assist the notion that stories of the Mohocks could not be taken at face value and to further foment the terror that the Mohocks represented much more than small-scale rakery.[65] The people of London were left unsure of the truth, a lack of certainty that did little to allay their fears, instead making the danger appear far worse.

The Mohock scare was fueled by detailed descriptions of the men and the types of violence they had allegedly perpetrated. Due to the very possibility that these descriptions were invented, they are valuable to historians as evidence of wider social anxieties surrounding certain upper-class youth activities. The *Gentleman's Library* saw the rake as "a Man always to be pitied . . . for his faults proceed not from *choice* . . . but from strong *Passions* and *Appetites,* which are in *Youth* too violent for the Curb of Reason, good sense, *good Manners,* and *good Nature,*" but most Londoners had a less sympathetic attitude, particularly where the Mohocks were concerned.[66] Contemporaries were very aware of the Mohocks' identity with the aristocracy, and their elite status only made them appear more dangerous.[67] Historian Randolph Trumbach argues that aristocratic libertines were largely tolerated by their contemporary society, but the Mohock scare suggests otherwise.[68]

The 1712 press on the Mohocks invented them as unfettered ruffians who frittered away their excess funds on drinking, whoring, and—the worst fault of all to middling sensibilities—sleeping during the day and carousing all night.[69] The drunken Mohocks were in a "constant Toast" to one another's health, according to one ballad, and a wide variety of popular literature attested to their intemperance.[70] Legal officials seem to have internalized this, as few records of prosecutions for drunkenness can be found among those suspected of being Mohocks.[71] The Mohocks came out after all decent human beings were safely in their beds, and the official response ordered that the night watch be doubled and that watchmen stay at their posts until six in the morning to combat this new nocturnal danger.[72] More significantly, the Mohocks were depicted as sexual predators, though the official records of their offenses do not bear this out in reality. Women were attacked at night during this period, but no prosecutions mentioned attempted rape or any other violence of a sexual nature. Despite the lack of real evidence, pamphlets accused the Mohocks of a tendency to "set . . . Women on their Heads, misusing them in a barbarous manner," and another of "turning up [side-down] . . . of modest Gentlewomen."[73] (The sexual aspect of such attacks becomes abundantly clear when it is remembered that "drawers or underpants" did not come into vogue for the general female population until the nineteenth century.)[74] Another fictitious treatment remarked that "if [the Mohocks] ravish not our Wives, We have good luck withal," because the opposite was more often the case.[75] These allegations had no basis in reality, yet the pamphleteers and their eager readers created a danger around idle rich youth that was specifically sexual.

Most important for our purposes, the accounts of slashings and horrible mutilations were also not characteristic of the official record. Of dozens of prosecutions, only five offer descriptions that approach the level of savagery seen in the popular press. Lucy Goddard was said to have been "assaulted" by a man "as she stopped to give him the way, who also held up his caine & swore he would knock out her braines," but neither Goddard nor any of the other prosecutors in the Commission's report mention stabbings.[76] A ward constable for St. Anne's parish reported a man wounded "with a pennknife in four . . . places."[77] The most grisly accounts are in two informations taken for the Middlesex Quarter Sessions. In one, "two persons like Gentlemen" were said to have "with a violent force thrust a penknife or some other instrumt through the lower part of [Mary Ann Kilby's] face at some small distance from her lower lip into [her] mouth."[78] The other described a woman who "was cot shrow [*sic*] hear lower lip had a blow on the side of her head and had a blow in hear bak" and added that the perpetrators "as they weer going . . . laft mitly and thay aber [appeared] . . . like gentelmen very well drest."[79] The *London Gazette*'s request for information on the identity of the Mohocks included an attack on Grace Joyce, who was "much Wounded in her Head and Face," but she was the only victim other than Mary Ann Kilby listed with slash wounds.[80]

These accounts of real attacks were not nearly as severe as the violence attributed to the Mohocks in the popular press. The penny pamphleteers capitalized on the minority of violent incidents, broadcasting the Mohocks as prone to vile mutilations, especially nose slitting, which is mentioned in almost every literary account. John Gay parodied their exaggerations in a scene in his play, depicting constables conversing about their encounters with the legendary Mohocks. As one constable averred, "I saw them . . . hook a man . . . cut off his ears, and eat them up," and another constable said he saw "all the Ground covered with Noses—as thick as 'tis with Hail-stones after a storm."[81] The press reproduced the few real assaults as a highly distorted picture of serialized violence, and they eagerly grasped at hints of gentry assailants as evidence of the dangerous excesses of rakery. This tendency in the literature attests to its readers' appetite for negative accounts of elite masculinity.

The Mohocks' reputation for physical brutality was combined with a complete disregard for social and political mores, turning Londoners' fear to loathing. As the broadsheet purporting to be their ballad asserted, "[W]e Govern in our Way. . . . / For Crowns and Scepters we decry . . . / 'Gainst Monarchy, we do declare, / in *Lucifer*'s dread Name."[82] Another poem satirically referred to the Mohocks as the "Great Reformers, whose exalted souls Despise stiff formal Rules, and Knots of Law."[83] Mohocks were notorious for attacking watchmen, though almost all of the records of prosecution were for one attack on a single watchman, John Bouch.[84] One broadsheet also considered a popular target of the Mohocks to be "particularly . . . cheif Magistrates."[85] Much of the literature focused upon their complete lack of human decency, the indiscriminate nature of their attacks, and the fact that their violence was always without provocation.[86] Their actions were described as "Barbarities" perpetrated on "innocent Persons," and the same broadsheet added, with palpable sarcasm, that "when any Watchmen presumes to demand where they are going, they generally misuse" him.[87] Characterized by a general disregard for rules, both formal and informal, the Mohocks were called "mean and vulgar" and were said to perform "barbarass tricks, without any provocation."[88] Defoe wondered, with contempt, "what humour it gratifies to murder or wound an unconcerned stranger who has not given the least affront," and he placed the Mohocks only a slight "degree above the Devil."[89] Though most Londoners had not *directly* fallen victim to the Mohocks' violence, they all considered themselves as potential victims and—more than anything—considered their social values to be in grave peril before the assaults of this nefarious band of rakes.

The public readily believed in the existence of the Mohocks, even with evidence to the contrary, and the ease with which accounts of these lewd violent youths abounded shows that a general distaste for elite male excesses was already prevalent in London society. The Mohock scare simply fed this paranoia and turned it into a moral panic. The concept of a moral panic originated with sociologist Stanley Cohen and has since been used by nineteenth-century historians with great effectiveness.[90] Essentially, a moral panic occurs when a group is targeted by society as a particular moral danger, usually without just cause, and is starkly and unfairly represented in the press. Eventually, when the flames of moral panic have been fanned into a frenzy, the object of panic is usually curbed by a change in social or legal policy. By perceiving the Mohocks as fearsome and powerful, the public wanted to see them controlled. Though much of the literature on the Mohocks overstated the level and frequency of violence, added lewd acts where none were actually prosecuted, and projected the arrest of a few aristocrats onto an elite culture, the exaggerations met with a credulous audience.

The moral panic was felt by all layers of society, and Londoners responded en masse with a desire to curb the notorious excesses of elite youth. Defoe wished that "the gallows, the army, or the navy would . . . soon rid us of such a set of bloodhounds."[91] Lady Wentworth was even more disgusted, averring that "instead of setting fifty pound upon the head of a highwayman, . . . they would doe much better to sett a hundred upon the . . . heads" of the Mohocks.[92] More sympathetic, though no less critical, the *Spectator* believed a substantial proportion of the Mohocks to be "some thoughtless youngsters" who "out of . . . an immoderate fondness to be distinguished for Fellows of Fire, are insensibly hurried into this senseless scandalous Project" and must "stand corrected by . . . Reproofs."[93] The violence in the Mohock stories coincided with a growing distaste for the practice of dueling, and the other aspects of libertinism—lewd behavior and disrespect for authority—were also receiving increased attention from the middling sorts.[94] The moral panic created by the Mohock scare thus represents the power of a brief event to align popular opinion in condemnation of genteel male excesses.

This power is most visible in subsequent prosecutions of elite men. The data from the assault recognizances for Westminster suggest that the Mohock scare did cause Londoners to consider upper-class men more dangerous than they had before. In the four years following the stories about Mohock violence, the number of upper-class men bound over for assault rose from approximately twenty per year in the preceding four years to about thirty-eight per year from 1712 to 1715.[95] This increase was not due solely to the sudden influx of prosecutions at the time of the scare itself either, as the proportion of gentlemen prosecuted was higher in eight of the fourteen subsequent sessions.[96] Recognizances are the most reliable measure of this phenomenon, as Robert Shoemaker has found their information on the identity and location of the defendants (which includes their occupation or status) to be more accurate than indictments.[97] Fluctuations in numbers of prosecutions, of course, are not a window into true levels of violence, but legal records can at least reveal popular *attitudes* toward crime. Though the numbers of recognizances binding gentry are small, we can see in these few prosecutions a much wider aversion to certain aspects of elite male behavior. The informal policing, in other words, was likely even greater than the formal policing of genteel masculinity constituted by the growth in recognizances. Whether gentlemen were genuinely becoming more violent or not, the rise in prosecutions indicates that they were more often *perceived* as a danger.

England had been treated to stories of youth gangs in previous generations, and the organized rake violence of the Mohocks was not the first of its kind to find its way into the popular press or the courts. Neil Guthrie opened his article on the Mohocks by citing references to "the heyday of the Roaring Boys in the reign of Elizabeth I" and "the ancient Mohocks" from the time of King Charles.[98] An account in the *OBP* described "one Mr. Gerard, Nephew . . . to My Lord Gerard," along with a group of "several other young Gentlemen," becoming frustrated when they found a victualling-house closed late at night.[99] According to the victualler, "[T]hey knocked hard at the door, and bid him open it, the which he refusing, one or more of them began to break the windows, and . . . [then] they threw up lighted Links," setting a small fire in an upstairs room.[100] This account appeared in 1695, more than a decade before the Mohocks, and is another example of the existence of rakery prior to the events of 1712.

Generally, the attitudes toward earlier rakes tended to be fairly indulgent, in stark contrast to the moral panic surrounding the Mohocks. Anna Bryson discerned a dramatic decline in public toleration of libertinism, especially in the decades following the restoration. Even though there was elite violence before 1712, she argued, the "Murderous Mohock outrages against Londoners" constituted a "peak" in rake violence, which provoked a greater public response.[101] The "gallant libertine figure" which had emerged by the early eighteenth century was, according to Bryson "radically uncivil in a way unknown" to previous generations.[102] This notion also coincided with the intensive campaigns of the Societies for the Reformation of Manners, which had been operating in the capital since the 1690s. These societies, which targeted typical rake behavior such as drinking and whoring, among other things, also emerged as a response to the perceived depravity of the restoration.[103] The Mohock scare occurred when the reforming zeal was still very strong, before it had begun its steady decline to disappearance in the 1730s. The Mohocks can thus be seen as the source of a moral panic, drawing public animosity and fear in a way never before elicited by rake excesses.

The moral panic seems to have been effective in increasing public prosecution for years afterward. In the decade following the explosion of press on the Mohocks, there was a perceptible increase in the prosecution of similar forms of rakery. The assault recognizances exhibit the persistence, in the public mind, of the key characteristics of the Mohock stories. David Bowen had John Bentley, a "gentleman," bound "for saying whenever he met him he would cut his Nose off" two years after the Mohock scare.[104] Victims went before sympathetic law officials with tales of gentlemen assaulting and "affronting them in the street."[105] The account of a gentleman bound over for assaulting a woman adds sufficient description to leave little doubt of his reputation for rakery. Said to be "a person of an infamous character and a common disturber of the peace," he was also accused of "assaulting the Drawers of the Vine Tavern at Chairing cross and bilking the house of the Reckoning and . . . swearing he would Kill Englishmen, Frenchmen, and germans saying he was sorry his sword was not sharp enough to kill all the Rogues in Charing Cross."[106] Similar aggression was present in the recognizance for Daniel Langthorne, another gentleman, said to have been "a nightly Common disturber" of Elizabeth Gray, "at her door and windowes . . . swearing, cursing and threatning her in most sad prophane words, for putting her in great terror and fear . . . & for threatning to cane her & much more."[107] Elite males had a reputation for behaving aggressively, and for flouting the law as well as the rules of common decency, and they may have actually been more limited as a result. In other words, when London society considered itself a victim of the Mohocks in 1712, they reacted by prosecuting more genteel youth than they had before.

This chapter reveals a very significant, though often imperceptible, victim of male petty violence in early-eighteenth-century London: the general public. Society as a whole had a key role to play in curbing male violence. We have seen the press at work interpreting the legitimacy or illegitimacy of rape acquittals, and more prominently in churning out grisly accounts of Mohock atrocities. These pamphlets both responded to and fueled a public paranoia that already existed about the dangers of certain forms of male aggression and the need to keep them in check. Individual prosecutors of men's assaults served a similar role to the press, on a smaller scale. Their prosecutions gained power and significance when they reflected forms of masculine petty violence considered particularly repugnant by society as a whole. The courts, too, were part of this society and punished certain male assaults more harshly than others.

Sexual assault prosecutors understood the courts' discriminatory nature and strategized by going before a JP and asking for a recognizance against their attackers. Male and female victims of masculine sexual aggression found satisfaction (though slight) for the wrongs done them by accusing men of attempted rape, sodomy, or fathering a bastard. Though lesser offenses, they often subjected those accused to more constraints than they faced when on trial for rape at the Old Bailey. Even the latter, however, experienced a certain amount of policing. Young girls and elderly women brought rape charges to court more than other women. This suggests the existence of an unwritten societal attitude that defined male sexual conquest as violence when it was directed against women of extreme age or youth. The courts and society felt that the death penalty was too severe for rape, but they found other ways to condemn and punish male sexual violence.

Even surrounded by skepticism of the truth of their existence, the Mohocks evoked very real fear in their contemporaries, indicating that the public was ready to condemn rakery and see it punished. The press took the tenuous connection between genteel attackers and a relatively minor spate of assaults and transformed them into a very marketable narrative, ridden with hints of conspiracy. The Mohock scare escalated into a moral panic. In subsequent years prosecutors of elite male violence were able to draw strength from the memory of 1712, and more men and women came forward with complaints of this type of youth violence than they had previously.

Moral panic, along with rape and sexual assault prosecutions, reveals the diverse and subtle ways in which eighteenth-century male aggression was confined within legal and ideological boundaries.

4

Female Assault Victims: *Pregnant Women and Battered Wives as Prosecutors*

Although the female victims of rape often met with more sympathy outside the courts than within them, as the previous chapter has shown, other female assault victims had more success in both spheres. Pregnant women and battered wives who prosecuted assault by binding over their attackers made use of cultural and medical ideas of the appropriate conduct due wives and expectant mothers. Pregnant women were far better able to elicit sympathy and gain satisfaction before the courts than assault plaintiffs with other physical vulnerabilities. Similarly, battered wives had more success than many previous histories of domestic violence have allowed.

Early-eighteenth-century medical opinion still had great difficulty in diagnosing pregnancy with certainty. In the first trimester, doctors and midwives relied almost entirely upon the word of the woman herself as to whether or not she was pregnant. The first section will show that women benefited from this medical uncertainty, along with the scientific view that pregnant women's cravings and fears must be taken seriously in order to avoid injury to the developing fetus.

As we shall see, battered wives also took advantage of extralegal attitudes condemning almost all husbandly violence as inappropriate. These female prosecutors even went to Justices of the Peace with tales of their husbands' adultery, and a recognizance was issued even though adultery was not a crime under the common law. Acknowledging that recognizances are a mediated source, constructed through a complex and varied process of communication between the prosecuting victim and the JP, this chapter illustrates that recognizances are a prism through which we can see their contemporary society.

Generally, historians have seen the state's involvement in defining motherhood and wifehood in a very negative light.[1] This chapter will alter this negative picture somewhat by showing that wives and mothers were sometimes able to benefit from their status in their interactions with the state. The latter, personified by the Westminster JPs, gave them sympathy as assault victims and granted their complaints legitimacy by binding over their attackers. We will see that, as assault victims, battered wives and pregnant women were empowered.

From 1685 to 1720 the Westminster JPs took eighty-seven recognizances for assault where the victim's pregnancy was specifically noted. These recognizances were fairly evenly spaced throughout the period and were taken by many different justices. As a percentage of the total Westminster recognizances for assaults upon women in this period—more than three thousand—those mentioning pregnancy are minimal. There were probably far more women of childbearing years assaulted in this group, and probably more than eighty-seven were pregnant at the time of the assault.[2]

However, almost no other recognizances list *any* aggravating circumstances in an assault. Only nine other cases mention victims having some sort of condition that increased the severity of the attack. All nine specify the victim's youth or old age, describing them as "infant," "child," "minor," "old," or even, in one case, "auncient"; and unlike those for expectant mothers, these recognizances do not go on specifically to relate this unique quality in the victim to the damage sustained by the assault. Gabriel Thomas, for example, was bound to appear "for violently assaulting and bruising Eliz Foster an auncient woman," while Timothy Corker's recognizance for assaulting Elizabeth Smith reads "she being great with child *whereby she is dangerously ill.*"[3] Clearly, a victim's pregnancy was given more attention by the Westminster court, and perhaps by society in general, than age or infirmity.

As assault prosecutors, these women were empowered; by stressing their identity as mothers, they strengthened the case against their assailant. Again, we can see these prosecutors as participants in the self-fashioning perceived by English literary scholars for the early modern period. By fashioning themselves as wronged mothers, these women could take advantage of a widespread cultural awareness of childbearing. Pronatalism was a key part of empire building in England.[4] Assault prosecutors knew that they were acting at a time when a large population was one of the central criteria for determining the health of a nation. These pregnant assault victims knew that they had special value in society, and this reinforced their claims of victimhood.

This type of assault was designated a special crime in several JPs' handbooks, but the JPs' opinions diverged as to its severity.[5] Giles Jacob stated, "If a Man happen to beat a Woman big with Child, and the Child when born hath Signs and Bruises in his Body, receiv'd by the Battery, and afterwards the Child dies; this is Murder in him that beat the Woman."[6] Richard Burn's *Justice of the Peace and Parish Officer*—a classic magistrates' manual, variations of which were used in the eighteenth and nineteenth centuries—digressed from this view. In a section on bastardy Burn wrote that "if a woman be quick or great with child . . . [and] if a man strike her, whereby the child within her is killed, *tho' it be a great crime,* yet it is not murder nor manslaughter by the law of England."[7] Joseph Keble instructed JPs that "to hurt a Woman great with-child, whereby the Child either dieth within her body, or shortly after that she is delivered of it . . . will not wrap a man within the danger of" being charged with "Man-slaughter."[8] Thus, although an assault on a pregnant woman was not always a felony, it was a significant crime, and many Westminster JPs took note of a victim's pregnancy.

While many of the women listed in the recognizances were "bigg with child" (visibly pregnant), some women prosecuting assaults would not have had their condition immediately noticed by the justice. In several cases, the agency *had* to have been the women's because the information would not have shown up in the recognizance unless they had volunteered it. For example, in 1701 Margaret Steward bound William Smith to appear in court for "assaulting & frightning of her & threatning to throw her downe staires whereby she hath miscarryed of a child wherewith she was about two months gone."[9] At two months, pregnancy was a very personal experience, which most women determined only by two months' absence of menstruation. At such an early stage even physicians had to rely on the woman's self-diagnosis. Apart from the cessation of menstruation, early-eighteenth-century doctors could determine a pregnancy only by a woman's enlarged abdomen and breasts or actual fetal movement, none of which would be apparent in the first two months.[10] In fact, we cannot even be sure that Margaret Steward was indeed pregnant, but her recognizance shows that she had successfully convinced the JP, and her prosecution was strengthened by having this factor included.

It is more difficult to see empowerment in the charge brought by Mrs. Williams against her husband in 1708, yet by prosecuting him at all, she was showing some agency. The recognizance says that he had "many times assaulted, beate and bruised her, whereby she has several times miscaryed."[11]

Williams convinced the JP that her husband had a long history of appalling violence, so at this stage, the record of her many miscarriages could only increase her ability to gain satisfaction for her husband's abuse. While a large belly may attest to pregnancy without the expectant mother saying a word, women like Steward and Williams had to speak before justices would know of a miscarriage after two months or a past history of miscarriages.

Women could also gain advantage from contemporary medical views of the fragility of childbearing women, even while they themselves internalized them. The good mother took care of her baby long before the birth. She had to control her very thoughts, making sure to be "chearful; for this doth exhilarate the infant," and, at all costs, to avoid "anger, troubles of the mind, affrights and terrors."[12] Pregnant women were subject to bizarre cravings, and this could affect their babies. According to Levinius Lemnius, if an expectant mother "by chance fasten her eyes upon any object, and imprint that in her mind, the child commonly doth represent that in the outward parts."[13] Nicholas Culpeper echoed this, saying that a child's harelip "is well known to be [caused by] the mother in the time of her conception being affrighted either with sudden starting of an Hare or Coney, or by losing her longing to eat a piece of such a creature."[14] The serious effects of prenatal diet were widely accepted in medical circles and in society as a whole. William Gouge advised husbands to "procur[e] for their wives to the uttermost of their power and abilitie, such things as may save their longing" because grave danger would befall "both . . . mother and childe" if the former was denied her cravings: "the death sometimes of the one, sometimes of the other, sometimes of both hath followed thereupon."[15]

Women themselves used these perceptions to their benefit before the courts.[16] In 1726 Mary Howard went before the Surrey Assize officials and claimed to have stolen a shoulder and breast of mutton because "she was big with child and long'd for the meat."[17] Significantly, she alluded to popular bewilderment about the whims that came with pregnancy by saying that "it would not have done her half so much good if it had been given to her, as if she had stole it."[18] Regardless of whether Mary Howard's plea succeeded, the fact that she attempted to garner sympathy by playing upon the conceptions of the importance of the mother's needs to the developing infant is very interesting. Pregnant women were regarded as both valuable and fragile by eighteenth-century society, and they used that perception to their own ends.

That they did so is visible in the Westminster assault recognizances. Mary Wakemen bound James Johnson to good behavior for "disturbing her and appearing before her house in a white sheet in the night time and frightening hir thereby that she miscarryed."[19] Francis Nevvil brought William Swift before a JP because Swift had made "a disturbance . . . at his house at an undue time of night and threaten[ed] Judith his wife thereby putting her in Bodily Fear she being pregnant with child."[20] Frightening a pregnant woman was supposed to have very dire consequences for her developing fetus.[21] As virtuous mothers, Nevvil and Wakemen experienced only mental anguish from those they accused, yet acting within the prescribed cultural and medical norms of the eighteenth century, they sought satisfaction for the physical harm these harrowing experiences may have inflicted upon their babies.

Paradoxically, while women were physically weakened by being pregnant, they were strengthened as assault prosecutors if they had had a miscarriage. One French doctor recognized this power and complained that certain women claimed a false pregnancy in order to take advantage of it:

> women, who having been ill treated, send for the chirurgeon that he may give them a certificate, the better to be revenged on their adversary; which that they may the easier obtain, they also affirm themselves with child, and having received blows on their belly, feign they feel great pain, and if by chance they have at that time their courses, they endeavour to perswade it is a flooding . . . , wherefore he must be careful not to be decieved.[22]

In the French context an assault upon a pregnant woman that caused her to miscarry brought the death penalty if the child had been quick, and a fine if the fetus had not developed to that point.[23] At least one literary example suggests that English women faked pregnancies and miscarriages as well. John Dunton's moralizing tale of a woman's descent into sin recounted her plan to extort money from her lover by pretending to be pregnant:

> I thought it now high time to feign my self with child, and therefore I would ever anon pretend I had qualms come over my stomach, and if I did eat anything, I sometimes made a shift to vomit it up again; then I would complain I had lost my taste, and that all sweet things seemed bitter to me, and at length would eat nothing but what was extraordinarily rare and dainty; and when I pretended to Long, which was done now and then, there maist be sure it was not for common things. These things maid him firmly conclude I was with child, and his belief having been confirmed by . . . a Doctor of Physic whom he consulted for that End. . . . When I thought I had got a sufficiency of both Goods and Money, I caused my Mother . . . to tell him . . . that I had . . . fallen down almost a whole pair of Stairs, and that thereupon I had Miscarried.[24]

This account strikingly illustrates the way in which a woman could make use of the mysteries surrounding the diagnosis of pregnancy and its bizarre cravings for her own ends. Clearly, early modern women could find empowerment before the courts in the guise of a wounded mother.

Some angered mothers laid their case before the justices by emphasizing their alleged assailant's *knowledge* of their pregnancy to compound his or her offense. Elizabeth Jones's recognizance against Thomas Biby carefully lists his cruelties. She accused him of "assaulting her, in throwing a pint pott of drink upon her, striking her severall times, & kicking her in the belly, *knowing* her to be with child."[25] Jane Johnson said that Joseph Hicks "threatned to make an example of her she being bigg with Child," and Dorothy Lumby accused Amy McCarty of "threatning to Murther the child she goeth w[i]th all."[26] Elizabeth Jury must have convinced her JP that Timothy Parrish had "swore he would stamp the Bastard out of her Belly."[27] Jury, a married woman, probably told the justice about Parrish's threat in order to strengthen her assault prosecution. As an assault prosecutor, she could claim that Parrish had hurt her physically and damaged her reputation as well. As prosecutors of assault, early-eighteenth-century women could take advantage of cultural and medical opinions of pregnancy to fashion themselves as very special victims before the court and command its sympathy and protection.

Although few have previously written about the extra sympathy accorded pregnant assault victims, many historians have written about women assaulted by their husbands. These previous histories of domestic violence have made use of the richer depositions in church court records at the expense of recognizances. The binding-over method of prosecution "was almost certainly available only for very serious cases" of domestic assault, they argue.[28] As we shall see, however, recognizances were generated for even relatively mundane forms of spousal assault. This may seem surprising, because on the surface recognizances did not appear to offer much in the way of punishment.[29]

Husbands bound for assault and forced to pay a fee to Quarter Sessions officials would probably have been more, rather than less, hostile to the wives whose prosecution caused this inconvenience. Furthermore, these angry husbands walked the London streets with relative freedom, especially as the recognizance's stipulation to "keep the peace" or "be of good behaviour" toward the complainant may have been only rarely effectively enforced.[30] Yet Westminster wives came out in relatively high numbers to see that their husbands received the "slap on the wrist" constituted by a recognizance. Simply put, these women must have felt that recognizances would make the violence stop, and by convincing JPs to bind over their husbands, these Westminster wives were empowered.

Over the thirty-five years between 1685 and 1720, the Westminster JPs bound 154 husbands for "assault" on the complaint of their wives, and an additional sixteen for "beating," two for simply "threatening" violence, and four to "keep the peace unto" their wives. Though perhaps not dramatically greater in *volume* than the evidence base of previous historians of domestic assault, these recognizances, in sheer numbers of cases, dwarf the research upon which past work has been based.[31] Recognizances were probably the most popular weapon of prosecution among abused wives in this period. It seems reasonable to suppose that none of these 176 women would have approached a JP to bind over their husbands if they felt the abuse would escalate as a result. There may well have been a substantial number of wives who were unable to prosecute for this very reason, whose identities we shall never know, but the significant portion of women who *did* come forward reveal some instances of spousal violence where remedy was actively sought and possible in the courts.

Similar to pregnant women prosecuting assault, the descriptions that appear on the recognizances for wife beating bear evidence of both the victims' and the recording officials' voices. Many of the statements are likely the result of direct questions from JPs, fueled by knowledge of the law and general public attitudes surrounding appropriate husbandly chastisement. As the recorder, the presiding justice (or his clerk) had the most obvious influence over the exact words that found their way into the record. Complainants, nevertheless, had some ability to influence the narrative—in the ways that they answered the questions or the information that they volunteered—bringing their own knowledge of public—and even legal—attitudes to domestic violence into the process. The detail of the recognizance binding a husband for "thrusting his caine into [his wife's] Belly, then stricking her on the nose with the said caine wch made [it] . . . bleed & also striking on her arme, that she thought it was broke" could have come only from the complainant's own knowledge of her injuries.[32] We can see similar agency in Jane Watson's reappearance before the law in 1698 to encourage Justice James Dewy to bind constable William Nichols "for refusing to Execute a warrant signed by three Justices of the peace, for the taking the husband of Jane Watson for barbarously . . . beating" her.[33]

Extreme characterizations of violence or barbarity occur in much higher proportions for assaults by husbands than they do for assault recognizances as a whole over the period.[34] As Hunt, Foyster, and Amussen have argued, husbands could physically correct their wives in early modern England, but they were constrained within certain widely understood bounds. Thus, Dorothy Williams had her husband bound for swearing he would "murder her," and her testimony must have convinced the JP to add that the man had "already stab'd at her with a knife against her side, which by reason of her stays did not enter but broke in two pieces."[35] The extensive history provided by Elizabeth Steel also convinced a JP to bind her husband for "assaulting her . . . with a mopstaff & a pair of Bellows that she is therewith made black & blew & her flesh much bruis'd wth other barbarous usage she receives of him & in the 15th instant [five days before, he] miserably beat her wth an oaken stick whch has put her in fear he will take away her life."[36]

These descriptions resonate with the law that allowed a wife to prosecute her husband if he "*outragiously* beat her" or at least gave her "notorious cause to fear it."[37] Husbands were allowed to prosecute their wives, presumably under any circumstances, but wives—according to the letter of the law—were expected to accept a certain amount of physical correction from their husbands.[38] The above examples show that wives nevertheless assertively deemed some "physical correction" to be unacceptable, and the recognizances prove that the JPs allowed them to prosecute.

Even more significant than the bloody tales that found their way into recognizances for wife assault is the equal number of recognizances where wives do *not* appear to have been beaten excessively. The law allowed JPs to take seriously the complaint of "the Wife if she be threatned to be killed, or" if she had been "outrageously chastised by her Husband," even without any evidence of *physical* violence.[39] Seventy-six recognizances use no evaluative terminology, describing the offense only as "assaulting" or "assaulting, beating and bruising," similar to the words used for *any* run-of-the-mill assault recognizance. An obvious assumption might be that these recognizances were written by lazier JPs, who simply recorded every assault recognizance in the briefest way possible and thus, unsurprisingly, failed to distinguish domestic assault from any other. However, of the seventy-six recognizances with no evaluative terminology, sixty (79 percent) were issued by JPs with a history of using *both* graphic and standard descriptions in recognizances against husbands, so they probably really were more run-of-the-mill assaults.[40]

"Assault," according to the justicing handbooks, could range from full-on physical attacks to acts as minor as aggressive *talk*. The assailant did not actually have to come into direct physical contact with the victim, nor did the victim have to be injured in any way.[41] With the potential for relatively mild acts to be labeled assaults, the standard terminology in these spousal assault recognizances becomes interesting. In a section entitled "In what cases assaults may be *justified*," some JPs' handbooks (though, interestingly, not *all*) guaranteed the husband's right to correct his wife "in a reasonable and proper manner," but many recognizances binding husbands for assaulting wives bear no description to indicate that the husband had, in fact, gone beyond what was "reasonable and proper."[42] Indeed, these recognizances look no different from those for regular assaults between individuals where no physical damage needed to be present at all. In *half* of the complaints brought to Westminster justices by wives against their husbands, neither the wives nor the court appears to have needed the wide range of derogatory terms available to indicate *excessive* violence.

Many of these cases were similar to that of Thomas Beard, who was bound by his wife for "assaulting and beating of her," or that of Thomas Pigings, charged to answer his wife simply "for an assault."[43] In some recognizances extreme violence had not yet occurred but was only threatened or feared as probable in the future. Jane Radford said that her husband had "threaten[ed] her life," and Thomas Graham had to answer his wife in the next Quarter Sessions for "treatning to cutt of[f] her nose."[44] In accordance with the legal definition of assault, if a wife even suspected that her husband's violence might reach unacceptable levels, she could prosecute him. Clearly, some of the women of Augustan London did so, and the violence of which they complained did not always have to be characterized as outrageous. As assault victims, these Westminster wives were more empowered than historians such as Amussen and Hunt have suggested.

Both the pregnant woman and the battered wife who were prosecuting assault were particularly empowered by the court's obligation to protect them. Good husbands, according to the early modern conduct literature, were expected to "be a tower of defence to protect" their wives and children from outside harm.[45] When a husband failed in that duty by correcting his wife too harshly, or when someone else committed a crime against his wife and unborn baby, the courts had to step in and assume the role of the protective patriarch. Courtroom decoration, such as that in the Thetford Guildhall, reminded the presiding officials to "plead the cause of the poor and needy"—those, such as assault victims of "the weaker sex," who required a champion.[46] In a society where men were cast as women's protectors, female assault victims had special, unwritten rights in the eyes of the male Justice of the Peace, which enabled them to convince him to issue a recognizance against their attacker.

Pregnant women prosecuting assaults could take advantage of the English legal tradition that granted special protections to unborn children. Unlike any other crime, those accused of infanticide were presumed guilty until proven innocent, as an attempt to deter people from taking babies' lives.[47] Pregnant women who had been convicted of a capital offense were granted a reprieve until the birth of their baby, and reports abounded of women getting pregnant to try to evade an execution sentence.[48] Misson's travel guide alluded to "a set of wags [in the prison] that . . . are diligent to inform [condemned women] the very moment they come in, that if they are not with child already, they must go to work immediately to be so . . . and so perhaps save their lives."[49] In the French context, historian Stephanie Brown has even argued that condemned women who used the *déclarations de grossesse* (declarations of pregnancy) were empowered because they could then at least "construct the circumstances of their own death and its remembrance."[50] The courts went to great ends to protect fetuses, and pregnancy sometimes granted women special advantages within the English legal system.

Unlike the investigations of pleas of the belly or infanticide, the pregnant women in the Westminster recognizances were victims rather than offenders. Coming to the court as a needy victim seeking retribution instead of a transgressor desiring mercy, the assault prosecutor "bigg with child" was even more powerful. The dozens of pregnant women who prosecuted assault left records of the danger that such attacks posed to both their own health and the health of their babies.[51] Miscarriages were known to be caused by "any blow received on the Belly," and medical opinion held that women who were forced to miscarry could become barren as a result.[52] This special group of assault victims drew upon these extra vulnerabilities to gain the courts' sympathy. In one example outside the eighty-seven in our study, Katherine Winter's recognizance for assault added that the offense had occurred "after fourteen Days lying in by which she reced much damage."[53] Her baby had been born and was presumably healthy, and the only person of concern to the courts here was Winter herself. We should not, of course, lose sight of the fact that pregnancy really *was* traumatic and weakening for women's bodies and that the tales of pain and suffering that these women brought to Westminster JPs were probably very real. What makes their cases empowering is that no other group of assault victims with equally real vulnerabilities (such as the very old or very young, the sick or the infirm) received such consideration from JPs for their special circumstances. The English legal system had a very specific concern for the reproductive health of women, which could work to the latter's advantage.

The same is true for battered wives. Although servants were in a similar position of vulnerability to "correction" from the master of the household, wives received more sympathy than servants from Westminster JPs. Of fifty-one recognizances brought by servants and apprentices against their masters for assault between 1685 and 1720, 61 percent used run-of-the-mill language to characterize the violence. This might seem to suggest that servants enjoyed even more judicial sympathy, because they did not have to show that the physical correction had been "extreme." However, unlike wives, the majority of servants prosecuting relatively minor forms of assault also had to stress their employers' simultaneous violation of contractual obligations.[54] In other words, servants' claims of abuse probably did not receive as much judicial attention as their claims of loss of wages or training.[55] While public and legal condemnation of wife beating arguably increased with the approach of the industrial age, a recent study of the law of master and servant by Douglas Hay revealed a growing tendency to favor the employer through the eighteenth and into the nineteenth century.[56] As prosecutors of relatively commonplace forms of assault, women beaten by their husbands had more power than servants beaten by their employers. Clearly, these women benefited from JPs' desire to protect battered wives and expectant mothers more than any other group of assault victims.

Although they represented themselves as weak yet valued females, these women were simultaneously able to argue that *other* women could be powerful and menacing antagonists. Twenty-seven pregnant women accused female, rather than male, assailants. This is not as high as the proportion of women assaulting other women in regular assaults, but it suggests that pregnancy did not always unite women.[57] The cultural ideals of appropriate motherhood, though gendered, were held by both men and women and were used by women against one another as well as against men. When pregnant women were successful in persuading a JP to bind another woman over for assaulting them, they were defining themselves as wronged and their maternity as legitimate. In this way, pregnancy could be empowering for women.

In certain recognizances, battered wives were also able to define their enemies and co-opt the courts into defining their husbands as passive pawns. In eleven recognizances these wives convinced the justices that their husbands' new lovers had caused the violence. Justice James Butler had a recognizance drawn up on the complaint of Margaret Gross against her husband which stated that he was "deluded and seduced . . . from his family" by Elizabeth Pickering.[58] Several recognizances that charged a husband with assaulting his wife specifically mention his adultery.[59] Adultery per se was not a common law offense, and thus its inclusion in domestic assault recognizances is another example of the triumph of cultural over purely legal concerns.[60] Wives vehemently pursued their husbands' lovers and imbued these rival women with a danger that surpassed that posed by their husbands, often professing themselves to be "in fear" of these women.[61] We might be tempted to think that wives prosecuted rival women only because they had a better chance of being believed. However, the greater number of recognizances against husbands suggests that wives had little trouble convincing the Westminster JPs that their husbands had illegitimately attacked them. Instead, wives made use of the cultural distaste for adultery and brought these tales to JPs when they genuinely believed in these women's guilt over that of their husbands.

Some of these recognizances used terminology that completely reduced the husband's power, simultaneously making the rival female appear even more powerful and conniving. Anne Atkins had to answer Dorothy Pressick for "assaulting her . . . & stricking her sev[era]ll Blowes" but also for "Delewding her Husband to Keep Company with her."[62] Even when the violence came directly from the husband, he was not always the one prosecuted. Elizabeth Gaudott was bound for "persuading" Ann Heydon's husband to beat her "in a Barbarous manner," and Sarah Roach for "causeing" Mary Ross's husband "to assault beate and bruise her."[63] Ellinor Kaliff was also said to have been "making a difference between" Dorcas Young and her husband "& causeing him to assault, beat and abuse her" along with "Insulting and abuseing her" herself.[64] These prosecutions present an interesting gender reversal in which the husband was the passive object who was fought for and was perceived by his wife (and her sympathetic JP) to have been manipulated. That so many more recognizances exist against the husbands themselves, however, casts doubt on the assumption that wives, or the courts, or both, bought into the image of fallen women as evil seducers or simply sought to preserve the marriage by deflecting blame from the real culprit, the husband. Indeed, in some of these cases at least, wives genuinely believed that the lovers had caused the abuse, and they made use of the courts' contempt for adultery to reinforce their prosecution.

To speak of empowerment for women who were victims of assault may seem somewhat perverse. Beneath the vague statements preserved in the recognizances listing the complaints of expectant mothers and wives, there was undoubtedly often excruciating physical pain, emotional agony at the loss of a child, or fear of a husband's unceasing abuse. Nevertheless, historians are left with only the records of the suits they brought in protest—and these provide evidence of empowerment. These records of female prosecution present an image of femininity not often portrayed by historians. These women went before the Westminster justices with tales of victimhood, and they were sufficiently *believed* to generate a record of prosecution. Wives and mothers, together with the JPs, created a record of contemporary judicial and cultural attitudes toward very specific aspects of eighteenth-century femininity.

The latitude in the recognizances indicates that both the Justices of the Peace and the victims who came before them brought extralegal considerations to their suit, revealing the prevalence of social and judicial attitudes that were fairly sympathetic to mothers and wives. Justices recorded victims' pregnancies in assaults, although legal handbooks were vague on exactly what sort of crime these types of assaults constituted, and wives were able to secure recognizances against their husbands for even minor assaults. In both cases the JPs were taking the role of protective patriarch, but the women used this to their advantage, stressing their fragility as childbearers or their weakness as wives. Their prosecutions were reinforced by contemporary medical views on prenatal care, and by eighteenth-century cultural views on the physical and sexual conduct appropriate for a married man.

These women constitute a unique category of female victims. As we have seen in chapter 3, rape victims were not nearly as empowered. These pregnant women and battered wives themselves served to *dis*empower other women by accusing them of assault. However, when battered women secured a JP's cooperation in issuing a recognizance against their husband's lover for beating them, they succeeded in emasculating their husbands, depicting them as mere pawns of their female lovers. Pregnant women and battered wives prosecuting assault were not opposing contemporary attitudes to appropriate feminine behavior, yet by stressing their own special identity as mothers or their vulnerability as wives, they were able to gain a narrow margin of power before the courts.

Part Two
Perpetrators

5

Forms of Petty Violence: *The Nature and Circumstances of Masculine and Feminine Assaults*

Now that we know that victims persistently brought assailants to court, we can explore the types of petty violence that were being prosecuted in early-eighteenth-century London. This chapter examines violence as a sort of physical language, recognizing that a variety of factors, such as gender and culture, have an impact on the form an assault will take in its particular historical context. While the subsequent two chapters will investigate more politically motivated petty violence, this chapter will look at *all* of the assault prosecutions to discern more general patterns. We will observe what physical languages were available to assailants in the period 1680–1720 and whether gender had an impact on the forms of violence assailants used. The locations and causes of assaults are also a part of their physical language, and we will explore whether gender was a factor here as well.

Alexandra Shepard has insightfully pointed out the difference between violence and what she calls "violation."[1] In our modern society almost all violence is perceived as violation, but in early modern England certain forms of physical aggression were socially acceptable. Husbands, parents, masters, mistresses, and the state used violence daily to chastise and correct errant wives, children, servants, or citizens, and this "violence" would not have been viewed as violation in most cases.[2] For violence to become violation, Shepard argues, it had to exceed the boundaries in some way—because of the gender or status of the perpetrator in contrast to that of the victim or because of the assault's excessive force. Only those forms of petty violence that constitute "violation," then, would be prosecuted as assault. At the same time, victims had to bring a *plausible* case before the JPs, so they also had to describe assaults that fell within appropriate forms of misbehavior. For example, of the 7,234 assault recognizances between 1685 and 1720, there are only *two* in which a husband had accused his wife. Most husbands knew they had a lesser chance of being believed than their wives bringing a similar tale of spousal abuse. We must remember, then, that this chapter is discussing only the petty violence that was prosecuted. Each recognizance reveals an episode of violence that the victim perceived as violation—but a form of violation that fell within particular norms. Assault victims may have been motivated by anger or by fear of future violence, but they all would have had to construct a believable account—making use of popular notions of gender—in order to prosecute their case. Laws reinforced norms of *mis*behavior as well as behavior, and we are investigating the gendered forms of violent misbehavior.

One of the most significant contributions of this chapter is in revealing women's perceived capability for violence. Historians of nineteenth-century violence have characterized violence as distinctly masculine.[3] Shani D'Cruze admits that women employed violence but argues that, unlike for men, violence did not "have specific resonances for their identities as" women.[4] Many more women were prosecuted for violent crime in the early eighteenth century, however, and we simply cannot assume that they were all transcending their gender to act in masculine ways.[5] This chapter will argue instead that, if we look at early-eighteenth-century petty violence through the eyes of its contemporaries, we will see that much of it was *ungendered*. We established in previous chapters that the Justices of the Peace had a great deal of freedom in describing the offenses in recognizances and that the record was at least as much the product of the victims' accounts of the acts against them as it was of JPs' concern for appropriate legal terminologies. If recognizances are evidence of popular perceptions of misbehavior, the fact that they used the same descriptions for assaults by men as they did for assaults by women shows that petty violence was perceived as a tool for women as well as men. Recording officials did not make a point of describing female assailants as "barbarous" or "inhuman," though such terms were available to them.[6] By characterizing violence as masculine, we would be forced to dismiss women's violence. By showing how much of the physical language of assault was ungendered, we can also find the few significant forms of petty violence that were masculine—and those that were distinctly feminine. *One-third* of all of those bound over for assault in the City of Westminster were women, meaning that JPs and victims believed that female violence was prevalent and worth prosecuting.

The first section highlights the most basic forms of assault. It asks whether assailants were described as kicking or scratching their victims, whether they had weapons, or whether they issued threats. In many cases men and women assaulted in similar forms, though their violence differed in a few significant ways. The same is true of the second section, which examines the special category of assaults whose specific goal was to humiliate their victim. Humiliation tactics tended to involve skirt lifting if the victim was female or dewigging if the victim was a gentleman, but both male and female victims could have their noses cut, be drenched with urine, or be subjected to a host of other indignities. The final two sections investigate the broader contexts of these assaults. The records are examined to discern whether particular parts of the city were considered more dangerous than other parts. It shows that women were not the only ones viewed with suspicion when they were out after dark. Men, too, could be subject to interrogation and arrest for being out at night, and both male and female assailants could be perceived as more dangerous when they assaulted after dark or in the theatre district. Assaults resulted from a wide variety of causes, but many were due to a dispute over money, to neighborhood tensions, or to drunkenness. These causes were equally plausible whether the assailant was masculine or feminine. However, men were more prone to petty violence during street sport. Many of the languages of petty violence were available to male and female assailants, and these languages were understood and prosecuted by their victims with the court's assent.

When the records are broken down into five-year periods, feminine assaults almost always comprise one-third of the total (table 5.1). The proportion of women dropped by 10 percent between 1696 and 1700. The anxiety surrounding an influx of unemployed soldiers with the end of the Nine Years War in 1697 may have caused a disproportionately high number of men to be brought before the courts for assault during this time, but by the end of our period the proportion of women accused of assault had climbed to even more than one-third.[7] Clearly, women were considered capable of a significant degree of physical aggression.

Eight-hundred fifty assaults were characterized as "violent"—recognizances binding people over for "violently" assaulting their victims.[8] Of these, the proportion of female defendants is only 4 percent lower than that of the male defendants (table 5.2). At first glance it may seem as if women were not as violent as men but were rather subjected to a much "easier" double standard in assault prosecution. In other words, JPs and victims might

Table 5.1
Total Number of Assailants: Breakdown of Defendants by Gender over Time

Time*	Female Defendants	Male Defendants	Total	Females as % of Total
Apr 1685–Jul 1690	292	617	909	32
Oct 1690–Oct 1695	281	525	806	35
Jan 1696–Oct 1700	242	720	962	25
Jan 1701–Oct 1705	253	564	817	31
Jan 1706–Oct 1710	265	560	825	32
Jan 1711–Oct 1715	380	837	1217	31
Jan 1716–Oct 1720	706	1232	1938	36

Note: Recognizances to prosecute assault have not been included.
*This column is broken down into seven periods of exactly twenty sessions each, corresponding roughly with every five years. Note that rather than four there are only two extant sessions for 1689 (27 Jun and 2 Oct) and three for 1693 (9 Jan, 19 Apr, and 4 Oct).

have considered a kick, for example, as "a violent assault" when it came from a woman but the same sort of kick as simply "an assault" when it came from a man. However, if this were the case, other, more suggestively evaluative words such as *barbarous* or *inhuman* would also have been frequently employed to describe women's assaults. Men's assaults were just as likely to be characterized as barbarous or inhuman, however, so the significant proportion of women "assaulting violently" means that the court really did see this feminine aggression as similarly dangerous to men's.[9] Novelist Henry Fielding, a Westminster JP shortly after this period, appears to have accepted violence as a female characteristic, judging the only gender differences to be in tactic rather than in propensity to fight. According to Fielding, "It is lucky for the Women, that the Seat of the Fistycuff War is not the same for them as among Men; . . . when they [women] go forth to Battle, . . . they never so far forget,

Table 5.2
Those Accused of Assaulting "Violently": Breakdown of Defendants by Gender

Defendants*	Violent	Total	%
Female	200	2038	10
Male	650	4683	14

Note: Recognizances to prosecute assault have not been included.
*Assault recognizances where there were multiple defendants both male AND female have not been included.

as to assail the Bosoms of each other; where a few Blows would be fatal to most of them," concentrating instead, he avers, on punching their opponents in the nose.[10] If women's actions had been measured in vastly different ways by court officials, the descriptive language surrounding them would probably have been more gendered as well, and words such as *violently* and *barbarously* would have appeared in much more gender-specific contexts.

Feminine assaults could also be seen to damage the victim only 10 percent less than masculine assaults according to the recognizances. Table 5.3 measures the proportion of recognizances for male and female defendants where the victim of the assault was said to be in danger of his or her life; was bleeding, wounded, or cut; or was made ill or harmed in any other of a vast range of ways. In recording such damage, the JPs and their clerks were influenced by more than purely legal considerations. The closest legal imperative affecting the wording of recognizances in such cases was the instruction that JPs ask victims to "swear that you are in Fear of your life, or of some bodily Hurt to be done, or to be procured to be done to you by" the defendant.[11] However, this rule applied only when victims were binding the defendant to keep the peace toward them. In other words, if victims wanted "to swear the peace" against their assailants, they had to, by law, also swear that their assailants had inflicted lasting emotional, if not physical, damage. This rule could then mean that the JPs who were recording damage were influenced less by the appearance of a visibly wounded victim than by blind application of the rules. In fact, however, the rules rarely applied because many recognizances mentioning damage bound the defendant only to appear and answer the charges and did not mention his or her keeping the peace toward the victim. Thus, JPs were clearly influenced by victims who convincingly demonstrated—either by their bloodied appearance or by their tearful testimony—that the assault had been particularly damaging. JPs and prosecutors saw female

Table 5.3
Those Accused of Inflicting Damage: Breakdown of Defendants by Gender

Defendants*	Inflicting Damage	Total	%
Female	420	2038	21
Male	1435	4683	31

Note: Recognizances to prosecute assault have not been included.
*Assault recognizances where there were multiple defendants both male AND female have not been included.

assailants as capable of inflicting serious damage, though men were considered even more likely to wound their victims.

In many ways, then, petty violence does not seem to have been distinctly gendered. Men assaulted in much greater numbers, according to these records, but when women *did* assault, they were seen to be almost as violent and as dangerous as male assailants. The strongest gender divisions appear in their choice of victims (table 5.4). Both male and female defendants tended to assault victims of their own gender, but women targeted other women to an even greater degree. This suggests two possibilities: either men were often too embarrassed to bring assault prosecutions against women who attacked them, or women simply did not generally assault men. Either way, it is safe to suggest that attacking men was not as feminine a form of misbehavior as attacking other women.

The physical forms of attack were somewhat gendered according to the recognizances. Compared to male assailants, women used their hands more than their feet. Almost one-quarter of all of the assaults by "striking" had female defendants.[12] In contrast, only one-eighth of all of those accused of "kicking" were women.[13] According to the *Oxford English Dictionary (OED),* "striking" had the same meaning as it does today, usually implying blows using the arms or hands, and the meaning of "kicking" has always indicated assaults by the feet.[14] Interestingly, face slapping, a recognized form of insult in early modern Europe, does not appear to be a popular practice in England, being entirely absent from the descriptions in the assault recognizances.[15] Women may have been less inclined to use their legs because they were trapped under layers of petticoats, and actions which might expose the leg to view were much less appropriate to feminine behavior than to masculine, though like most other forms of etiquette, this social dictum was more easily indulged by gentry women.[16] Invariably involving the use of one's foot, kicking showed

Table 5.4
Gender of Assailant vs. Gender of Complainant-Victim: Number of Recognizances

	Female Victim*	%	Male Victim*	%	Male and Female Victims*	%	Total (*n* =)
Female** Assailants	1492	77	372	19	62	3	1926
Male** Assailants	1387	34	2453	61	203	5	4043

Note: Recognizances to prosecute assault have not been included. The figures show the number of recognizances, not the number of complainants; the totals would be slightly higher because some recognizances named more than one complainant.
*Cases where the recognizance was clearly brought by the complainant on behalf of another individual who was the actual victim have been excluded.
**Assault recognizances where there were multiple defendants both male AND female have been excluded.

more contempt on the part of the assailant for his or her victim. For example, one gentleman kicked Francis Key, matching this physical insult with a verbal one by calling Key "a popish priest."[17] Women did not kick as often, but kicking held the same meaning for them as well. Ann Clond kicked John Foresight along with "spitting in his face & also . . . scandalizeing & aspersing false things of him the said John Foresight."[18] Elizabeth Henly kicked Mary Lithgol "in the face & other parts whereby she is very much disabled."[19] Kicking, though occasionally part of the physical language of assault for women, was reported more frequently for male assailants, while the proportion of women allegedly "striking" their victims is much higher. Assaulting with the upper body was considered a more appropriate form for feminine violence.

Robert Darnton has already shown the strong folklore connection between early modern femininity and cats, and some feminine assaults did have particularly feline qualities.[20] Though very few recognizances mentioned clawing, spitting, and biting at all, when they did, they tended to bind female perpetrators. Though one man assaulted a gentleman by "scratching him in the face," the remaining six recognizances bound women for using their nails on their victims.[21] Only 27 percent of the thirty recognizances for spitting bound male defendants. Compared to their overall participation in assaults, women were much more likely to be recorded as spitting at their victim than men. John Camden and his wife Dinah were bound to answer an assault on Jane Garten, and it was Dinah specifically who was described as "spitting in her face, beating upon her head & tearing her head cloths in pieces."[22] Mary Maccommow was accused of assaulting another woman, "spitting in her face and putting her fingers in her eyes."[23] Margaret Wilden, a coffeehouse keeper, allegedly spit upon Judith Gyles as she was raising the mob on her.[24] Of a total of fourteen incidents of "biting" where the gender of the defendant can be determined, four were clearly binding women. This number is slightly less than one-third, so biting cannot be shown to be as exclusively feminine a language of assault as scratching or spitting. In principle, early modern men were expected to use their teeth in battle, though, in practice, biting—like scratching—was considered unmanly.[25] Thus biting was far from exclusively masculine. Alice Stedman was charged with "making a Rout & Disturbance" at a man's house and "assaulting him and biting his thumb."[26] One woman assaulted another by "biteing her by the finger."[27] Elizabeth French was recorded as "assaulting, beating, bruising and biting," and Elizabeth Rawlings of "assaulting and biteing [Mary Rawlings'] arme, whereof she is disabled to follow her business."[28] Two other women, Katherine and Elizabeth Birt, were bound with Nicholas Palmyre for "assaulting & beating [Wm Griffith] in a Riotous Manner and biteing him by the *Legg*."[29] Short of arching their backs, by spitting, biting, and clawing their victims, women reinforced the early modern association between feminine and feline qualities.

While women were relying on their teeth and nails, men were reaching for their swords in many assaults. When a weapon has been mentioned in an assault recognizance, clear patterns emerge depending on the gender of the defendant. Table 5.5 shows the slightly smaller likelihood of women to be depicted with a weapon in comparison with men. Prosecutors and justices clearly considered a weaponless woman a worthy opponent, sufficiently strong and menacing to merit an assault charge.

Greater gender differences emerge when the data are broken down into *types* of weapons. In contrast to female defendants, almost 60 percent of the men accused of assault with a weapon used traditional arms (table 5.6). Of those men, 91 percent were using swords. Possession and use of swords were legally restricted to gentlemen.[30] Only 8 percent of the women using weapons were described as having conventional arms. Women appear more inclined to

Table 5.5
Total Weapons Named in Assault: Breakdown of Defendants by Gender

Defendants*	With Weapon	Total	%
Female	80	2038	4
Male	327	4683	7

Note: Recognizances to prosecute assault have not been included.
*Assault recognizances where there were multiple defendants both male AND female have not been included.

have used whatever they could get their hands on. In 1716 Rachell Bliss was described as stabbing with scissors, a chisel, and a knife; and hitting with a quart pot, a hand brush, and an iron poker.[31] Elizabeth Burn was accused of using the "iron pinn of a window," and Catherine Bach the "Barr of a Doore."[32] Not surprisingly perhaps, women were proportionately far more likely than men to use objects associated with food preparation and cleaning, such as pots, dishes, and brooms (table 5.6). Even in the general category of knives, some recognizances bear additional description to place the weapon in the kitchen or scullery. One woman was described with a "chopping knife," and another with a "cheese knife."[33] Anne Quinton was accused of striking her male victim with "a Ladle full of Scalding greese."[34] This may overemphasize the connection between women and domesticity, however. In early modern London, workshop was intertwined with home, and completely separate spheres were largely unserviceable for most of the middling and lower classes.[35] Gabriel Pilkington, a pastry cook, allegedly used his rolling pin, "striking [his victim] on the face and neck . . . so that he went in danger of his life."[36] John Richards had his male assailant bound for "assaulting of him by pushing a broome in his face," while Susan Robertson's recognizance listed a "hammer" as her weapon.[37] In the language of the recognizances, resort to a weapon was more a masculine action, and women tended to use domestic objects. However, swords or hammers were not beyond their grasp; nor were brooms and rolling pins inconceivable objects to be wielded by male assailants.

In addition to physical weapons, verbal weapons could also be launched at victims, and we might expect women to have a much stronger role in this form of assault, given Laura Gowing and Tim Meldrum's work on defamation in early modern London.[38] In fact, the proportion of men issuing threats was almost equal to that of women (table 5.7).

Table 5.6

Types of Weapons Named in Assault: Breakdown of Defendants by Gender

Type of Weapon	Female Defendants with Weapons*	Male Defendants with Weapons*	% of Total Females with Weapons	% of Total Males with Weapons
Traditional arms[a]	7	201	8	59
Knife	19	20	22	6
Food prep'n tools[b]	13	15	15	4
Candlestick &/or candle	9	6	11	2
Cleaning tools[c]	7	3	8	1
Stone(s)	4	4	5	1
Firetending tools[d]	4	9	5	3
Building tools[e]	3	9	4	3
Driving tools[f]	0	13	0	4
Stick/club/stake	3	18	4	5
Pattens[g]	3	0	4	0
Cane	1	16	1	5
Tobacco pipe	0	5	0	1
Glass bottle	0	4	0	1
Misc.[h]	12	20	14	6
Total**	85	343		

Note: Recognizances to prosecute assault have not been included.

*Assault recognizances where there were multiple defendants both male AND female have not been included.

**These totals are of ALL types of weapons used. Totals will be larger than the sum of the figures in table 5.5 because some defendants were listed as using more than one weapon.

[a]Sword, gun/pistol/musket, bayonet, cudgel, brickbat (contemporary term for broken pieces of brick used as projectiles).

[b]Rolling pin, pot (pint/quart/pewter), dish/mug/earthenware, fork, ladle, cleaver.

[c]Smoothing iron, broom/mop/broomstick/mopstaff, water tub.

[d]Spit, fireshovel, bellows, poker, shovelful of coal.

[e]Saw, mallet, hammer, trowel, chisel, adze.

[f]Whip, pole/coachpole/chairpole, vehicle (coach/cart).

[g]Clog or overshoe to keep the wearer out of the mud.

[h]Objects named in only two or fewer recognizances for both male and female categories: pail, basket, pair of shears/scissors, stool/chair, iron pin, pump handle, pricking instrument, handbrush, church keys, porter's knot, brick case, whalebone, shovel, pitchfork, chamber pot, bar of a door, nine pin

Table 5.7
Total Assaults with Threats: Breakdown of Defendants by Gender

Defendants*	Threatening	Total	%
Female	192	2038	9
Male	371	4683	8

Note: Recognizances to prosecute assault have not been included.
*Assault recognizances where there were multiple defendants both male AND female have not been included.

Female assailants' threats could also be as bloodthirsty as male assailants' threats. Threats against the victim's life or threats of bodily harm appeared in similar proportions for both male and female defendants, and both were far less likely to resort to the more innocuous threat of property damage (table 5.8). Men were more likely than women to threaten to "stabb," "stick with a sword," or shoot their victims, but this is probably the result of weapons such as swords and pistols being gendered male. Gore was ungendered, however, and feminine assailants possessed an arsenal of grisly imagery equal to anything their male counterparts could invent. One woman was said to have assured the complainant she would "pull out her eyes," another threatened to "run a knife down [her victim's] throate," and two other recognizances recorded female defendants as each desiring "to wash her hands in her [victim's] harts blood."[39] Twelve recognizances at diverse times for threats involving bashing, dashing, or beating out their victims' brains were equally divided between six female and six male defendants, though such language was favored in a slightly greater proportion of the female threats as a whole (table 5.8). Elizabeth Furnell reportedly assaulted a man and threatened to "have his blood," and a man who had Elizabeth Taylor bound for striking him on his head also accused her of pledging "to doe the same to his wife."[40] The feminine assailant's imagination was equally capable as the masculine of conjuring gory fates for victims, when threats accompanied assaults.

A small but significant group of the assaults described in the recognizances were primarily intended to humiliate, rather than physically harm, their victims. Assailants particularly attacked women by tearing their clothes and exposing their breasts or genitalia in order to question their sexual respectability.

Table 5.8

Types of Threats with Assault: Breakdown of Defendants by Gender

Type of Threat[a]	By Female Defendant[b]	By Male Defendant[b]	% of Total Females Threatening	% of Total Males Threatening
Life	39	99	20	27
Murther	30	71	16	19
Cut Throat	2	3	1	1
Have Blood	3	2	2	1
Stabb/Stick with a Sword	3	14	2	4
Shoot	0	8	0	2
Injury to Brains	6	6	3	2
Further bodily harm/mischief	33	44	17	12
Damage to property	4	5	2	1
Unspecified[c]	48	97	25	26
Misc.	24	22	13	6
Total	192	371		

Note: Recognizances to prosecute assault have not been included.
[a]Includes threats to victims AND associates (relatives or employers) of victims.
[b]Assault recognizances where there were multiple defendants both male AND female have not been included.
[c]Refers to recognizances listing only that the assailant "threatened."

Recognizances that mention damage to clothing were fairly numerous and were overwhelmingly brought by female victims against other women (table 5.9). We must, of course, take into account the likelihood that much of the damage to clothing was inadvertent and was not part of a sexual humiliation ritual.[41] Unlike today, clothing was a significant piece of property to eighteenth-century Londoners, and victims often mentioned damage to clothing because of the economic loss it represented. Also, in a pitched battle it would be natural for clothing to become ripped and headgear to be thrown off. However, in several assaults the damage to clothing was not an inadvertent outcome, and the sexu-

Table 5.9
Assaults with Loss/Damage to Clothing: Gender of Complainants vs. Gender of Defendants

Defendants**	Female Victim*	Male Victim*	Male and Female Victims*
Female	103	15	2
Male	65	36	4

Note: Recognizances to prosecute assault have not been included.
*Cases where the recognizance was clearly brought by the complainant on behalf of another individual who was the actual victim have been excluded.
**Assault recognizances where there were multiple defendants both male AND female have been excluded.

al element was clear. For example, "Mrs Sydney Colhone single woman of good repute," said that two women had purposely torn her clothes while "calling her Bitch and whore, etc, to the loss of her Reputation, etc."[42] Ann Barber assaulted and beat Sarah Mathews and also threw "her Coats over her head."[43] Women did not wear underwear beneath their petticoats in the early eighteenth century, so Barber, by displaying Mathews' genitals, symbolically questioned her respectability. A mother and daughter were called "Bitch Baw'd and many other vile names" while their clothing was torn in the middle of the street in 1717.[44] Clearly, in some attacks on women, assailants purposely tore their clothing or lifted their skirts in order to humiliate them and question their sexual respectability. When men were attacked in this form, the sexual element is not as clear. Where female complainants describe being stripped or having their dresses lifted, there are no recognizances where a man was stripped below the waist or had his breeches torn.[45]

If the goal of the assault was to humiliate a *male* victim, it was better to expose his bald head than his genitalia. Perukes and periwigs were a mark of social class, but they also symbolized their owner's masculinity. Male honor was associated with the head in early modern Europe, whether it was "bowed, bared, touched, or cut off," and exposing the shaved heads men kept hidden under their wigs would have left them feeling naked and vulnerable.[46] *A Scene from "The Careless Husband"* (figure 5.1) shows how the husband's wiglessness symbolized his exposure and humiliation in being caught by his wife after an obvious infidelity with her maid.[47] Lady Easy, his selfless and devoted wife, covers his head to hide his disgrace. Assailants recognized the shame a man could feel when bereft of his wig. One woman was accused of

Figure 5.1
Philip Mercier, *A Scene from "The Careless Husband,"* 1738 (oil on canvas, 101.6 by 127.0 cm). York Museums Trust (York Art Gallery).

"pulling off [the complainant's] crevate & perriwigge in a violent manner," another woman allegedly attacked two men and took "away their Hatts and perruques," and a man was bound by a mercer for assaulting him "in the street in the night, whereby he lost his hatt and periwigg."[48] We must remember that perukes and periwigs were valuable property, and assailants may have removed them because they were *stealing* them, not because they particularly wanted to see their victim shamed and bald. In at least one case, however, it is very clear that shame was the only goal.[49] Mary Houghor and Jane Pollard removed John Buriously's "hatt and periwig" and deliberately threw them "into the Fire."[50] There could be no other benefit served to these women than the satisfaction of destroying Buriously's expensive property and seeing him hatless and wigless. This form of assault is very much a part of its historical context; in the seventeenth century when wig wearing was not yet the fashion, hat removal or hair and beard pulling were the preferred tactics.[51] If one wished to disgrace a gentleman in the early eighteenth century, however, one only had to remove his wig and expose his shaved head to public view.

Other forms of humiliation were less gendered. Both men and women might be ducked, splashed, or showered with water by assailants. Drenched, with clothes clinging in a bedraggled fashion, victims of such assaults would have felt the injury to their dignity far more keenly than anything water could do to their bodies. Susanna Furz flung water on Alice James while "calling her bitch and other opprobrious names."[52] John Maddox raised a mob upon Hannah Bowers in the street and flung water on her, and Alice Nevill threw water at Samuel Jones "twice in his face in the Streete."[53] Just as those found guilty of certain crimes could be ducked or "cucked" by the state, private citizens punished their victims by dunking.[54] Mary Singleton would have drawn her female victim "through a horsepond" if she had not been rescued, and Tom Taylor, caught pickpocketing, was turned over to the mob who "unmercifully pumped him and ducked him in a horsepond."[55] The horsepond, as the name suggests, was a pond from which horses could drink, but it was also, according to the *OED*, a "proverbial . . . ducking-place for obnoxious persons." Water was a widely recognized tool of humiliation and punishment and was used by male and female assailants on their victims of both genders.

Though London water was anything but clean, there were even dirtier projectiles in eighteenth-century assailants' arsenal of humiliation. With privies and chamber pots in full and ready supply, it is not surprising that they were employed against enemies. As the ones who emptied the night's excretions, women used these weapons more than men. Elizabeth Wells threw "a pisspott upon" a woman (along with throwing "salt in her eyes & spitting in her face"), and another woman flung "a Chamber pott and water in it" on her victim.[56] After she had stolen Abram Edwards's breeches, Sarah Squibb replaced the money from his pocket with human feces and returned the breeches to his room."[57] A surgeon's wife was bound for "tearing [her victim's] hood, assaulting & throwing of fowle water upon her."[58] James Farr suggested that people probably hurled such missiles at their enemies because "the very uselessness of garbage and household wastes . . . symbolically reinforced the association of the valueless with the dishonorable."[59] Male assailants did not use chamber pots, but they could still ensure that their victims were dishonored by filth. A plasterer seized a gardener's wife "and push[ed] her into the mud," and Josia Blake, a baker, was bound for "throwing dirt" at his victim.[60] Though the early modern period is notorious for its aversion to bathing, historian Sara Matthews Grieco stressed that this was not synonymous with an aversion to cleanliness. In fact, she argued, even before bathing came back into vogue in the mid–eighteenth century, "a clean appearance was a guarantee of moral probity and social standing."[61] Prosecutors before the Westminster Quarter Sessions sought retribution for attacks that had made them appear unclean, both physically and morally.

The use of unpleasant missiles is also connected to London's public life. London crowds demonstrated their scorn for and disapproval of convicted prisoners by pelting them with rubbish. In a 1716 poem John Gay described a culprit in the pillory "elevated o'er the gaping croud" who was hit with "turnips, and half-hatch'd Eggs (a mingled show'r)."[62] John Beattie refers to accounts of Southwark men in the pillory being bombarded with sticks, stones, and dirt by the derisive crowd.[63] People seem to have been more sympathetic to convicts on their long procession to Tyburn, but when they were to be hanged for the more despicable crimes, crowds were known to throw mud and stones.[64] These actions seem to have been played out in smaller theatres of interpersonal conflict—as when three women were bound for "riotously assaulting beating and bruising [another woman], flinging dirt upon her in the public market, and raiseing a great tumoult of people about her whereby she was in danger of her life."[65] Everyone—assailants, observers, and victims—associated the pelting of rubbish with the mockery accorded prisoners at the pillory or gallows, and it was a prominent tool in the assaults involving humiliation.

One could also shame one's victims by disfiguring their noses.[66] The nose had many symbolic associations in early modern culture. Syphilis was popularly known to cause nasal disfigurement, and nose slitting was a state punishment for certain crimes.[67] In 1731 *Fog's Weekly Journal* described an execution for forgery where "the hangman . . . with a pair of scissors, slit both nostrils" of a convict in the pillory.[68] Having one's nose slit meant a permanent and highly visible deformity because noses were one of the most exposed parts of the body, giving them great power to humiliate.[69] Ann Jones's nose was a special target for Mary Morgan, who was bound for wounding it with her iron patten.[70] Audrian Scroop "caught [a man] by the nose with his teeth" in a tavern brawl, and two men assaulted a third by removing "a piece of his nose."[71] Religious hatreds prompted one gentleman to use the language of nasal disfigurement. Fulke Grosvenor, a non-Juror, "slitt" Susannah Hayes' nose while "calling her Low Church Presbiterian Bitch & raising a mobb upon her."[72] At a trial in the Old Bailey, John Francis prosecuted Michael Dobson for an attack that bore many of the elements of humiliation seen in the assault recognizances, including nasal injury. According to Francis's testimony, Dobson "came with a drawn sword and . . . cut him on the Nose, took his Wig, and turn'd him out" of his home.[73] Whether for its association with illicit sex or convicted felons, the injured nose symbolized humiliation and seems to have been used in several assaults for such a purpose.

In recent decades historians have become fascinated with the idea of internal notions of temporal and geographic space.[74] Rather than simply representing the backdrop for the more prominent historical "event," space has taken on a significance of its own. Closely connected with discourse on modernity, these analyses link urban spaces with gender and class, showing how, as modern institutions developed, an ideology of subtle self-constraint developed simultaneously and jointly. According to Judith Walkowitz, for example, respectable middle-class women of nineteenth-century London "developed personal maps and proscribed zones to organize their walks around the West End" in order to avoid harassment from men, who enjoyed much broader access to the city.[75] Almost all of these spatially focused histories describe the new significance of space in the modern world, but space also held significance in the *pre*modern world, and this section will explore early modern perceptions of space. Victims and law officials must have found space to be a factor in certain assaults, as the place of the assault was mentioned in 415 recognizances, and the time in which it occurred was mentioned in 115. Contemporary laws made place and time a significant factor in particular crimes, which both reflected and reinforced popular norms.[76] When specific places or times were recounted in recognizances, they sometimes meant that prosecutors and JPs felt that the location added to the significance of the assault. Put simply: certain places and times were more dangerous than others.

The highway was a very dangerous space in early-eighteenth-century London. Early modern travelers were advised to avoid the highways and take instead the "petty By-roads" in order to avoid violent robbery by a highwayman.[77] Though a "house" or "street" was the location most often recorded in the assault recognizances, the highway was mentioned more often than any other specific location, such as a market, park, or workshop, and the attacks on the highway were overwhelmingly perpetrated by men (table 5.10). Thus, we can see the highway as a place imbued with an especially masculine form of danger. The highwayman was seen as a sort of genteel rogue. Legends of Dick Turpin, one of the most famous highwaymen, recounted his gallantly refusing to rob "pretty girls" or to take sentimental objects (in this case a mourning ring) from his victims.[78] Highwaymen who did not embody this chivalrous form of masculinity would probably have been judged more

Table 5.10
Place of Assaults: Gender of Complainants vs. Gender of Defendants

	Female Defendant*			Male Defendant*		
	Female Complainant	Male Complainant	Mixed	Female Complainant	Male Complainant	Mixed
"Private" home[a]	15	11	4	37	51	14
Street	19	8	4	40	73	12
Shop/workshop	6	1	0	4	6	2
Market	4	2	1	2	7	0
Highway	0	0	1	5	14	3
Park/field	1	0	0	2	5	0
Outside door[b]	6	6	3	6	8	3
Misc.[c]	4	6	0	1	18	2

Notes: Recognizances to prosecute assault have not been included. Cases where the recognizance was clearly brought by the complainant on behalf of another individual who was the actual victim have been excluded.
*Assault recognizances where there were multiple defendants both male AND female have not been included.
[a]Where "quarters" or a "house" belonging to a particular individual have been specified.
[b]Where recognizance describes assault as occurring "outside" or "about" an individual's "house" or "door."
[c]Recognizance gives only the name of the parish or only vague descriptions (such as "near" particular places)—anything that cannot easily be categorized as one of the above.

harshly. Officials noted that John Axton treated his victim especially "uncivilly" when he assaulted her on the highway and violently prevented her husband from rescuing her.[79] The very assumption that Axton could have behaved more civilly was probably informed by these popular images of genteel highwaymen. The highway was not exclusively male space, but the *dangers* of the highway were masculine, and the potential for violence increased if these male attackers did not adhere to certain masculine ideals.

Just as those transgressing masculine ideals made the highways seem more dangerous, those transgressing feminine ideals made certain streets and lanes seem more dangerous in early modern London. The parts of the city associated with "fallen women" were considered dangerous in popular mentality. Many recognizances mentioning a location described it only as "the street," suggesting that the location was significant to the assault only for its public nature, but occasionally specific streets were named in the recognizance. The theatre district, the Strand, and Drury Lane were explicitly noted in thirteen recognizances, more than half of those that mentioned streets by name.[80] The "mazy Courts, and dark Abodes" of Drury Lane were notorious as the "guileful Paths" of "Harlots," who were also known to ply their trade in the surrounding theatre district and on the Strand.[81] Prostitutes held many attractions for their male clients, but they also evoked danger: male clients felt vulnerable to venereal disease or robbery when they had transactions with London whores. In the context of assault, prostitutes were threatening not only for their own violence but also for the potential violence of the many lascivious men they attracted. Normal rules of civil conduct could not be expected in these dark and dangerous alleys. Two constables on night patrol in the Strand were assaulted and wounded by Evan Hughes.[82] In a "mobb neare the Playhouse in Drury Lane," Ann Uttim accused Walter Watkins of assaulting her and tearing her headclothes, and she herself was bound on the same day by John Robinson for "assaulting and stabbing him in the shoulder neare the Playhouse."[83] When one ventured into the fleshpots of Drury Lane and the theatre district, danger was omnipresent.

Whether in Drury Lane or otherwise, all women out after dark risked being arrested for prostitution, making the night a very significant temporal space in the early eighteenth century. The law against "nightwalking" targeted those who "sleep in the day and walk in the night, . . . and such as might haunt any house suspected of bawdery, or use suspicious company, or committ other outrages or misdemeanours."[84] In practice, this legislation tended to confine women much more than men and assumed that their very presence out-of-doors made them prostitutes. The record of a thirteen-year-old girl's charge of rape against James Peirson in 1707 reveals the situation facing women after the sun had set:

> [A]bout the hours of twelve and one in this morning a stranger who calld his name James Peirson came to this Informant she sitting upon a pair of staires and being afraid of the watch being a late hour the said James Peirson told her he would take Care of her and secure her from the watch [if] she would suffer him to lay upon her.[85]

By being caught out-of-doors at night, regardless of the circumstances, women brought their respectability into question and were vulnerable to sexual predators. However, the recognizances for assault suggest that men were not entirely exempt from these temporal constraints.[86] The recognizances that mention that the assault had occurred at night, or those that used particular-

Table 5.11
Time of Assaults: Gender of Complainants vs. Gender of Defendants

	Female Defendant*			Male Defendant*		
	Female Complainants	Male Complainants	Mixed	Female Complainants	Male Complainants	Mixed
"Night"	1	2	0	13	48	2
Early morning[a]	0	0	0	0	9	1
Late evening[a]	0	0	0	3	4	1
Evaluative[b]	2	1	0	2	18	1
"Sabbath"	0	0	0	0	5	2

Note: Recognizances to prosecute assault have not been included. Cases where the recognizance was clearly brought by the complainant on behalf of another individual who was the actual victim have been excluded.
*Assault recognizances where there were multiple defendants both male AND female have not been included.
[a]Recognizances that list a specific time.
[b]Recognizances that do not list a specific time but instead employ evaluative terminology, such as "very early/late," "in the dead of night," "unreasonable hour," etc.

ly evaluative language, overwhelmingly bound male assailants (table 5.11). Joseph Powell was accused of "being a Loose Idle disorderly person taken at an unseasonable time of night" in his recognizance for assault.[87] A constable of St. Margaret's Parish brought one man before a Westminster JP for an assault "in the dead time of the night," and Isaac Green was bound for assaulting a man "at an undue time of night."[88] The Middlesex Sessions papers recount an event after an "Outcry" and a "hubub" in James Street Covent Garden "about tenn of the Clock," when the parish Constable felt it his duty to search and examine all of the men he found in the dark street.[89] He "seized" Richard Jenkins and Samuell Eades who refused to sign statements about what they were doing in Covent Garden at night.[90] Eades and Jenkins reveal the way in which men could face official intervention when they moved about the streets at night. Though lower-class women out after dark probably tended to be more often suspect, the use of evaluative language in the recognizances for assault shows that middling men were also not impervious to temporal constraints.

The commercial areas, the workshops, marketplaces, and taverns of the metropolis, were also sites of violence. Along with churches, streets, and highways, commercial space would seem to be public space. This was not necessarily true in the minds of Augustan Londoners, however. Many shopkeepers or public housekeepers lived and ran their business under the same roof.[91] The line between shop and private dwelling in early-eighteenth-century London was not as firm as it later became, as seen in the 1716 recognizance for an assault that describes the defendant "comeing to her house" where she claimed to have "her customers," who were assaulted along with herself.[92] Nevertheless, many assaults occurring in Westminster taverns and markets may have been motivated by a desire to *publicly* air grievances. Many disputes between men began over an insult shouted in the tavern. John Wincles was "violently assault[ed]" and "knock[ed] downe twice at the Crowne Ale house," and "the Dogg Tavern" was the site of "a Riott and Disorder" where a constable was beaten.[93] The London markets were mentioned even more often as the place of assault. Three women were bound for "riotously assaulting beating and bruising" another woman "in the public market, and raiseing a great tumoult of people about her wereby she was in danger of her life."[94] Two gentlemen and a tailor allegedly assaulted a shopkeeper "in a riotous manner entring into his booth at May fair & throwing about his meat and Provisions," and a "market woman" was accused of "disturbing [the] business" of a fellow retailer by "Raiseing a mobb about her . . . in covent Garden Market."[95] Francis Roche may have chosen to assault Mathew Fury "while he was working in his shop window" because of the visibility such space allowed, which enabled Roche to "rais[e] a mob" against him.[96] Market stalls and shops were the scene of heated exchanges at the base of several defamation suits. One woman was standing in her husband's shop door when a neighboring shopkeeper "took an occasion to fall out with" her, calling her "a Dirty Bitch" and accusing her of adultery before several witnesses.[97] Thirty years later, the Bishop of London's Consistory Court was still hearing cases of defamation which had occurred between neighboring shopkeepers.[98] As a form of public conflict, the scenes depicted in defamation cases resonate closely with the assaults described in the Westminster Quarter Sessions recognizances where a tavern, shop, or market was named as the location.

Though public and private had not become ideologically separate and gendered in the way they were by the nineteenth century, the recognizances that mention the place of an assault nevertheless reveal an anxiety when the public intrudes into the private, and vice versa. The threshold of a dwelling as the border between home and street—between public and private property—seems to play a key role in some violent incidents. Laura Gowing discerned the significance of doorsteps in defamation suits. She described women standing on their doorsteps to conduct arguments with one another. This location, she argued, "reinforced their position in the households from which stemmed their standing in the community."[99] Garthine Walker has also recognized the cultural significance of breaching the threshold for early modern victims of assault.[100] By assaulting people in their doorway, or dragging them across the threshold into the street, assailants used space to shame their victims. Three men "pulled" William Dawson "out of his house" during a riot, and Christian Ross was "dragg[ed] by the hair of her head out of her own habitacon."[101] Rice Owens assaulted Jane Ross "by Kicking & pushing her Downe" his master's steps.[102] Similarly, Margarett Dyer was reportedly assaulted by two men who "violently thrust . . . her onto the street."[103] Even the *threat* of removal from private to public seems to have been socially and legally significant in alleged victims' complaints. Anne Staples's assailant pushed her down and dragged her through the house, "intending as she beleeveth to throw her into the street."[104] Augustan householders were aware of their right to their own private space, and they prosecuted those who crossed their thresholds uninvited. JPs' handbooks reflected and reinforced this perception, stating that "every mans house is (to himself, his family, and his goods) as his Castle, as well for his defence against injury and violence, as also for his repose and rest. And therefore the law doth give to dwelling places diverse privileges."[105] John Stockwell, a bailiff, was asked to answer charges of "attempting to forceably Enter" the home of John Frances.[106] Even women protected their right to control the space within their homes. Mary Davis went before a JP and caused him to bind John Dubain "for assaulting her and forcing himself into her apartment."[107] The threshold played an important role in the recording of some assaults, and movement across it in either direction was of interest to the Westminster recording official.

Though not the majority, a distinct number of assaults were directed at victims from outside their homes or the homes of their relatives ("about" their houses) (table 5.10). Several assaults clearly damaged the houses themselves, such as the alleged assault prosecuted by Catherine Warrman against three men for "breaking her windows in the night time" or the "ryott in St. James Square where his grace the duke of Norfolks windows were broken."[108] Targeting the victim's home as another way of openly publicizing his or her perceived disgrace appears to have been fairly effective, generating a number of prosecutions. Mary Lemon was bound for "assaulting [a woman] & her dau[ghte]r & raising a Tumult & mobb about her house soo that she cannot live with peace & quiet in her neighbourhood."[109] James Calowne was accused of "raising the mobb abt" a woman's door during his assault on her, and Mary Coleman assaulted Anne Davison "about her shop."[110] Another woman was prosecuted for assaulting her "with all manner of abusefull and approbrious Language" and "causing a great disturbance about her house in breach of the Peace."[111] Attacks against Londoners through their dwelling place provided assailants with a public forum, and this was probably a key part of their attraction as an assault tactic. Several cases show men shouting from the street at the victims' doors, issuing challenges to fight.[112] The physical language of assaulting victims in the streets or in front of their homes was available to both men and women. Early-eighteenth-century violence made use of clearly understood spatial customs.

Now that we have a sense of the various forms of assault, and of the spaces in which assaults took place, we can investigate the circumstances behind them. Special categories of violence, such as rape, rescues, domestic violence, or assaults on government or law officials, are dealt with in other chapters, so this chapter will focus on other causes of violence. Alcohol, of course, probably played as prominent a role in assaults in the early eighteenth century as it does today. Henry Fielding observed in *Tom Jones* that "no Nation produces so many drunken quarrels, especially among the lower People, as *England* (for, indeed, with them, to drink and to fight together, are almost synonymous Terms)."[113] The *Gentleman's Library* sardonically deemed it necessary for a "man of *Gallantry* to get immoderatly Drunk, and break a Drawer's Head," and, in a murder trial at the Old Bailey, witnesses testified as to one man's propensity for violence "when in Wine."[114] The courts recognized this. JPs were warned, "The English Blood is very easily Irritated. . . . Especially if it be inflamed with Drink."[115] Several recognizances indicate that beer or other intoxicants were involved in the attack. William Playdell assaulted Peter Taylor by "throwing Beer in his face," and Edward Ambler "spurt[ed] Ale from his mouth" into a man's face.[116] Susan Amussen characterizes tavern brawls as distinctly masculine forms of violence, but women participated in some of the assaults involving alcohol.[117] Jane Bond assaulted Damarass Buss and threw "a Glass of some Sort of Liquor in her Face."[118] Dorothy Porter accused Eliza Phillips of "being an Idle Drunken women [*sic*] who has assaulted her," and a man flung "drinke" in Margarett Anderson's face.[119] Women's presence in taverns at this time is discernible in Consistory Court records as well.[120] Anne Fletcher was "in a publick house knowne by the signe of the Catt" when she was defamed, and Mary Cope was sitting with her husband "by the fire side" of "a publick house" when another woman entered and uttered the insults that brought them before the church courts.[121] Both women and men could be involved in rising tensions in the tavern, and both were susceptible to increased aggressiveness as they imbibed.

Given the crowded living conditions of Augustan London, it is not surprising that many assaults occurred between neighbors.[122] Of all the recognizances listing sureties for both the prosecutor and the defendant, more than half (60 percent) appear to have been from the same parish.[123] Living in close proximity, tenants would be all too aware of one another's distasteful habits. Witnesses to one defamation case speculated that the insults were sparked by a woman sweeping dirt onto her neighbor's front step, and in another case the argument was suspected to be due to a neighbor's mastiff dog barking.[124] In one recognizance Eliza Riggs's neighbors complained that she kept a bawdy house in their neighbourhood and that she frequently disturbed them by "keeping bad hours & by Railling & curseing at those that Reprove her."[125] Disorderly houses figured prominently as a source of neighborhood animosity, but people also came to blows over discipline of neighborhood children. When Jane Bentley hit Mary Sumers's child, Sumers went next door "and asked her the reason," which led to a heated argument and a defamation suit.[126] James Thatcher reportedly assaulted Mary Taylor's children "Till they were forced to cry out Murther," so John Taylor found Thatcher "& broke his head."[127] Tension built up visibly within the neighborhoods of the metropolis, and disputes over territory, noise, or errant children could escalate into violence.

As the root of all evil, money also was the cause of several assaults. When we think of assaults over money, the first thing that probably comes to mind is armed robbery, but even the most conventional economic relations could result in bloodshed. Barthia Gotherid reported a violent assault and "Barbarous" beating when she came "to demand money of the said Robert Reed which hee owed her," and Elizabeth Battersby also met with violence "when she came to demant her rent" from tenant Isabella Mimroe.[128] An irate customer murdered a tailor's assistant with "a pair of sheers" for not having his clothing ready on time.[129] William Brown was bound for "assaulting, and strikeing" another man "and threatning to run him through the Body, for not lending him fifty pounds," and William Warner assaulted another man during a high-stakes card game.[130] One form of financially motivated assault uniquely targeted women. Elizabeth Appric, "an unmarried person of good fortune & Heiress to her father," was "violently assaulted & forced away" by a man intending "to marry her against her will."[131] As loan and rent collectors, tradespeople, gentlemen, card players, and eligible heiresses, the men and women initiating recognizances reveal how disputes over money sparked violence.

Certain circumstances behind assault were more distinctly gendered. Though dueling was illegal by this period, insults might still be met with a challenge to fight. John Camden stood outside Captain William Courtnay's door and "challeng[ed] him to fight," saying "that he would have satisfaction out of his fatt sides."[132] Accepting the challenge to armed combat could be proof of one's masculinity. In one of many fatal tavern encounters, a man drew his sword and said to his opponent, "*D—n you, are you a Man? If you are, draw, and shew yourself so.*"[133] According to William Lee, Thomas Guinton's "abusive language . . . provoked him to fight."[134] Thomas Miller was killed after "he resolved to take satisfaction" for "scurrilous words" that William Tindall had spoken of him and he "bid him draw."[135] These "challenges" were almost overwhelmingly issued by men against other men, but it is interesting to note the exception in one defamation suit. Standing in the street, Katherine Sanderson reportedly challenged Joan Phillips to "come out [of her house] and fight me if you dare," a challenge which Phillips accepted, and the two grappled in the street until they were pulled apart.[136] Nevertheless, men seem to have goaded one another much more often and made violent engagement a proof of masculinity.

Street football was another occasion for male violence. The impromptu (and violent) nature of the London street football match was recounted by John Gay:

> I spy the Furies of the Foot-ball war:
> The 'Prentice quits his shop, to join the crew,
> Increasing crowds the flying Game pursue.
> Thus, as you roll the Ball o'er snowy Ground,
> The gath'ring Globe augments with ev'ry Round;
> but wither shall I run? the Throng draws nigh,
> The Ball now Skims the street, now soars on high;
> The dextrous Glazier strong returns the bound,
> and gingling sashes on the Pent-house sound.[137]

Apprentices and other male artisans were drawn into this raucous game of football, and its masculine ferocity probably made more observers than Gay anxious when "the throng" drew "nigh." The potential danger of men mobilized in a football match can also be seen when "a Mach of Futtball was Cried at Ketring of five Hundred Men of a side, but the desighn was to Pull Down Lady Betey Jesamine's Mills."[138] Westminster Quarter Sessions heard prosecutions from people injured during a street football game. Richard Ellis and Jacob Nevill assaulted a woman while "w[i]th many others to the number of near an hundred persons Royetously & Tumultuously gathered together at football wch Ball they kick'd ag[ains]t the kitching Windows of Mrs Askews house in Vine Street and broake them and also at the same tyme by throwing a stick at broak the sash windows one Story high of the said house."[139] Though not exclusively, this sort of violence was distinctly masculine.[140]

Other nonpolitical forms of mob violence appear to have been more *feminine* environments for assault, however, a phenomenon that is treated in detail in chapter 7. Men's nonpolitical group violence was generally caused by situations involving rough street sport, such as those described above.

The assault recognizances, teamed with evidence from contemporary literature and testimony before the Bishop of London's Consistory Court or the Old Bailey, offer a complex view of the construction of masculinity and femininity in Augustan London. The high participation of women in defamation cases has allowed historians to see women as verbally aggressive, but women also had the potential to be physically aggressive. It was not impossible for assault prosecutors and Quarter Sessions' officials to characterize petty violence by women—even weaponless attacks—as dangerous and damaging. They vehemently humiliated their enemies, making use of popular symbolism associated with shame, and their presence in London's criminal underworld, as prostitutes and thieves, struck fear in the hearts of complainants and recording officials.

Just as femininity cannot be exclusively equated with weakness, so Augustan masculinity cannot be seen as all-powerful. Though often allowed more freedoms than women, eighteenth-century men were limited in significant ways. They were vulnerable to humiliating assaults, and elite men were inclined to prosecute assaults where their periwig was removed. Men could be subject to questioning when they were out at night, and even as highwaymen they were judged more harshly if they not did operate chivalrously. In pitched battles, if they did not rise to a challenge, they risked being considered less manly; if they did, they risked prosecution or injury.

The Westminster Quarter Sessions recognizances present an image of a city full of people who were well aware of their role in the state's criminal punishments and the importance of their homes in guaranteeing safety from trespassers. They reveal women's perceived potential for aggression and men's vulnerability to certain types of attacks, but they also allow us to blur the line between masculinity and femininity, and they show the ways in which the men and women of Augustan London did not always constrain themselves to act in gendered ways. Similarly, in their recording of assaults, the Quarter Sessions officials did not always have gendered expectations of their defendants. In both instances we are left with a sense of the many physical languages of assault in the metropolis between 1680 and 1720.

6

Petty Violence against the State: *Assaults on the Government, Military, and Police*

The period between 1680 and 1720 was fraught with religious and political turmoil in England. Catholic King James II was forced to flee the country in 1688, and the Protestant Stadholder of the Netherlands, William of Orange, and his wife Mary were invited to take over the throne. Though the English people were fairly eager to stem the growing tide of Catholicism launched by James II, William III did not inspire deep-rooted affection among his new subjects. He involved England in an expensive war against the French that was motivated primarily by his Dutch interests. The Hanoverian succession in 1714 was also hotly disputed. The new German King was popularly disliked, and the feeling seems to have been mutual. Like William III, George I used England's resources to pursue foreign interests. These European wars brought an equally contentious rise in taxation, and John Brewer has described the extensive development of the fiscal state over the eighteenth century.[1] The taxes levied during the reign of James II *doubled* under his immediate successors.

Given the political and religious upheaval of the *fin de siècle* environment, one would expect to see a significant amount of petty violence against the state in the capital. In fact, London (and the rest of England, for that matter) was surprisingly peaceful. Despite widespread opposition to the monarchs and their advisors, there was no large-scale assault upon the state in this period. Ian Gilmour argues that the English government was able to cast a veil of hegemony over a people ripe for revolution. Notwithstanding a substantial undercurrent of popular dissent throughout the century, Gilmour observes, the government was consistently able to "engineer consent" among its people. Because English men and women believed that "they were a uniquely free people," they did not feel the need to violently overthrow their government.[2] This desire was also fueled by the fear of repeating the disorders of the interregnum and restoration era and by the reluctance of some to frontally attack the government during wartime. The public demonstrations and petition drives that occurred during this era also served as an escape valve for violent antigovernment sentiments.

One would probably think that riots comprised the most significant form of violence against the state in this period. However, although Londoners rioted against everything from high theatre prices to French alehouse keepers, there was remarkably little violence in eighteenth-century riots.[3] E. P. Thompson has written extensively on the organized and disciplined character of the eighteenth-century crowd, and many historians have remarked upon the largely defensive nature of the English riot.[4] Chapter 7 examines the more violent aspects of riot to highlight the little-studied fact that riot was an avenue for female assaults on the state, and it focuses especially on the violent elements of female Jacobitism. The current chapter could deal more generally with the violence of Jacobitism as a whole, but because the topic has already received substantial attention in other histories, it seems unnecessary to reiterate their well-known findings.[5]

Instead, this chapter will show that the vast majority of petty violence against the state was expressed in small-scale conflicts with individuals. Although Sir Robert Walpole himself was attacked in 1733, there were almost no attacks on high government officials in the early eighteenth century, and there were no assassination attempts.[6] Londoners' violence was confined to much smaller theatres. We will explore the state as it was personified in tax collectors, soldiers, press officers, constables, watchmen, bailiffs, and marshal's men. These officials came into contact with Londoners in the course of their official duties, and they were attacked for a wide variety of reasons, ranging from their individual personalities to the government policies they enforced. Londoners assaulted soldiers not only because they were inconsiderate and unruly, but also because they represented growing state intervention in daily life. They attacked army and naval press gangs because they violated the principles of freedom held sacred by the English. They struck out at constables and other policing bodies who exceeded their authority or attempted to enforce unfair laws. Aside from Jacobitism—where historians have focused most of their attention—violence against the state was perpetrated mostly at an individual level, provoked by immediate concerns; it very rarely took the form of organized, sustained attacks.

Although women participated in political demonstrations and specific forms of violence against the state in this period (as chapter 7 illustrates), the vast majority of the attacks on the state appear to have been largely restricted to masculine participants. Women certainly had their own opinions about taxation, military recruitment, and the policing of the city, but they rarely allowed their opposition to escalate into physical violence. Aside from a few significant areas, depicted in the following chapter, the one-third of assaults perpetrated by women observed in chapter 5 stemmed mostly from neighborhood disputes. While men became violent over neighborhood disputes as well, they were much more likely than women to become aggressive with state officials as they conducted their duties.

One might think that Westminster, as the seat of national government, would have seen many Quarter Sessions assault prosecutions from those associated with parliament. In fact, only three recognizances for assault were brought by Members of Parliament or their assistants. The Speaker of the House of Commons was stopped "in his passage to the parliament house" in 1708, and his servant was assaulted as he rushed to protect his master.[7] Mr. Edward Arnold was assaulted "in his office in Whitehall" in 1720.[8] In 1701 a "cowkeeper" stopped an MP's coach "in the open street" and assaulted him. The law took such assaults very seriously, and Queen Anne passed a statute in 1710 particularly to protect her Privy Councillors. The statute made an "assault . . . strike or wound" punishable by death without the benefit of clergy.[9] Whether frightened by the severity of such laws, or simply because parliamentary officials were well guarded, there were few attacks on these representatives of the state.[10] All of these assailants were male, but with only three attacks we can only hesitantly characterize assaults on MPs as a masculine form of petty violence.

The same is true of attacks on the state's tax agents. Although our period in Britain's history saw the beginnings of a dramatic expansion of the fiscal state, with high taxation, John Brewer has observed that there was surprisingly little popular resistance.[11] The Westminster recognizances show, however, that there were a few rare occasions when Londoners' ire against the heavy taxation did erupt in violence. Indeed, even contemporaries who defended the nation's taxes admitted that it was "very much in Men's mouths, that the Taxes are . . . grievous," and several pamphlets were published between 1680 and 1720 which demanded reductions in various taxes.[12] Despite the likelihood of some resentment among the populous, no large-scale tax riots swept

London at this time. Instead, anger was expressed against taxation at its most personal level, against the tax collector himself, and again only very rarely.

There are only five recognizances for tax-related assaults in Westminster. Thomas Rush assaulted the collector of the hearth tax in 1688; Rebecca Marson assaulted "one of the collectors for the highways" in 1693; James Barron attacked an overseer of the poor in 1705; Thomas Clarke assaulted a Land Tax collector in 1709; and John Shoplin assaulted an excise officer in 1717.[13] Aside from the latter, all of the recognizances indicate that these officials were attacked while they were demanding money from the defendants. The records make clear that it was the men's very role as tax collectors that had provoked the assault.[14] Though Rebecca Marson was the only woman prosecuted for such attacks, her presence among the men suggests that women could and did question the legitimacy of certain taxes or the conduct of the collection officers. In her study of seventeenth-century Cheshire, Garthine Walker observed women's opposition to taxation, arguing that "this area of female concern over household goods was widely acknowledged."[15] Nevertheless, it is likely—even given our small numbers—that men were more inclined than women to be violent with tax collectors in eighteenth-century London. It seems clear that tax collectors were not assaulted with any frequency in this period, as no laws had to be drawn up to protect them. Though legal handbooks had special procedures for people who refused to pay the poor rates, for example, there was no special penalty for physically attacking an overseer when he was collecting.[16]

Even though Shoplin's recognizance is not explicit, it seems likely that his assault was also motivated by his victim's identity as an officer of the excise. Shoplin was described as "beating" the officer, "tearing his neckcloth & creating a riott" around him.[17] Excise tax collectors may have been especially despised among the populace. Excisemen could conduct inspections at any time, day or night, and many Londoners found their visits highly intrusive. One pamphleteer referred to "the unspeakable disquiets and disturbances" associated with the excise collector in his "daily execution of this duty."[18] The exciseman's very character was questionable; Brewer found "ample evidence" to substantiate the "exciseman's reputation as a roué and philanderer," preying upon the wives and daughters of the tradesmen he visited in executing his office.[19] There are no accounts of women attacking these excisemen to avenge their honor, however; nor did the tradesmen themselves attack excisemen in any significant numbers (Shoplin is the only man to appear in the Westminster recognizances). The records suggest instead that there was not one particular type of tax or tax collector that roused Londoners to violence and that attacking tax collectors was a fairly masculine form of misbehavior, if it was gendered at all.

Londoners clashed with the state's military more often than with its Members of Parliament or tax collectors. There had long been opposition to a standing army in England, and John Childs has argued that it stemmed as much from civilian antipathy to the soldiers themselves as it did from "fears for the survival of the constitution."[20] When Daniel Thorne, a "Lifeguardman," stopped to water his horse, a horsecar driver assaulted him with his whip and called him "one of King George's Rogues."[21] Similarly, a fishmonger told a soldier that he was a "vilain" and "one of King George's Rouges."[22] The fishmonger also said that "they were all Rouges that wore the Cloath"—in other words, that the soldiers' very uniforms tarred them all with the same brush.[23] The uniforms allowed civilians to attack individual soldiers while voicing opposition to the army as a whole. One man assaulted a soldier specifically because he was "wearing the king's coat," and another man threw rocks at soldier John Poin on the highway while calling him "Lobster" in derision of his uniform.[24]

These attacks were symptomatic of many clashes between Londoners and their military. Though the army enforced law and order on various occasions, soldiers had a reputation for lawlessness, and John Childs argues that this was exacerbated by state policies encouraging soldiers to misbehave.[25] The record of a soldier prosecuted in 1706 for threatening a constable and "being known to be a common guinea dropper [purveyor of counterfeit coins]" is just one of countless examples of troops who preyed upon the community wherever they were stationed.[26] The government attempted to minimize this antagonism between civilians and their standing army by passing new laws requiring only alehouse keepers, victualing-house keepers, or innkeepers to quarter troops.[27] Quartering troops meant lost trade, unpaid bills, and damaged property at the very least, and it is not surprising that this became a source of violent conflict. One Westminster victualer struck the soldier who was supposed to be quartered with him.[28] Two other publicans focused their violence on the constables who brought the quartering orders, assaulting them and refusing to take the soldiers under their roof.[29] Yet another proprietor ignored the court's order to quarter a soldier, saying that "he car'd not a fart for the Justice, nor for the whole Bench" who issued the quartering order.[30] Women kept inns and alehouses in the early eighteenth century, yet there are no records of female victualers violently protesting a quartering order. More often, according to John Childs, publicans resisted more subtly, by convincing more impoverished private householders to take their unwelcome guests.[31] Violent protest against quartering soldiers was another uniquely male form of attack on the state.

Violent opposition to the military was not always directed at soldiers, however. New recruits or deserters were often united with the civilian community in opposing the harshness of military recruitment and discipline. Women had a slightly greater role in this form of petty violence against the state. There were two wars during the period 1680–1720, and the operations of various press gangs in the capital aroused particular ire. Impressment was seen as a direct attack on English liberty, and Londoners of both sexes could become violent in their resistance.[32] During one naval press, John Richin "abused and threatened" Gervis Forster because Forster had told the authorities "where one . . . able seaman had concealed himself."[33] Such strong popular contempt for impressment was most visible in the many attacks on press officers. A group of watermen assaulted Lieutenant Charles Russell, rescuing the man he had already pressed into the navy. They removed his hat, wig, and cane—the accoutrements of his status—and beat him severely, dragging him through the mud of the Thames River. The recognizance describes him as "in a sad blody condition . . . much endaingered" of his life.[34] The mob that had gathered focused all of their hatred of impressment on Lieutenant Russell, with some people crying "pull out his Liver, whilst others threw Coals out of the Lighters at him."[35] When officers rushed in to disperse the crowd, the watermen continued to resist, telling one another not to divulge anyone's identity and "to hyde the number of their boats" from the authorities.[36] Given the vehemence of popular hatred for impressment officers, it is not surprising that in 1709 Constable John Eason refused to execute the JP's press warrant unless the justice could guarantee his safety.[37]

Aside from the waterman who was arrested, we cannot determine the identity of the vast majority of those who participated in the attack on Lieutenant Russell, yet it is clear that opposition to impressment united all sorts of people. A "gentleman" was bound for "opposing the pressmasters in the Execution of their office" and concealing a man from being pressed, and a *soldier* was even bound on one occasion for "wounding" two members of a press gang.[38] As the wives, mothers, or sisters of the men who might be taken, women were also vehement opponents of impressment, and there are several examples of women who violently resisted press officers. Elizabeth Desternell caused "a Ryott & Tumult to be made about" a constable enforcing a press warrant.[39] William Walker's wife Johanna barred impressment officers from entering her home, though they had "a search warrant" to execute an impressment order.[40] Nicholas Rogers recognized women's participation in anti-impressment riots, suggesting that they could be very "militant," particularly when the male providers for their households were in danger of capture.[41]

Londoners continued to attack military officials even after the soldiers and sailors had been successfully impressed. Alexander Yates assaulted and abused a press officer and rescued a new recruit in 1707, and Edward Bowers raised a mob against another official "by which means a new listed Soldier deserted" nine years later.[42] These attacks resonate with that on Lieutenant Russell, where the desertions took place in the heat of an anti-impressment riot. However, men and women assisted with desertions long after the initial recruitment. Anne Vance helped two other men rescue a third from his service as "a foot Soldier in Brigadeer Stearness' Regiment."[43] Vance had a different surname from that of the soldier, but she may have been his sister or lover, and the family connection was the likely motive for another assisted desertion. William Bodily concealed his son from officials after he deserted another infantry regiment several years earlier.[44] Desertion seems to have been a more serious problem than ever before, if we are to judge by the plethora of statutes related to mutiny and desertion by this period.[45] The most significant catalyst for clashes between civilians and the military was the act of impressment itself, however, and any official enforcing a press warrant was vulnerable to attack by Londoners of both sexes. Hatred of soldiers or military recruitments was a fairly common source of petty violence in early-eighteenth-century London.

Assaults on constables and watchmen were even more common, however. Not surprisingly, the law gave constables special authority in situations where people attempted to resist them with violence. The *Guide for Constables* stated that "if an . . . assault be made upon the Constable himself, he may not only defend himself, but also put the parties offending in the stocks, till such time as he can carry them to a Justice of Peace, or to the Gaol" if they had no sureties.[46] There were 343 recognizances to appear and answer assaults upon constables or watchmen at the Westminster Quarter Sessions between 1685 and 1720, constituting 5 percent of all the recognizances to answer an assault. Of the 388 people bound in these recognizances, 17 percent were women.[47] Though constables' prosecutions of assaults by women fluctuated throughout the period (table 6.1), they were consistently lower than the 19 percent of female defendants accused of assaulting males as a whole (table 5.4 in chapter 5). The proportion of women was especially low in the five-year periods of 1696–1700 and 1701–5 (table 6.1). These periods cover the end of the Nine Years War (1697) and the beginning of the War of Spanish Succession (1702). It is likely that the influx of newly unemployed men in the capital

Table 6.1

Recognizances for Assaults on Constables and Watchmen: Breakdown of Defendants by Gender over Time

Time[a]	Total Assaults on Police*	Female Defendants*	Females as % of Total	Male Defendants*	Males as % of Total
Apr 1685–Jul 1690	39	6	15	33	85
Oct 1690–Oct 1695	34	4	12	30	88
Jan 1696–Oct 1700	44	2	5	42	95
Jan 1701–Oct 1705	32	2	6	30	94
Jan 1706–Oct 1710	53	10	19	43	81
Jan 1711–Oct 1715	59	6	10	53	90
Jan 1716–Oct 1720	60	11	18	49	82

Note: Recognizances to prosecute assault have not been included.

*Assault recognizances where there were multiple defendants both male AND female have not been included, and the numbers reflect recognizances rather than defendants. Thus, the number of defendants may be slightly higher because some recognizances named more than one defendant.

[a]This column is broken down into seven periods of exactly twenty sessions each; this roughly corresponds with every five years. Note that rather than four there are only two extant sessions for 1689 (27 Jun and 2 Oct) and three for 1693 (9 Jan, 19 Apr, and 4 Oct).

with demobilization and the rise in impressments following close on its heels at the start of a new war caused a corresponding proportional increase in clashes between authorities and male Londoners. Though slightly higher in other decades, women's involvement in assaults on the police was still consistently lower than their participation in one-third of all assaults discussed in chapter 5, which suggests that assaulting constables or watchmen was much less "feminine" (or, conversely, more a "masculine" form of behavior) than assaulting in general.

Many of the assaults upon constables and watchmen resulted from heightened tensions during an arrest, such as the recognizance binding Charles Ewers to answer two beadles and five watchmen "of the same parish for assaulting and obstructing them in the execution of their office."[48] A chairman was part of a riot "where the head Constable of Westm[inste]r and several others were wounded," and a baker attempted "to shoot John Mathews Constable for executing [a] warrant."[49] Indeed, the violence directed at constables and watchmen could be quite serious. One constable and his assistants vowed that they were "in danger of their lives" from one malcontent.[50] Constable Thomas Addison also professed himself "in danger of his life" after an assault by Roger Mackmanus, a gentleman.[51] Two constables were murdered in Turnham Green when they stopped a peer's coach and asked the occupants to identify themselves. The aristocrats' widely publicized response was "*God Damn um, . . . they would make* [the Constables] *know who they were,*" and the constables were stabbed in the resulting melee.[52] Many assaults upon watchmen and constables occurred in the heat of an arrest or a similar conflict relating to their policing duties.

Before offering more evidence of the hundreds of assaults upon London's policing bodies, I should acknowledge the possibility that these accounts might be false. Although assaults on constables and watchmen would have been taken very seriously at Quarter Sessions, and cases of assaults on policing officials were less likely to be settled by informal mediation, very few of the assaults on Westminster constables and watchmen were prosecuted by the more serious method of indictment.[53] Three hundred forty-three constables and watchmen had their assailants bound over during this period, but only twenty-nine of these recognizances went on to indictment—1 percent less than that for assault recognizances as a whole.[54] The lack of indictments for this period may be partially explained by the possibility of venality among constables and watchmen. Many legal historians have acknowledged the potential for corruption in England's eighteenth-century legal system.[55] If a constable or watchman brought false actions against Londoners, generating recognizances and forcing payments from the innocent parties in order to drop the assault charge, he would have had no interest in prosecuting by the more expensive indictment method. In order to combat such venality, one constables' manual counseled the constable "never . . . to make himself a party in a complaint, unless he is called on by a magistrate."[56] The 343 assault recognizances prosecuted by constables illustrate that this advice was rarely followed and also indicate an increased possibility that corruption motivated some of the officers' prosecutions.

As many as 50 percent of the 343 recognizances to answer for assaulting constables and watchmen may have been false—created by a corrupt officer swearing that an assault had occurred, having the alleged assailant bound over to show his sincerity, and then dropping the charges in exchange for payment after the recognizance had been issued.[57] However, whether these recognizances were genuine or were stories manufactured by corrupt police, they can still provide valuable insights of the *types* of assaults directed at officials and the assailants' possible motivations. We will be looking mostly at recognizances that offer descriptive detail of the assault, as it is more likely that detailed recognizances record an actual assault—or, at the very least, were an account of a believable form of assault on constables or watchmen. Whether true or not, these recognizances document *probable* scenarios of attack on law officials, which allows us a sense of the types of violence that might be perpetrated on constables and watchmen.

Given the nature of the constables' duties in the early eighteenth century, it is not surprising that they faced some violent confrontations. The tensions behind arrests gave rise to several defamation cases at the Bishop of London's Consistory Court, and, in the absence of Quarter Sessions depositions for this period, these church court depositions offer a rare view of the anger and public attention involved with law enforcers' activities. Mary Pettyfer deposed that she was with her sister and her nieces "in the parlour" of her sister's house when "an officer br[o]ke open the door upon them on pretence of arresting" her sister.[58] Pettyfer's sister did not go willingly, however, and "many words arose between" the officer and Pettyfer's sister, following which "a great mob was soon gathered ab[ou]t the doore."[59] Even more public was the scene when William Wiltshire came "to arrest Joseph Fletcher, . . . then sitting in a roome below staires in a publick house," surrounded by its many patrons.[60] Wiltshire entered the room with the man at whose suit Fletcher was to be arrested, and "presently afterwards some [hot] words arose between" the parties.[61] Two recognizances tell a similar story. One woman and two men beat Constable Thomas Shepard for trying to extricate them for staying too long in a public house. All three defendants were "found in the Publick house of Simon and Jane Prichard of Drury Lane . . . at an unseasonable time of night."[62] The unwelcome guests at the alehouse "instead of going assaulted and beat . . . Shepard . . . and his assistant with a Red hot Poker and Tongs causeing a Great Disturbance so their lives were in danger Thereby."[63] In the normal execution of their duties as arresting officers, constables faced the constant threat of violent resistance, and their activities were often carried out in the public eye.

Indeed, the publicity of constables' and watchmen's work seems to have encouraged a sense of popular vigilance, and Londoners were not afraid to alert law officers when they overstepped their authority. One woman, charged with "raiseing a mob, and making a Riot in St. James Park," had also opposed "two constables in the doing of their duty, saying, the constables had no power in the park."[64] Similarly, a constable before the Old Bailey deposed that rioters threw rocks at him and told him "that he had nothing to do there, not being a constable of that Ward."[65] John Bowden abused the High Constable and "contemn[ed] his authority."[66] Londoners were well aware of the limits of the various governing bodies in the metropolis. Buildings along parish boundaries were marked with lead plates, "so that the limits of a parish's responsibility could be clearly defined."[67] A constable was prohibited from arresting a felon outside the county, unless he was "in fresh [pur]suit," that is, only if the felon fled over the county boundary while the constable was chasing him.[68] Justices were told that their "first care," when a case was brought before them, "must be to consider diligently, whether the Case be within [their] Jurisdiction."[69] A combination of factors, not the least of which being poverty and filth, made certain districts in London able to openly defy legal authority and serve as a shelter for all sorts of lawbreakers.[70] Each year, hundreds of couples took advantage of the liberty of the Fleet to marry without a license.[71] Similarly, the area within the "Rules" of King's Bench was known to be the site of gambling, coining, prostitution, smuggling, and various other illegal activities, unhampered by outside law officers.[72] Londoners knew the restrictions of constables' and watchmen's authority and were not afraid to remind them with violence if necessary.

This resistance to constables must be understood in the context of the voluntary nature of the office in early modern England. As a private citizen temporarily holding the office, the eighteenth-century constable may have faced more public defiance than would a professional police force. The armament of constables and watchmen was probably not intimidating, nor, probably, were their numbers.[73] It is likely that there were a few "professional," full-time constables in London at this time because the constables' handbooks allowed a constable to "make a Deputy" who could serve in his place as a substitute.[74] Several Londoners eligible to serve found it worthwhile to simply pay a deputy to take over their constableship, resulting in a number of constables who had served many consecutive terms and had essentially adopted policing as a profession.[75] However, even in the city many constables would have had their own trade, entirely separate from their law enforcement duties. (This is most obvious in the recognizance binding Constable Gabriel Pilkington, a pastry cook who once refused to serve an arrest warrant because he "was then making Pyes.")[76] Watchmen and constables came from all walks of life—and are recorded in various trades from fishmongers, tailors, and distillers, to lowly laborers.[77] In most cases, constables had to continue their other employments while they held their office.

In some cases Londoners attacked their police because of their lower social status and coarse behavior. A constables' handbook warned these officers of the hypocrisy of drinking in a tavern when their job was to arrest unruly drunkards, and the handbook even warned that it might provoke violence among parishioners.[78] Nevertheless, some constables appear to have spent a fair amount of time in the tavern rather than on their duties.[79] Legislators understood the problems that constables with low social status could create. In principle, a constable had to "be an honest, understanding and able Man, both in Body and estate, and not of the meaner sort," but in practice London had a reputation for the low social standing of its law officials.[80] The most obvious way that Londoners showed their contempt for constables and watchmen was by mocking the very symbols of their authority. One man assaulted Constable Jacob Duhamill by pushing him out of his own house and "taking his staffe from him."[81] The staff, of course, was both a tool and a symbol of office, and City officials' repeated requests that London's constables attach their staff of office to the outside of their homes attest to the staff's importance as sign of constableship.[82] A group of men attacked Constable Richard Brothers by ripping his "Constables staff" from his arms, and beating him with it "in a violent manner."[83] A watchman was murdered in 1680, the result of being "struck . . . with his own Watch-staff."[84] The symbolism of using the officers' staffs may have been the result of inadvertent, rather than calculated, attempts to humiliate, because the staff would have probably been the most obvious weapon at hand, seized during a struggle. Nevertheless, it seems likely that all of the defendants mentioned in these records would have found a certain satisfaction in assaulting law officers with their own symbol of office. This form of assault on constables and watchmen was a way of showing contempt by assailants who labored under the popular perception that the London police were of lowly status.

Attacks on bailiffs and marshal's men also form a special category of assaults on police, and the men serving in this office were viewed with far more contempt than were constables or watchmen.[85] The main responsibility of the office of bailiff, which could be held in various courts, was to serve writs and carry out arrests.[86] Marshal's men had similar responsibilities but served only the Palace courts, which were known interchangeably to contemporaries as the Marshalsea Court, the Court of the Verge, or the Palace Court, among other titles.[87] These courts had jurisdiction over a twelve-mile radius surrounding the royal household (the verge), and their authority was a bone of contention to the Londoners who found themselves before any of them, as this section will show. Unlike constables, bailiffs and marshal's men were paid for their duties, and their reputation for venality also seems likely to have been at the base of many of the attacks upon them. Although they served other courts, a significant number of bailiffs and marshal's men came before the Westminster Quarter Sessions JPs to report assaults by irate Londoners.[88]

Popular literature encouraged violence against these officers, with one bloodthirsty pamphleteer stating that corrupt bailiffs "commonly die with their Guts ript up, or are decently run through the lungs; and as they liv'd hated, die unpitied."[89] Another depicted a bailiff rightfully attacked by a mob who "wash'd" him under every pump in the vicinity, ducked him "Head over Ears thrice" in the ditch, and finally forced him to take an oath which stated "I . . . do confess my self a Rogue by my profession."[90] The actual prosecutions for attacks on bailiffs and marshal's men are not as sensational, but they nevertheless reflect Londoners' distaste for the activities of these law officers. Edward Cole attacked George Extone, "one of the under Bailiffs of . . . Westminster," because he was "Whipping . . . Martha Jones along Peter Street in the Parish of St. Margaret."[91] Extone was whipping Jones as part of his official duties, having been ordered by the court to execute this particular punishment on Jones, but Cole was clearly not pleased with either the punishment or the way that Extone was executing it, or both. A man assaulted Bailiff Phillip Brag in order to take Brag's prisoner from custody.[92] Two men and two women assaulted marshal's man John Brown, and a woman attacked another marshal's man several years later, and both events occurred while the officers were escorting prisoners to jail.[93] As we shall see in chapter 7, women assaulted officials who held prisoners more often than any other official, so bailiffs and marshal's men faced violence from women as well as men when they arrested and guarded prisoners. Mostly, however, attacks on bailiffs and marshal's men were masculine, as with all of the other attacks on the state. Every rescue mentioned above was accompanied by a riot, which suggests that assailants had no trouble stirring the crowds to oppose these infamous officials. As the takers of prisoners and the executors of punishments such as whipping, bailiffs and marshal's men provoked Londoners' anger and violence.

Bailiffs and marshal's men had a reputation for being extremely violent themselves, which probably explains many of the assaults on them. One pamphlet depicted bailiffs "with swords drawn, hangers and other weapons, as if they intended a murder," rather than merely an arrest.[94] Marshal's men were called "savage Cattle," prone to "Cruelty and Barbarousness," in the *Proceedings* account of a marshal's man who murdered a little girl with a cudgel while he was arresting her father "for a Debt of seven shillings."[95] The Westminster Quarter Sessions saw virtually as many prosecutions for assaults *by* bailiffs and marshal's men as they did *on* these officers. One bailiff violently assaulted his own wife,[96] and several bailiffs assaulted constables and watchmen who questioned their authority.[97] The recognizances binding bailiffs and marshal's men for assault, along with publicized accounts referring to their notorious aggressiveness, suggest that the violence against these officers was motivated by a desire for revenge over their many acts of brutality.

This was further exacerbated by their reputation for corruption.[98] Marshal's men were particularly hated for serving a court that many considered to be illegitimate.[99] Alternative courts, like the Westminster Quarter Sessions, denied the authority of the marshal's men in several cases and allowed those they had arrested to turn around and prosecute the marshal's men for assault.[100] In addition to persisting in arrests despite their perceived lack of authority, marshal's men also had a reputation for corruption, which further alienated the general public. These officers were said to be "false," encouraging malicious prosecutions in order to make more money.[101] Bailiffs had a similar reputation for venery. One pamphleteer assured readers that the bailiff's "first business is to bait you for money," and another declared that bailiffs were "addicted to Perjury" and would "tell more Lies than a Traveller."[102] Sixteen bailiffs arrested a gentleman and picked his pocket "under pretence of searching for pistols."[103] Another bailiff confessed that he "very much wronged" the poor "by Extortion."[104] Westminster bailiff Joseph Succliffe was prosecuted for "fomenting quarells and Lawsuits and arresting in sham actions."[105] Both bailiffs and marshal's men notoriously used their office for immoral financial gain.

One of these officers' key responsibilities was to arrest debtors, and given bailiffs' and marshal's men's reputation for corrupt financial practices, this irony was probably not lost on their fellow Londoners.[106] In arrests for debt, officers were constrained by several rules, which may have given Londoners more incentive for resistance and vigilance. Bailiffs "could not make arrests at night, nor on Sundays, nor could they break into a house in order to make an arrest, and if they did infringe any of these conditions then they were acting without legal authority and could be resisted by force."[107] Julian Hoppit summarized the advantage accorded debtors: "if the debtor was obstinately strong willed, he could defeat all attempts to get at his property by keeping his front door firmly shut."[108] Despite these restrictions, arrests for debt took place frequently. Lord McGregor affirmed a nineteenth-century parliamentary committee's report that "in many cases the decision whether a debtor is actually conveyed to prison or not rests effectively not with the court but with the creditors and the bailiffs," and McGregor argued that this principle applied equally to the eighteenth century.[109] Indeed, after creditors had convinced a court to issue a writ for debtors' arrest, debtors could find themselves in prison if they were unable to put up bail. Not until the suits came to trial might debtors have a chance to speak in their own defense.[110] The Palace Court had the authority to try "Debt, Trespasse, Battery, Slander, Trover, and all other actions personal," according to its constitution, but it seems to have dealt mostly with minor debtors.[111] Both marshal's men and bailiffs in general, therefore, were especially associated with arrests for debt, and the combination of their restrictions and powers in this area probably evoked particular hatred among many Londoners.

Indeed, such arrests were deemed unjust in popular literature. Early modern sentiment held debt apart from other crime. Debt was "an honest man's" offense, in the words of one pamphlet, and many felt debtors deserved better treatment than other prisoners.[112] This sense of the injustice of arrest and imprisonment for debt provoked many of the assaults on bailiffs and marshal's men. Aside from one woman severely beating a marshal's man for arresting a man for a debt of £10, there are no other records of feminine attacks over debt.[113] This does not mean that women did not share the popular contempt for bailiffs' and marshal's men's cruelty and corruption. It does, however, indicate fairly strongly that women were unlikely to let their hatred escalate into real violence. The men had no such restraint. "Youth" William Buckley murdered a "bailiff's assistant" who was trying (along with "a Marshall's court-officer" and four assistants) to arrest Buckley's master for debts "amounting to £112." [114] Roger Swiny murdered another bailiff's follower when he came with a party of "five or six Bailiff's and their followers" to arrest his brother "for a debt of sixty pounds."[115] William Carman, along with "foure or five men with naked blades and pistols," assaulted arresting officers when they came to arrest Anne Tener "for a Debt of 600l."[116] One officer was wounded in the shoulder, and another officer's injuries were so serious that, according to the surgeon, he "was in danger [of] his life."[117] As custodians of debtors, and notoriously violent and corrupt themselves, bailiffs and marshal's men were popular targets for masculine petty violence in the early eighteenth century. Male Londoners would stop at nothing to prevent the arrest of debtors, and their violence was solidly rooted in a popular sense of the illegitimacy of debt as a crime.

Despite mounting taxes and recurring succession problems, none of the violence against the state in the early eighteenth century came close to a large-scale revolution. Aside from the Jacobite riots, historians have generally assumed that there was almost no violence against the state. However, Londoners—in their more everyday interaction with the state through its officials—could become physically aggressive. This aggression was generated almost entirely by male Londoners. Women were markedly hesitant to assault officials at any level of government, though the next chapter will suggest that they did so in a few significant contexts.

These records do not contradict previous histories that underscore the English government's almost hegemonic control of its people. When we look at assaults on the state, we see very few against taxation, one of the most burdensome elements of the contemporary regime. Even the attacks upon the military were less in protest of the principle of a standing army and more against the everyday nuisances of quartering soldiers or losing able-bodied men to the press. The vast majority of assaults on the state were perpetrated, not surprisingly, against London's policing officials—constables and watchmen especially, but also bailiffs and marshal's men. Similar to the attacks on MPs, tax collectors, and soldiers, the assaults on police occurred mainly in the heat of an arrest, out of contempt for these officers' lowly birth or reputation for venery.

That being said, there are echoes of bigger woes. The press gang flew in the face of every English man and woman's belief that they were born free. Londoners also had a very deep-seated sense of the injustice of debt as a crime. These concerns motivated them—particularly the males among them—to physical aggression.

7

FEMALE ASSAILANTS:

Women as Rioters and Rescuers

Just as we looked at special categories of assault *victims* that were particularly feminine in the first part of the book, we will now examine two categories of assault *perpetrators* that tended to include a significant number of women. We will explore women's involvement in group assaults, especially riots of all kinds. Women form a very high proportion of all of those prosecuted for "raising" riots, which suggests that they were very comfortable with this form of public violence. Indeed, riots were a significant avenue for women's petty violence. Women rioted with other men, but they also rioted in groups of their own. Where eighteenth-century riot is largely seen as nonviolent and peaceful, the London rioters who were prosecuted were actually highly aggressive, and female rioters are no exception.[1] Although we are interested in the causes of these riots, JPs rarely were, and the records are largely silent on the circumstances behind riots. Nevertheless, they *do* describe the violence perpetrated by rioters, which allows us to explore the phenomenon of feminine mob violence.

Many of these riots seem to have been the result of neighborhood tensions rather than demonstrations against the state as discussed in the preceding chapter. However, female Jacobitism, the subject of the second section, is a significant exception. Female Jacobites have traditionally been viewed as equal in vehemence to their male counterparts, staunchly voicing their desire for the restoration of the Stuart monarch, but no one has looked at female Jacobite *violence*.[2] Even women's seditious words were at least as violent as men's, and women often participated in Jacobite riots but were rarely caught. As a result, they rarely found their way into the historical record, but we can obtain fleeting glimpses in the recognizances which suggest that their participation was actually much higher than most sources indicate.

These "glimpses" might lead us to broader conclusions. We have seen, in chapter 6, that women were not prominent among the attacks on the state. However, perhaps non-Jacobite women also assaulted the state but were not prosecuted for it, and thus have not found their way into the historical records. It would be tempting to argue that petty violence against the state was a perfectly viable form of female misbehavior. However, while there are at least *glimpses* of female Jacobite violence, there are almost no hints of female assaults in other types of political violence in the early eighteenth century. Because constables and other prosecutors rarely charged women with such attacks upon the state, they clearly did not consider these attacks realistic forms of female misbehavior. As a matter of fact, John Bohstedt concluded that female rioters were probably *not* ignored by authorities, and the higher numbers of men arrested for food riots likely indicated there were simply a higher number of male participants.[3] Nevertheless, this puts female Jacobite violence in a special category, as a unique area where women were sufficiently moved to physically oppose the state.

Rescues are another such area. Although (as we know from chapter 6) women did not assault police officials in as high proportions as they perpetrated most other assaults, they *did* become violent with police in rescues. Women attacked jailers and arresting officers to help their husbands, sons, and a host of other men related to them in various ways to escape. Again, because of the vagueness of the records, we cannot determine whether women rescued these men for only particular types of offenses. We cannot trace the patterns from chapter 6 to uncover whether female rescuers sprung into action only if, for example, someone was arrested for debt or had been newly impressed. Most of the recognizances give little detail of the escape or suggest that the rescue had occurred while the prisoner was being conveyed to jail, but they give no indication of the offense for which he was arrested. Nevertheless, the phenomenon of the female rescuer—never before observed or studied—is fascinating for a variety of reasons. Rescues were another narrow avenue for female petty violence against the state, of course, but they also dispel many myths about early modern women being restricted to the role of the rescued.

Although John Bohstedt and Robert Shoemaker both conclude that women were more prominent in urban riots in eighteenth-century England, neither they nor any other scholars have conducted a detailed study of women's violence in London's riots.[4] I shall do so here. In the early eighteenth century, riots were legally defined as *violent* group activity. Indeed, violence was a key ingredient in order for an offense to be characterized as a "riot." If twelve people assembled and plotted to disturb the public peace, they were only an "unlawful assembly," but if they put their plot into action "with violence," it became a riot.[5] The law is somewhat more confusing about female rioters, however. One JPs' handbook said that a group of women could not be punished for riot "unless a man of discretion moved them to assemble for the doing of some unlawfull act."[6] This implies that women were prosecuted for riots only if they had rioted with men. However, the many recognizances binding only women for the same riot suggest that this rule was rarely followed. While historians have found many eighteenth-century riots to have been surprisingly peaceful, with the only violence directed against property, many of the rioters who were prosecuted committed significant acts of violence.[7]

Aside from Jacobite riots, which are discussed in detail in the next section, the "riots" mentioned in the Westminster recognizances generally seem to be nonpolitical, in the sense that they occurred spontaneously at a neighborhood level, usually with one person as their target. The recognizances rarely give any details of the event or behavior that made someone the target of a riot, so we are forced to study all non-Jacobite riots together, in complete ignorance of their cause. The recognizances also lack details of the forms that Westminster riots took, so it is impossible to determine whether particular types of riot were gendered. We know that Edward Coalsworth rioted by kicking a tub down the street.[8] The noise of the reverberating tin tub on the cobblestones probably served as a form of rough music, similar to that seen by E. P. Thompson and Martin Ingram in charivaris, and Coalsworth was probably not the only Londoner who used elements of rural demonstrations in urban riots.[9] Robert Shoemaker has found that women frequently rioted around their victims' houses[10] probably as a way of drawing neighborhood attention to the transgressor and shaming him or her within the community, as when Katherine Pendelton raised a riot around Elizabeth Plunket's house in 1708, or Mary Davis made a riot both "within and without" Dennis Obryan's house.[11] Overall, however, it is impossible to discern distinct or gendered patterns in Westminster riots because they are described so vaguely.

Regardless of their causes or forms, riots *were* an occasion for female violence of all kinds. Mary Gillham, Willomine Driscoll, and Elizabeth Banwell tried and threatened to do great harm to Edward Burridge when they had made a riot around him, but—for whatever reason—they were unsuccessful at inflicting any real damage.[12] The violence from many other female rioters was much more immediate. Dorothy Murray, Elizabeth Molloy, and Elizabeth Walker "assaulted and beat" Elizabeth Gumblton "in a very barbarous manner" when they rioted against her in 1717.[13] Elizabeth Herbert assaulted John Whitlamb while she was "causeing a ryott and disturbance" around him, and Sarah Griffith perpetrated a "Riot and assault on the bodye of" William Willis.[14] Ann Edwards assaulted and "grosely abused" Theodosia Wharton when she rioted against her.[15] Elizabeth Price stripped Dorothy Oakley and assaulted and beat Sarah Sparrow while "causing a riot" about Oakley "in the street."[16] Although two-thirds of all of the assaults with a riot were perpetrated by men, women were responsible for the final third, showing that riot was a significant avenue for feminine violence in London at this time.

Women also rioted *with* men in violent demonstrations. In several instances, married couples rioted jointly against a single target. Catherine Hutching and her husband Emanuell assaulted Lovell Detwiga and made a riot against her in 1705.[17] Similarly, Ann Richardson rioted with her husband John and "violently" assaulted Isabell Kitlewell so badly that they "frighted her into a sound [swoon or fainting fit] and put her in feare they will doe her some further Bodily harme."[18] Female rioters were not limited to rioting with their husbands, however. Women's participation in large riots with men was probably much more frequent than the records attest (an important point of the next section), and there was at least one occasion when a single woman took part in a very violent riot. "Spinster" Jane Jordan was bound, along with four men, for participating in "a ryott and assault" on Sir Richard Buckley "with sev[era]ll Hundreds more unknown."[19] In addition to injuring Sir Richard, the rioters also broke his windows and seriously damaged his house.[20] There were probably many other female participants in this riot, who eluded arrest and thus do not appear in the records. These examples, though few, are sufficient to indicate that both men *and* women found riots an appropriate outlet for petty violence in the early eighteenth century.

Though women made up the standard one-third of all assaults with a riot, they formed a much higher proportion of assaults when they "raised a mob." Women were bound for more than *half* of all of these assaults.[21] In a recent article on the riots against Gin Act informers, Jessica Warner and Frank Ivis acknowledge women's unusually high activity as mob raisers in the eighteenth century. For Warner and Ivis, however, "raising a mob" was a way for women to participate in group protest *without* being violent.[22] "Raising the mob" implies leadership and assertiveness, and the Westminster assault recognizances show that—contrary to Warner and Ivis—female mob raisers *were* physically aggressive.

In fact, prosecutors and recording officials had no qualms suspecting female defendants of violently mobilizing their fellow Londoners in attacks. Jane Gibson was bound "for an assault and breading a Riot of near 100 persons aboutt" her victim.[23] Two women "Gather[ed] the Mobb" around their victim, "swearing they would Tear her heart out & pull her out of her house insomuch that she was forced to Leave her house shop & buissiness & is affraid of further Disturbance."[24] As mob leaders, these female defendants evoked images of power. While Sarah Ceake assaulted and beat Thomas Rack, she loudly proclaimed that his wife Hannah "had two Bastards and that she knocked them on the head in her Masters Garrett."[25] Women did not limit themselves to initiating riots over sexual indiscretions. Mary Bissett raised "a Mobb and Tumoult of people" around Mr. John Jullion because he was from France. She struck him "in the Face" and rallied her countrymen to her side, exposing Jullion's identity to the passing crowd by shouting that he was a "French Rascall."[26] Women had an arsenal of effective words which allowed them to "raise the mob" to assist them in their violence. Clearly, mob raising was a highly significant source of feminine petty violence.

Although many assaults perpetrated by groups were not explicitly designated as "riots" by law officials, group assaults can nevertheless be studied in a similar context. Again, the Westminster recognizances reveal that women could be prominent leaders in assaults perpetrated by groups—even groups mainly of men. In my look at forms of assault in chapter 5, I ignored those assaults perpetrated by groups of men and women acting together in order to know for sure which acts had been committed by male, and which by female, assailants. These records of group violence are best examined anecdotally rather than quantitatively because most of these 391 recognizances do not contain enough information for us to characterize who was perpetrating which aspect of the assault.

As chapter 5 has established, women generally attacked other women and men generally attacked other men. Nevertheless, several recognizances reveal interesting exceptions to this pattern. In one example a man and a woman had Thomas, Ann, and Mary Smith bound for assaulting them, and Thomas and his wife Ann were clearly named as the woman's assailants, while Mary was designated as "assaulting and beating" the man.[27] Women were occasionally singled out as inflicting more damage and constituting a greater danger to the prosecuting victim than a male codefendant. John Ross was bound only for "assaulting," but Christian Ross (likely his wife, though she is not explicitly identified as such) was bound for "assaulting . . . & dragging [the victim] by the hair of her head out of her own habitacon."[28] William Parsely only "ayd[ed] and assist[ed]" Elizabeth Eason, who was accused of "assaulting and breaking [her victim's] arms with a fireshovel."[29] A few prosecutions identified one of the multiple defendants as having the more passive role of simply not preventing the attack, as when, for example, James Simms held "the

Door" while a woman was beaten.[30] When the passive partner was male and the person identified as doing the actual beating was female, the recognizances again underscore the potential for violence in Augustan femininity. Henry Lanster faced assault charges for "holding [a woman] whilst Jane Evans did beat and bruise her," and Robert Saint John was similarly bound for "standing by and frequently suffering Anne . . . his wife to assault beate and bruise" their apprentice.[31]

In other cases, the defendants were described as actively instigating the assault. Women were present among such defendants, suggesting that—in the eyes of the law, at least—they were quite capable of leadership and control over men, even their own husbands. Elizabeth York was charged with "Encouraging and comforting one Joseph Silver at the same time that the sd Silver was assaulting cutting and wounding [the victim] with a naked sword," and Elizabeth Emmes was bound for "occasioning & provoking of her husband Richard Emmes to assault & wound [the victim] with his drawne sword on the head."[32] Another recognizance bore even stronger imagery. William Burley, a bailiff, had Thomasine Windrum bound for "assaulting him by pulling him Backwards by the haire of his head, crying out to her husband stabb the Rogue, which he Endeavoured to doe, and swearing she wou'd cutt his Throate."[33] Wives and other women perpetrating assaults with men could be represented as more violent in their attacks or as the controlling agents behind them, revealing the breadth of feminine misbehavior in Augustan London.

Historians are well aware of the existence of female Jacobites in the capital in the early eighteenth century.[34] However, aside from Nicholas Rogers's study of female involvement in eighteenth-century crowds, historians have never given Jacobite women special attention or investigated whether they used violence in expressing their views.[35] An equal number of women as men were bound over for uttering seditious words in Westminster between 1689 and 1719, but considerably fewer women were charged with more aggressive Jacobite activities.[36] We might be tempted to argue, then, that women tended to choose more passive forms of political resistance than men. Perhaps female Jacobites did not move beyond verbally questioning the legitimacy of the monarch, while their male counterparts participated in the more aggressive activities that we have heard so much about. This is certainly the picture we get from a superficial reading of Jacobite prosecutions, yet if we look at the records more closely, we can see that women could and did become violent supporters of Jacobitism.

Women were active at every level of Jacobite unrest. Not only did Ann Amy refuse to take the oath of allegiance to the Hanoverian dynasty, but she also helped to unite other dissidents. She was prosecuted for holding meetings in her house "where one Arch-Deacon Fitz-Gerald a Non-Juror preaches and prays for the Pretended Prince of Wales."[37] Elizabeth Campion, who was probably related to Henry Campion, a Tory Member of Parliament and recognized Jacobite, sent "letters into France of Dangerous consequence."[38] Jane Mosson, possibly Campion's accomplice, was accused of "bringing letters . . . from France suspected to be of dangerous consequence to the government," and Mosson confirmed her Jacobite allegiances by saying that "the Prince of Wales was her king and she hoped to see him here shortly."[39] The recognizances are tantalizingly vague, and though they suggest that these women were involved in very serious illegal activities, there is no record of either Campion or Mosson as defendants in state trials. The recognizances for Amy, Campion, and Mosson offer a rare glimpse of eighteenth-century women who had strong political views and the resources to attempt real political change.

Many women of much poorer backgrounds could also launch significant attacks on the state. Elizabeth Tarding, a laborer's wife, sang Jacobite ballads "in order to Raise and Encourage Sedition amongst his Majesties Liege subjects," according to her recognizance.[40] Elizabeth Humphries was caught hawking a Jacobite pamphlet in the street.[41] Many female ballad singers would sing whatever their customers wanted, and their political allegiances could probably be bought and sold, so we must remember that not all of those caught singing or hawking Jacobite material were necessarily Jacobites. In at least one case, however, a ballad singer's hatred of the Hanoverians may have been genuine. A soldier's wife was caught singing two Jacobite ballads and was heard to say "give the Cuckold's Curr a Crust, he is one of the Low Church, Let 'em all go to Hell and sow Turnips."[42] Nicholas Rogers cites another example of a ballad seller with strong Jacobite sympathies. Though she claimed to be selling the anti-Hanoverian literature "purely for Want of bread," in utter ignorance of its political ramifications, both Rogers and the magistrate hearing her case found sufficient evidence to believe otherwise.[43] As ballad singers, even the poorest of London's women could participate in seditious culture.

Often, of course, women's Jacobite sympathies fall below historians' radar because they were not prosecuted nearly as frequently as men. As we have seen, Jacobite women appear most often in the *OBP* and the Westminster Recognizances between 1689 and 1719 as the speakers of seditious words. After the Hanoverians ascended the throne and the Whigs took power, they were very anxious about curbing Stuart supporters and shoring up their very shaky new regime. The authorities pursued all dissidents tenaciously, including those who were heard to ridicule the Hanoverians or praise the Stuart Pretender.[44] Though one who uttered seditious words faced the death penalty in the medieval period, by the seventeenth century the crime was a misdemeanor, and those found guilty faced a range of lesser penalties, from fines to imprisonment.[45] A distinction was made between seditious words that were spoken and ones that were written, the idea being that there was much more danger of hearers "mistak[ing], pervert[ing], or mis-remember[ing]" spoken words, so the accused should not be punished as severely.[46] Indeed, it is difficult to tell how genuine these accusations of seditious words were. The words may have come entirely from the imagination of a malicious prosecutor. Alternatively, an individual might really have drunk to the health of the Pretender or damned King George without having strong Jacobite allegiances.[47] Regardless of their authenticity, the gendered patterns of seditious words are reliable as evidence of what prosecutors and authorities believed women *capable* of uttering.

We must not simply regard the larger number of women uttering seditious words as evidence of feminine passivity. Though women were more likely to be charged with *speaking* seditiously than with putting their words into action, women were no less aggressive than men. In fact, women were proportionately more likely than men to issue *violent* threats against their monarch.[48] In the words they chose, therefore, women were at least as—if not more—aggressive than their male counterparts. Ann Murkott spoke of cutting off King William's head, and Elizabeth Lindsay said that if she were that "Devill" King George's cook, she "would poison him."[49] Margaret Hicks had a thirst for King George's "Heart's Blood" and said that "the first time [he] came by the door she would stick him."[50] In contrast, there were only two violent male threats in this small group. William Colthurst vowed to "dash" King George's "brains . . . against the wall," and Jonathan Lane promised to cut a Whig JP "in two" if the Duke of Ormond ever returned to England.[51] The character of the women's threats was at least as violent as the men's, and the former were just as likely to lay out specific scenarios where their bloody acts could be carried out. William Colthurst imagined himself "in the room with the king" so he could perform his deadly deed, but Elizabeth Lindsay also pictured herself with the king, as his cook. Margaret Hicks added reality to her threat by waving a knife that she had in her hand. Hicks also brazenly asserted her sobriety when her words were dismissed as drunken ravings by her companions, insisting that she would "rather be hang'd" than retract her threats. Because Hicks's, Lindsay's, and Colthurst's words were not merely idle but rather "set forth a means of actually accomplishing the murder of the king," Hicks and her counterparts could indeed have been hanged, under a charge of uttering treasonable words.[52] That they were charged only with the misdemeanor of seditious words should not mitigate the fact that the women were at least as aggressive as the men in asserting their hatred for their monarch. Of the few recognizances for seditious words at Westminster Quarter Sessions and the Old Bailey, a higher proportion of Jacobite women used violent imagery.

Though Jacobites *threatened* violence against King William or King George, the physical vent to their anger was directed against the kings' supporters. Mobs smashed windows that had been illuminated in honor of King George's birthday on May 28, 1715.[53] The Hanoverian loyalty of a group of men "crying out God Bless King George" so incensed Phillip Stevens that he assaulted them.[54] After William Griffin voiced his loyalty to King William in 1694, James Singleton assaulted him and damned him along with the king.[55] Again, Jacobite women participated in these violent forms of protest. Jane Cornwallis assaulted four constables because they were "searching her house for disaffected and dangerous persons against the government."[56] Sarah Coggs joined her husband Richard in assaulting a mother and daughter for "rejoicing on king George's birth Night."[57] Ann Wronng abused a woman in the middle of the street, by raising a mob against her, calling her "a Presbeterian Bitch" and damning her "and [her] King George too."[58] On the anniversary of Charles II's restoration, Hannah Wilson wore "Oak Leaves and Green Knotts" as "distinguishing favours to stir up sedition," and she attacked Eliza Goodman, calling her a "Presbyterian Toad and Inform[an]t."[59]

Although women were rarely tried at the Old Bailey for Jacobite riots, the testimony at the trials of male rioters makes it clear that women were active perpetrators of mob violence. The most prominent Jacobite riot in London during our period occurred July 24, 1716. A Jacobite mob composed of more than one hundred people attacked the Salisbury Court mughouse, a recognized symbol of Hanoverian loyalty.[60] Witnesses deposed that the mob included "Women, and Children," all crying "*High Church and Ormond for ever,* and, *Down with the Mug-house.*"[61] Women were in the front lines of the riot and helped to breach the back door of the mughouse and drag out one of its occupants. The women then "struck him over the Head with their Patens till they cut him to the Skull."[62] At another point during the riot, a woman threw brickbats at the mughouse windows and shouted, "*High Church and Ormond, Damn all the Hanoverians, Down with the Presbyterians,*" to the male Hanoverian supporter who tried to stop her. He attempted to drag her into custody, but she was rescued by a fellow rioter. The fellow (male) rioter was then successfully captured, and his name appears in the record while her anonymity was preserved.[63]

Women rarely figure among the defendants for Jacobite-related offenses at the Old Bailey. Hester Gibbs, Eleanor Bomsky, and Anne Lane are among this small minority of women. They were charged for commemorating the hanging of one of the mughouse riot leaders. The three women were part of a group of "near a thousand" who met at the scene of the riot in Salisbury Court and planned to walk through the streets of London "drest with White Hoods and Favours" in honor of their deceased leader and the Jacobite cause in general.[64] They were caught fleeing in a boat with five others and were indicted as rioters. The record of their case suggests that there were many other women participating in the demonstration who would never find their way into the historical record.

Gibbs, Bomsky, and Lane are among the very small minority of women who can be found among the records of political demonstration in the capital for this period. A pamphlet promising to give *An Account of the riots, tumults, and other treasonable practices since his Majesty's accession to the throne* specifically mentions female Jacobites only twice in dozens and dozens of accounts.[65] However, by uncovering these rare glimpses of women who were prosecuted for Jacobitism, particularly in the Westminster recognizances, we can see the extensive political activity of countless other London women who evaded capture. Clearly, Jacobite violence was a much more significant feature of eighteenth-century femininity than has often been portrayed.

In the heat of riot, women assisted in rescuing other prisoners, and we have seen how at least one female Jacobite avoided prosecution because she was rescued by her fellow rioters. In chapter 6 we saw that women prevented their husbands, brothers, and fathers from being impressed by assaulting their impressment officers. The recognizances show women's participation as rescuers to be so significant that it merits separate study here. Early-eighteenth-century women found particular justification for assaulting the preservers of law and order if they had imprisoned their loved ones.

Aside from capital punishment, incarceration was one of the greatest punitive powers of the English criminal justice system. By removing someone from custody, a rescuer was effectively thumbing her nose at the power and authority of the law. It is interesting, therefore, that women were particularly active in this form of resistance. Even the more "passive" types of rescue, such as when Thomas Bliss's wife brought him a rope to enable his second escape from the Marshalsea prison, were taken very seriously for this reason.[66] In the pamphlet recounting the trial at the Kingston Assizes, Mrs. Bliss was reportedly "kept . . . an hour . . . and threatn'd to [be taken] before Justice Ladd, for bringing her Husband the Rope."[67]

The law placed the responsibility for preventing rescues on the jailers themselves. Constables had a vested interest in reporting escapes and in detailing the violence perpetrated against them by rescuers, because they were vulnerable to prosecution themselves if their negligence had allowed the prisoner to escape. Constables' handbooks voiced strong warnings that, should the responsibility for an escape lie with them, "it may produce a prosecution against the constable that may end in his ruin."[68] It was thus in the constable's best interest to explain fully how he had been rendered helpless in the escape, making the prosecutions for rescues likely to be detailed and copious. Given the likelihood of their comprehensiveness, it is interesting to note women's significant role in the rescue attempts prosecuted by recognizance.

Constables who "voluntarily suffer[ed] a Felon to escape" were guilty of a felony themselves if the individual had already been arrested, and they were guilty of a misdemeanor if the escape occurred before "he was actually taken."[69] Even when the escaped prisoner had been guilty of only a misdemeanor assault, if the victim of that assault "dieth . . . within the year and day," then the Constable who had let the assailant escape could be fined "to the value of his Goods, in the opinion of Some."[70] Constable Ralph Hambleton was bound for "suffering a prisoner to escape whom he had taken upon a private search," and William Hutchinson was accused of "suffering severall women to escape who were taken up by . . . [the] Constable."[71] However, there are considerably fewer recognizances against constables for escapes than there are those to *answer* constables for escaping or rescuing. Indeed, given the serious repercussions, it is possible that the constables involved in this offense would have taken great care to prosecute rescues or escapes, and it is possible that many of the recognizances would include descriptions showing the force used against the officers and showing their helplessness—and innocence. This likelihood was even greater in London, where constables were seen as prone to corruption. Here, constables would have had to make extra effort to show that they had not simply let prisoners escape for a fee.

If a constable *did* allow a prisoner to buy his way out of jail, the escape would probably never have been reported. Deveil's justicing handbook warned, "There is a great Evil carried on by the Constables for the county of Middlesex, and the City and Liberty of Westminster: and that is, when they have Prisoners in custody, and sometimes for great Offences, they take the

Liberty from their own Authority to set the Prisoner at large for . . . the sake of Lucre and Gain, which . . . well deserves the severest Punishments."[72] Only one recognizance gave evidence of this type of corruption among the London police, binding "John Keelman for letting Ann Spikeman make her Escape after she was delivered into his custody . . . & takeing halfe a crowne of her."[73] Justices John Chamberlayne and Francis Negus were prominently mentioned in the recognizance, and another officer bound for Spikeman's escape was also accused of "disobeying the Justices orders in not making a due return."[74] Such judicial vigilance is absent in most of the recognizances, however. There would be little incentive for an individual who had bought his or her freedom from a corrupt official to then prosecute the escape, so unless a JP or other officer (such as the upper marshal) discovered the constable's venality, these escapes would go unrecorded.[75] Thus, those that appear in the recognizances were likely the result of genuine rescue attempts.

Having established that the records of rescues are genuine, we can now examine the phenomenon of female rescuers. Not surprisingly, women tended to rescue male relations more than anyone else. As we have seen, women did not participate significantly in most assaults on state officials, but rescuing husbands, sons, or brothers was one of the few forms of such resistance open to them. A male relative in prison could pose a serious economic difficulty for his female dependents, making them highly motivated to attempt his release. These women must have considered this form of petty violence against the state as an acceptable type of female misbehavior because they were acting within their roles as their husbands' assistants and as family nurturers. The aggression and defiance of women toward the men imprisoning their family member is another example of the natural extension of female roles observed by Barbara Harris in early modern England. According to Harris, "[W]omen moved unselfconsciously" into roles commonly considered masculine when "they fulfilled their responsibilities as wives, mothers and widows."[76]

Rescues were one of the few unique situations, then, where women lost their reluctance to use violence against state officials. When William Ourd was arrested, his wife Maria "cruelly" beat and abused the arresting officer and rescued her husband from custody.[77] Katherine Green and Alice Williams made "a Riott and assault upon" an officer while rescuing Alice's husband "after he was legally arrested," and Catherine Shepheard was bound "for rescuing her husband . . . after he was arrested."[78] Shepheard also assaulted the arresting officer and set "mastiff Doggs upon him."[79] Mary Luty accompanied her son in "rescueing one John Luty a prisoner," and "Anne the wife of Edward Oakley" and her son Joseph were bound separately for rescuing

Edward "in a Riotous manner."[80] As wives, women were willing to go to any length to regain their husbands' freedom.

In other cases the existence of a relationship between the female rescuer and the prisoner was not stated but was blatantly obvious. Katherine Proctor, senior, Katherine Proctor, junior, and Anne Proctor were bound jointly "for Rescuing . . . Francis Proctor . . . and riotously assaulting beating and bruiseing" the custodial officer, "in which affray he lost his Hatt and Cane, and Edward Price his assistan[t], his Hat and Wigg."[81] Groups of women, on their own or with other men, were significant participants in this sort of rescue. Ann Lockett "with others" rescued her husband by "causing a Ryott and Assault when he was in custody," and Mary Shute "rais[ed] a Tumult and assault[ed]" a jailer "whereby Michael Shute escaped out of his custody."[82] Whether wives, daughters, sisters, or cousins, women rescued their male relatives and were not afraid to use violence against any officer who stood in their way.

It is not always possible to detect family relationships in rescues, yet it is still safe to assume that family connections motivated most of the rescues perpetrated by women. Rescuers with the same surname as the escapee make blood or marital ties clear, but unless women were unmarried or were rescuing sons or husbands, their surnames were different even when they were related. Married women's surnames were different from brothers' and parents'. Similarly, women may have cohabited with men in the equivalent of a modern-day common law marriage, and their "official" surname may then have been different.[83] Cousinship or an employer-employee relationship might also be undetectable when one is forced to rely only upon connecting surnames. In these cases we can only guess at whether such a relationship motivated the rescue.

For example, Deborah Barnes (for whom no marital status was given) may have been a sort of common law wife of John Dobel, whom she violently rescued from two officers, but the recognizance provides no information to clarify Barnes and Dobel's connection.[84] Similarly, we will never know for sure what caused Elizabeth Franklin, "wife of James Franklin," to "obstruct" an officer in his execution "of a warrant to Retake Harrington Sheepay who made his escape . . . after [being] arrested."[85] Sheepay may have been Franklin's brother, father, or cousin—or even her son from a previous marriage. It seems fairly clear that "widow" Hester Stephens and "spinsters" Elizabeth Cobb and Jane Flitt bore no family relationship to Francis Roach, yet they were bound for "rescuing" him.[86] Perhaps Roach was the live-in lover of one of the women or perhaps was at least betrothed to one of them. He may have been their cousin or Stephens's brother or father.

There is another possibility in all of the above examples where a relationship cannot be determined with any certainty. These prisoners may have had an economic connection to the women—as their apprentices or masters perhaps. There certainly was an economic relationship of sorts between Dorothy Hill and the "lewd wenches . . . which she rescued from the constable that took them."[87] Hill was a bawdy-house keeper, and she was clearly rescuing her workers in order to continue earning a living from their labor. Other female rescuers may have wanted to restore their apprentices' freedom because their labor was a vital contribution to the household economy. Conversely, some women may have been apprentices or servants themselves, rescuing the masters who fed, clothed, and housed them.

Regardless of their relationship to the prisoner, female rescuers were just as aggressive and assertive as their male counterparts. Male-authored rescue attempts were sometimes even *less* violent than those authored by women. Rather than confronting and assaulting the sheriff's officer who held Joseph Brown (presumably a relation) captive, Marmaduke Brown chose to file off "one of the Iron Barrs of the Room wherein [Joseph was] confined."[88] In one case a man even disguised himself as a woman to rescue a male prisoner. Richard Vincent went to the Westminster Gaol "drest up in women's cloaths & a Vizard Mask" and begged Mr. Anthony Church, the jailkeeper, to let him "see Mr. St. Legar who was a Prisoner in the said Goal."[89] Church detected his disguise and prosecuted him for attempting "(as is supposed) to endeavour the escape of Mr St. Legar."[90] Many reasons may have been behind Vincent's decision to adopt female dress. Natalie Zemon Davis has pointed out that sometimes men dressed as women in early modern France because "the disguise . . . exploit[ed] the expected physical frailty of women to prevent harm to the male or to disarm his victim."[91] It seems more likely that Vincent simply found the adoption of a cross-gendered identity the most convenient form of disguise, as the two women who accompanied him in the rescue attempt were themselves dressed as men.[92] Nevertheless, men were no more violent or aggressive as rescuers than women, and rescues perpetrated by males were not distinctly different in form from those perpetrated by females.

Perhaps one of the most fascinating insights from the gender analysis of recognizances for rescues is the lack of recognizances binding men for rescuing women. There are only three records of women being rescued (and that includes the "lewd wench" rescued by her female brothel keeper); most of the recognizances were for the rescues of men.[93] And frequently, as the examples have shown, these men were rescued by women. This is a remarkable reversal because rescuers are generally considered to be powerful, and those they rescue, weak and vulnerable. In early modern parlance, God "rescued" sinners, King William "rescued" England from popery and tyranny, strong armies "rescued" cities under seige, etc.[94] The Grimms's fairy-tale heroines were usually rescued by handsome princes.[95] Even the earlier folktale versions (from which the Grimms drew their inspiration) almost never have their heroine in the role of rescuer. When they do, the heroine vanquishes the villain not through her own violence but rather through magic, wiles, or simple good fortune.[96] However, the "damsel in distress" images of patriarchal society do not seem to have applied to the rescues carried out from the roundhouses, compters, and houses of correction in eighteenth-century London. As this section has argued, rescues were one of the few areas where women used violence against the state. Women assaulted constables and other jail officials to forcibly obtain freedom for husbands, brothers, cousins, employers, and masters. While they may have been motivated by dependence—by the need to have a male breadwinner in the household—these female rescuers paradoxically revealed a unique opportunity for feminine agency and empowerment.

Although chapter 6 has argued that women did not participate in petty violence against the state, riots and rescues were two significant areas where feminine opposition to officials became physical. Women attacked those who imprisoned their men; they assaulted people who claimed loyalty to a non-Stuart monarch. Jacobite women voiced their desire to inflict great harm on William III or George I, and they put their words into action when confronted with Williamite or Hanoverian supporters in London's streets. The fact that there is no discernible pattern to women's rescues (the fact that they were probably not rescuing only those men arrested for debt or taken by press gangs) suggests that female rescuers were motivated solely by personal ties to the prisoner. However, these ties brought them into direct confrontation with the state and transformed the personal into the political. Rescuing their men was one of the rare ways women directed violence against the state.

Although this form of feminine violence was rather narrowly constrained, women participated in a wide variety of group assaults. Far from being mute bystanders or obedient followers, female rioters were aggressive, eager participants and were often the leaders of riots. They incited others to violence while actively perpetrating assaults themselves. Men's presence did not deter female group members from aggressively participating in the attack, and occasionally these women beat their victim while the men merely held him or her down or guarded the door.

Women's conduct as rioters bears a unique irony. While the female presence in the eighteenth-century crowd was effectively smothered and masked by contemporary record keepers, the women themselves seem to have become energized and invigorated by the London mob. A high proportion of group violence was perpetrated by women.

8

CONCLUSION

This book began with the story of Thomas Taylor asking that Elizabeth Woosey be bound over for assaulting him with a pitchfork in 1692. In the chapters that followed, we saw that Woosey was not as unusual a woman as she might appear. Thousands of women were called before the Westminster Quarter Sessions in the decades surrounding the turn of the century to answer for assaulting other women and men. Indeed, the very commonness of Woosey's attack hid her from history until now. Her violence—though serious to modern Western eyes—was considered rather petty to early modern mentalities used to beatings as a natural way to maintain order.

Thomas Taylor did, however, feel that Woosey's assault was sufficiently unacceptable to merit a small prosecution. He approached the English criminal courts at their most accessible level: the magistracy. Taylor asked Justice Andrew Lawrence to bind Woosey over in a recognizance, the most popular method of dealing with assault on record. As a resident of the huge metropolis of London, Thomas Taylor felt that Woosey's recognizance was a formal way of ensuring that her violence did not escalate. Taylor did not need to prosecute Woosey again, like most assault complainants in this period, which suggests that he and other prosecutors were satisfied with the binding-over method.

As a man, Taylor was not ashamed to depict himself as vulnerable to attacks by women. Thousands of other men and women brought complaints to Westminster JPs and were empowered by vehemently professing their own victimhood, often stressing the severity of their injuries or the lack of provocation for the attack. Without a prosecution (even one as minor as a recognizance), these men and women are just passive victims, victimized yet again by having their stories silenced for all time. By prosecuting the crime against them, however, these thousands of men and women were empowered. All of these records of petty violence represent a victim who successfully convinced a JP of his or her victimhood and of the plausibility of the defendant's guilt. Their credibility was only as strong as their vehemence before a magistrate. The desirability of victimhood is most apparent in the significant minority of cases where two people competed for victim status—each trying to convince the same JP that the other was the true aggressor.

These were savvy prosecutors who knew how to gain satisfaction through the law. Shouts of "bear witness" and "stop thief" exemplified Londoners' knowledge of the lower courts. It was not uncommon for a prosecutor to resort to the law again, after once prosecuting petty violence in the past, and there were far more repeat prosecutors than repeat offenders. These persistent assault victims made London's legal system an effective deterrent. Astute prosecutors appear in surprising guises. Female sexual assault victims who characterized the attack as a misdemeanor rather than a rape knew that they would receive much more sympathy from the courts and society as a whole. Pregnant women and battered wives were also unlikely candidates for empowerment, yet they harnessed community and court sympathies by coming forward to prosecute assault. Similarly, the aftermath of the largely fictitious Mohock attacks revealed that even relatively groundless community fears could have very real repercussions on elite masculinity. In the records of petty violence in London, women and the lower classes—usually the most disadvantaged groups in early modern society—were able to overcome the obstacles of gender or social status and actively prosecute their social superiors who attacked them.

These records of the prosecution and perpetration of assault reveal much about early modern violence. Episodes of petty violence can be found in the *Old Bailey Proceedings;* in the defamation depositions of the Bishop of London's Consistory Court; and in many other pamphlets, letters, and treatises in early modern literature. However, recognizances document the fullest account of petty violence in the capital during this period. This book has built on the work of Norma Landau on the mechanics of recognizances and their value as a prosecution strategy.[1] It has also shared Robert Shoemaker's appreciation of recognizances as a source of broader social histories.[2] Even more than previous work, however, *Gender and Petty Violence in London* imagines recognizances as an episode in the meeting of elite and popular culture. Upper-class JPs met with Londoners of all walks of life and embarked upon a joint exercise in describing misbehavior and establishing victimhood.

It is important to remember that recognizances were not meant for the general public, in contrast to documents like the *Old Bailey Proceedings.* First and foremost, the Westminster assault recognizances were legal documents, informed by the law of assault and the rules governing JPs, clerks, and constables. The words found on the slip of parchment were not intended primarily for a mass audience, but rather for the legal bureaucracy that oversaw Quarter Sessions in the metropolis.

However, the recognizance had a public nature in practice. The alleged victims told their story to JPs and had to persuade them of its plausibility. If the complainants were successful, the JPs then summoned the accused assailants and had them bound over. The variety and detail of these relatively minor court documents show that JPs were highly influenced by the complainant's account of the assault. Recognizances were a very minor prosecution tool in the criminal justice system. This, along with the higher courts' general apathy toward nonfelonious violence, gave JPs and prosecutors virtually limitless freedom to describe the attacks in recognizances.[3] The resulting one- or two-sentence accounts are a record of extralegal attitudes to petty violence, showing that the public took such acts much more seriously than did the courts.

The preceding chapters have shown that men and women of *all* walks of life found even fairly minor acts of aggression worthy of complaint between 1680 and 1720. In most instances I have not worried about noting that the acts described in the recognizances are only alleged—that the "assailants" are only accused, and not necessarily guilty, and the assault may never have occurred or may have occurred in a different form from that described. Because these men and women were bound in recognizances, their guilt was presumed; establishing truth was not important to the courts, and we cannot presume to determine it hundreds of years later. The "assailants" depicted in the preceding pages can best be regarded as very convincing fictitious characters—as real as they needed to be in order for JPs to bind them over.

This book recognizes that JPs, constables, and other state officials could operate out of venality, and prosecutors' testimony could be more vengeful than truthful, but it argues that recognizances depict a *reasonable* image of violence. Other historians have lamented that malicious prosecutions distort our image of real crime levels.[4] In this study we have not tried to ignore malicious prosecutors but instead have accepted them as a part of the landscape of the early modern criminal justice system. Along with corrupt officials, malicious prosecutors reinforce the gendered norms of misbehavior. Because being believed was essential, these dishonest men and women constructed accounts of typical, plausible forms of petty violence. In addition, the very existence of malicious prosecutors reveals the power available to "victims"—real or imagined—when they approached their local magistrates.

Hitherto largely unheard, their tales of assault revise the traditional image of the role of gender in early modern violence. These records show that women were significant perpetrators of petty violence. Both men and women could do serious injury to their victims. Women were also as likely as men to issue bloodthirsty threats. Many assaults are comparable to a sort of physical language that was understood and used fairly widely. When shaming was the goal of an assault, there were often specific ways to humiliate victims, depending on the victims' gender. The location and circumstances of assaults could also be patterned. Highways, red-light districts, and the night were equated with danger in assault cases, and both the laws and public opinion seem to have caused them to appear as a factor in the official record of the crime. Not surprisingly, drink, money, or intrafamilial feuds were often the source of assaults, but violence could also erupt from street recreation, such as a sporting event. The violence that was prosecuted in Augustan London was highly varied in its forms and causes, and women were significant participants among the defendants.

Women were much less prominent in cases of violent resistance to the state. Although all Londoners were remarkably passive toward rises in taxation and increasing government involvement in their lives, much of the active resistance that did occur was perpetrated by males. Violence against government officials, the military, constables, bailiffs, and marshal's men was largely masculine. This is not surprising. The political arena was considered male terrain, and masculine petty violence in this arena can be seen to make statements about issues such as the illegitimacy of debt as a crime and the unfairness of military recruitment practices.

Women were instead more often mobilized to petty violence by immediate concerns, such as neighborhood tensions. Here, they were confident enough to lead the attacks, inciting crowds to riot against a particular individual or group. When their violence did stem from political concerns, as with Jacobite riots, women were not nearly so prominent. Nevertheless, they were present, and their threats against the non-Stuart monarchs could be just as bloodthirsty as those of their male counterparts. Women could also be driven to acts of violence against the state when their husbands, sons, or other relatives were jailed. Far from simply providing a rope or smuggling a file into the prisoner, these women were aggressive liberators, sometimes grappling with jailers to facilitate a man's escape. Female rioters and rescuers seem to defy the prescribed bounds of femininity in early modern society, yet they remained within them to a certain extent. Women tended to riot based on smaller community concerns rather than broader political reasons, and their rescues could have been construed (by them and others) as a natural extension of their role as assistants to husbands and protectors of sons. Though visible only on the peripheries of assaults on law officials or seditious words prosecutions, these women reveal a very interesting aspect of eighteenth-century femininity.

After summarizing the main contributions of this book, it is also important to consider the areas where further research is necessary. The study of assault needs to be extended to the end of the eighteenth century, enabling a sense of the changes in petty violence, and its prosecution, over time. Interesting insights might also emerge from a study of the changes in women's prosecution activity over time. More work also needs to be done to obtain a sense of the differences in experience of the poorest classes. Perhaps jail records might provide additional evidence of plebeian violence, or perhaps the poor had alternative means to gain retribution for the assaults upon them. The history of assault recognizances might also benefit from a more thorough overview of the other types of recognizances—those binding only "for the peace," for example, might be linked with those to answer assaults in a more systematic way than they have been here. The limits of space prevented my study from testing the data for a variety of factors that might affect petty violence and its prosecution: the different seasons, for example, or economic factors. Perhaps modern criminological studies of interpersonal violence might shed light on some of the causes of assault in the early eighteenth century. Petty violence is a new field of history, and many questions remain to be addressed.

Though perhaps the tip of the iceberg, this book has brought to light thousands of hitherto unknown episodes of petty violence in London between 1680 and 1720. The Westminster Quarter Sessions recognizances for assault are a powerful source in illuminating these stories. Taken alone, they communicate little, but together in these massive numbers, they reveal much more than crime patterns. They speak of the empowerment available to some of the least likely men and women of Augustan London and of the amazing degree of popular knowledge of the law and its potential to resolve differences. London stands starkly apart from the countryside, where conflicts were more often concluded informally. Some of the most captivating pictures of London life are also made visible through these records. At a time when the bureaucratic arm of the state was reaching ever further, Londoners protested only at a direct personal level, by attacking impressment officers and parish constables. Even more fascinating, the recognizances expose women as legal actors in their own right. Cooperating with JPs, thousands of female victims came forward to define the many varied forms that nonfatal violence could take in the capital. From these descriptions early modern femininity appears surprisingly assertive and aggressive. The accounts make it clear that *both* sexes were inclined to deploy violence in early modern London. Though not as prominent in political violence, women were valiant rescuers and wild rioters. This book has, hopefully, established beyond a doubt that neither the perpetration nor the prosecution of petty violence was entirely subject to gender limitations.

Appendix A

The Westminster Assault Recognizances

As a public wrong, assault was a misdemeanor rather than a felony. Certain types of assaults were labeled felonious and were thus theoretically subject to harsher penalties, though in practice many felonious assaults were treated as misdemeanors.[1] Misdemeanors could be punished with fines or imprisonment, in contrast to the capital punishment that might face those accused of felony. Felonies had to be prosecuted by indictment, but most people charged with assault could simply be bound over in a recognizance to answer their victims at Quarter Sessions.[2] These offenders had no trial to establish their guilt or innocence; in most cases they faced no punishment other than the inconvenience of having to appear at court. However, prosecutors probably knew that pursuing a trial would not serve their interests, as grand juries rarely found assault indictments to be "true bills."[3] Recognizances were probably the most popular form of assault prosecution in London in this period. Therefore, the recognizances for assault returned to the Westminster Quarter Sessions between 1685 and 1720 are our principal source;[4] the insights gained from a detailed study of these records form the parameters for the investigation of all of the other sources.

In form, a recognizance was a small slip of parchment that gave the names, addresses, and occupations of three sureties (often the offender was one of these sureties, but this was not required), signed by a JP.[5] Beside the sureties' names was a monetary amount, which they had pledged as a guarantee that the offender would appear at the next Quarter Sessions.[6] A brief but important statement below the sureties' information lists the offender by name and stipulates that he or she is required to appear at the next Quarter Sessions and answer the complainant (also almost always listed by name) for a specific offense. The phrase describing the offense is the most significant component of the recognizance for our purposes. In assault cases individual prosecutors had tremendous influence over JPs, often persuading them to record unique details of the alleged violent act.

As figure A.1 illustrates, recognizances relating to misdemeanors came in five basic forms, binding individuals (or groups), with sureties, for many different purposes: (a) to appear at the next Quarter Sessions and answer a charge; (b) to appear and prosecute or give evidence;[7] (c) to appear at the next (or some other specified) Quarter Sessions and keep the peace (to an individual or the king);[8] (d) to appear and be of good behavior in the interim;[9] (e) to appear to answer a charge and "not depart the court without licence;" or (f) to appear and answer an offense for which the defendant was also prosecuted by indictment. The latter category is subsumed under all of the categories to appear and answer in figure A.1, accounting for approximately 10 percent of the total 7,129.[10] Recognizances of types (a) and (c) or of type (d) were also sometimes combined, resulting in recognizances in which the defendant was asked to appear to answer a charge *and* to keep the peace or be of good behavior in the interim.

With a total of 7,129 binding defendants to appear and answer a charge or plead to an indictment, recognizances for assault clearly comprised a significant portion of the court's business. They were not the only prosecutorial option for assault plaintiffs, but they were probably one of the most popular. As we have seen, those who chose to press their case on to an indictment (seen in recognizances of type (f)), which could generate a trial, faced much higher costs and risked having the indictment thrown out by the grand jury. The majority chose the binding-over method instead.[11] An unknown number of Westminster's assaults may have been settled by informal mediation. Both magistrates and constables were encouraged to help the parties come to an agreement rather than tie up the court's time with petty squabbles, but such informal activities were very rarely recorded.[12] Similarly, those who were charged with assault but were unable to enter into a recognizance (because they did not have connections in the community to act as their sureties) would be imprisoned—and also often lost to historians.[13] Thus, in contrast to the absence of records of informal mediation and jail commitments, and the more expensive—and far less numerous—indictments, recognizances offer a rich source of insight into the early modern experience of petty violence.

Recognizances are particularly valuable for gender historians, because they were especially popular among female prosecutors.[14] Half of all of the assault complaints that were brought before the Westminster JPs and that generated

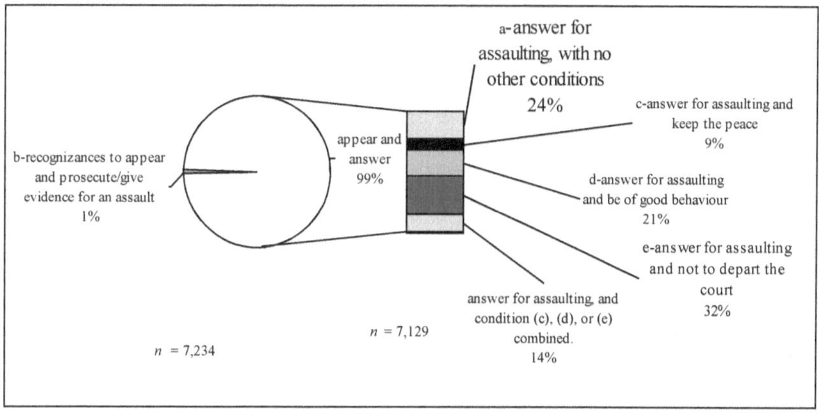

Figure A.1
Proportions: Recognizances to Appear and Prosecute vs. Recognizances to Appear and Answer Assault, Broken Down by Type

recognizances were from women. This is largely due to recognizances' affordability to both prosecutors and defendants.[15] Middling men and women appeared as prominently among defendants as they did among complainants in recognizances, but the laboring classes were represented as well. While poor and friendless defendants would have been deterred even by the standard bond sums, 5 percent of all of the defendants whose social status can be determined were listed as laborers.[16] Peter King's study of the Essex Quarter Sessions' records observed that "more than a fifth of felony prosecutors . . . were labourers," and "labourers were even more active in assault prosecutions."[17] Again, this makes recognizances an especially valuable source for historians.

A recognizance posed little real punishment upon those it bound, and it gave no insight into what happened to the defendant after he or she fulfilled its terms and appeared.[18] Many historians have ignored the recognizance for this very reason.[19] Despite the fact that they almost never resulted in a formal, court-ordered verdict or punishment, recognizances' unquestionable popularity among eighteenth-century assault victims suggests that this prosecution method *must* have held more possibility for satisfaction than the records themselves express.[20] Parties may have settled their differences after the recognizance had been generated. Steve Hindle has suggested that sureties might have put their own pressure upon the defendant because they themselves risked financial loss if the defendant continued to misbehave.[21] Vengeful prosecutors may simply have wanted to see their attackers inconvenienced by having to round up sureties, appear at Quarter Sessions, and pay legal fees.[22] We will never know for certain why recognizances were so popular among assault prosecutors, but the fact that they were means that historians must take them seriously as well.

Because a recognizance represents an interaction between a Justice of the Peace and a prosecutor, it can reveal much about the role of the courts in everyday life and, simultaneously, the influence of popular culture upon the courts. When a prosecutor brought an indictment for an assault, he or she simply went before a clerk, paid the appropriate fee, and had the indictment drawn up based on a very strict formula. However, to have someone bound over, the complainant had to go before the JP directly and convince him that the prosecution was legitimate.[23] Though some initiative rested upon the prosecutor in rejecting indictment as a course of action, the JP also played a significant role in generating the recognizance.

Because the eighteenth-century courts were not particularly concerned with assault, they encouraged magistrates to mediate between quarreling parties and bring about an informal settlement, but in London, as we saw earlier, most prosecutors preferred the formality of a recognizance. The greater likelihood of formal prosecutions in London caused the region to be associated with the nefarious "Trading Justice"—a JP who wanted to draw up a recognizance because he could then collect a fee.[24] There are many accounts of contemporaries accusing "Trading Justices" of actively stirring up tensions between people in order to profit from the resulting litigation.[25] These allegations do not bear out in reality, however. The assault recognizances reveal substantial time and energy given by JPs in describing the exact nature of each offense, which would not have occurred if justices were churning out recognizances purely for their own profit.

JPs (and, indirectly, complainants) had great freedom in drawing up a recognizance. The law did not impose many restrictions upon the form and wording of recognizances for assault, unlike indictments. Shoemaker considered recognizances "a difficult source to interpret . . . because the level of detail . . . was so dependent on the whim of individual justices (or their clerks)."[26] He went on to say that each JP either (1) had a propensity to state only "that the defendant was bound over for no more than 'to answer what shall be objected against him,' 'to keep the peace,' or 'to be of good behaviour,'" or (2) would instead be more inclined to "spell out the objectionable behaviour."[27] Contrary to Shoemaker's findings, *none* of the prominent Westminster JPs or clerks writing recognizances for assault in the period 1685–1720 consistently abandoned detail. During this period, 23 of the 153 JPs in the database issued more than 100 recognizances apiece for assault.[28] Rather than simply writing "assaulting" or "assaulting and beating," in every case, *all* of these JPs (or their clerks) used additional description at some time or other, despite their higher workloads. Ten of them—almost half—veered from this standard terminology in at least 40 percent of their assault recognizances. Of the 7,133 recognizances to appear to answer a charge of assault in the database, almost one-third defied simple classification because they used different wording or added detail.[29] What caused these variations in description?

At times, certainly, their digression from simply classifying the offender as "assaulting" was probably dictated by the law. Particular types of assaults were punishable by statute in more severe ways, such as assaults that took place in a churchyard or that severely disfigured the victim, so they would have to be described clearly in either a recognizance or an indictment.[30] Though there are no prominent rules in justicing handbooks (the reference manuals used by JPs in their work) about the wording of recognizances, much is made of the process behind writing indictments and warrants, and it is possible that the composition of the recognizance was informed by the warrant that preceded it, or in anticipation of the indictment that might follow. Indictments were entirely in Latin until 1731 (*4 Geo. 2 c. 36)* and were subject to petty conventions, such as: "if the Words *Vi & Armis* . . . are not put immediately before the *Insultum Fecit*, . . . the Indictment is naught, though these words are in the beginning of it."[31] Beyond recounting the assault to the point that the recording official could select an appropriate formulaic charge, the complainants had little influence over the written record of the offense.

The drafting of a recognizance allowed JPs substantial latitude, in consultation with the complainant, to describe the offense.[32] It was in the JP's own interest to ensure that recognizances gave a relatively full and detailed account, as one manual warned justices that they were expected to "not only . . . appear and return such Recognizances and Examinations as they have taken since last Sessions, but [also] give Information touching Persons and Things to facilitate the Prosecutions."[33] If a JP did not keep a notebook recording his daily business (and many did not, given the small numbers that have survived), the few short lines in the recognizance may have been enough to trigger his memory and allow him to adequately perform this function at Quarter Sessions. Detailed recognizances may have even substituted for the JP himself, as many Middlesex and Westminster JPs did not often attend Quarter Sessions.[34] In this case presiding officials would have been grateful for the recognizance that provided sufficient detail to allow them to effectively admonish the defendant and ensure that he or she did not commit the same offense in the future.[35]

The activities of a JP were theoretically monitored by the higher courts. In practice, however, historians have found that parliamentary statutes and

King's Bench served at least as often to *broaden* JPs' autonomy as to curb it.[36] Writs of *certiorari, mandamus,* and *habeas corpus* governed justices' activity but had no impact upon recognizances.[37] The closest mention of recognizances is with the writs of *supersedeas* or *supplicavit.* However, the former did not affect the description of the offense, which is the most significant element for our purposes, and the latter was almost never used.[38] Thus, we can safely assume that thousands of recognizances were created by JPs acting on their own judicial authority, subject to very few constraints.

JPs' handbooks meticulously outlined their duties relating to the amount and reliability of sureties, dictating that this portion of the recognizance be written in Latin to a standard format.[39] In contrast, the vernacular portion describing the offense—most significant to us—rarely bears mentioning.[40] Not surprisingly, given our sense of legal attitudes to petty violence in this period, the recognizance for assault was given the least attention of the many types of recognizances discussed in the justicing handbooks.[41] This lack of regulation enabled contemporary ideas and popular perceptions to find their way into the recognizances for assault studied here, and it makes them very valuable for historians, as evidence of both the active role of prosecutors and popular perceptions of violence and authority.

Appendix B

The Bishop of London's Consistory Court Defamation Depositions and Accounts of Felonious Violence in the *OBP*

The Bishop of London's Consistory Court met at the Long Chapel of St. Paul's with the vicar-general acting as judge.[1] Those convicted would face several possible punishments, "such as Monition, Penance, suspension from participation in the rites of religion, and even Excommunication," according to a nineteenth-century treatise on the church courts.[2] The same author did, however, grudgingly admit that they "are punishments which affect only the mind and conscience; they have little influence upon persons who have no respect for religion."[3] This seems to have been satisfactory for female Londoners, however, as many women came before this court to prosecute defamation.[4] Defamation could be prosecuted in the secular courts or at other ecclesiastical courts, but most people chose to prosecute defamation in the Bishop of London's Consistory Court.[5] Clearly, some Londoners found the Church Court a favorable alternative to secular justice, making its defamation records valuable as evidence of the interpersonal tensions within the metropolis, and more particularly of women's use of the law to resolve these tensions.

From the last quarter of the seventeenth century, virtually every individual tried at each session of the Old Bailey was mentioned in the diverse pamphlets published under a range of titles, known commonly to historians as the *Old Bailey Proceedings*.[6] Though the actual authors of the papers are difficult to determine, it is clear that they were hired by a fairly diverse group of publishers, ranging from "fairly low-key individuals" to the more established, based around the Old Bailey and nearby Fleet Street, some of whom plied their trade within the halls of justice themselves, and each issue was carefully policed for accuracy "as early as 1678."[7] Although the *OBP* attracted many readers from the legal community, the pamphlets also seem to have been popular among a much wider audience.[8]

Because versions before 1729 have survived only sporadically, the evidence used here has necessarily been a sampling, the parameters of which have been defined by those issues of the *OBP* that exist in microform.[9] The *OBP* give names of the defendants and an account of the crimes committed, usually with a summary of the evidence brought by each side and always with the verdict and sentence. Because they generally bear more description than recognizances, the *OBP* are a valuable supplement in the study of urban violence.

Consistory court depositions for forty-five defamation cases heard at the Bishop of London's court also supplement the recognizances. Like the *OBP*, they are too numerous for every case to be reviewed, and the forty-five have been taken randomly at five-year intervals from the collection of depositions for urban parishes in Middlesex.[10] The depositions could also be quite lengthy, giving detailed statements of the circumstances behind the slander from as many as five different witnesses. It is important to note that the direct statements of the plaintiff (called the *producent* in canon law) and the defendant (known as the *ministrant*) are not recorded in these depositions, which were a later stage in the process.[11]

Occasionally, the case documents might also include interrogatories, a list of questions formulated from the ministrant's story of the event—some of which have been found and included here, or ministrants might launch either a "counter-allegation," with corresponding statements from witnesses, or an "exception," which questioned the character of the producent's witnesses altogether.[12] The depositions list witnesses' names, addresses, and occupations or marital status, but they do not formally list those of the producent and the ministrant.[13] All in all, a defamation suit would generally have taken about a year—if producents saw it through until the end. The fact that few litigants actually pursued their suits to a sentence suggests that they probably came before the Bishop of London's Consistory Court with a similar goal to those prosecuting by recognizance at the Westminster Quarter Sessions: to make public the offense against them and cause the offender to experience embarrassment and remorse.[14]

The depositions were a mediated source, taken by trained scribes (usually registrar's deputies), and no doubt influenced by the "ecclesiastical lawyers, proctors, and advocates" who were regularly involved in church court litigation.[15] Each deposition represents a question-and-answer session between the scribe and the witness that sets the structure of the narrative, yet this structure was masked by the written text's appearance as a monologue. Nevertheless, the gist of their stories must certainly have originated with the witnesses themselves, and the slanderous words at the heart of the dispute were probably recorded exactly as the witnesses said them.[16] Eighteenth-century litigants generally brought only cases of sexual slander to these courts, although ecclesiastical laws prohibited many other kinds of insult, reflecting the church court's popular image as "the bawdy courts."

The Consistory Court depositions and the *OBP* are valuable supplementary sources for the Westminster recognizances. They offer more anecdotal information on the circumstances surrounding interpersonal disputes and their litigation, whereas the recognizance presents only a snapshot of an isolated moment in time. The *OBP* and the defamation depositions also help to hide some of the regional anomalies of the Westminster records, because the Old Bailey and the Bishop of London's Consistory Courts' jurisdictions cover the entire metropolis.

Notes

Notes to Chapter 1

1. MJ/SR1798 R27, 23 Apr. 1692.

2. See R. B. Shoemaker, *Prosecution and Punishment: Petty Crime and the Law in London and Rural Middlesex, c. 1660–1725* (Cambridge: Harvard University Press, 1991), 140–44, on the costs of indictments at Quarter Sessions.

3. Ibid., 6–7.

4. Norma Landau, "Appearance at the Quarter Sessions of Eighteenth-Century Middlesex," *London Journal* 23, no. 2 (1998), 35, 47n, lists these fees.

5. Although serious attacks like nose slitting or taking out an eye were defined as felonies under the law, they were often, in practice, treated as misdemeanors and prosecuted only by recognizance.

6. See, for example, Michael Dalton, *The Countrey Justice* (London, 1655), 203.

7. In addition to assault, the various "trespasses against the peace," are "Battery, . . . where any person hath violently struck another"; "Bloodshed, . . . where upon any such Battery Blood hath been shed"; and "Maihem," which involved mutilations of various kinds. W. T., *The Office of the Clerk of Assize . . . Together with the Office of the Clerk of the Peace . . .* 2nd ed. (London: Printed for Henry Twyford, 1682), 127. For a more comprehensive description, see Sir William Blackstone, *Commentaries on the Laws of England in Four Books,* Book Three (reprint, Philadelphia: Geo. T. Bisel Co., 1922), 120–22. As mentioned earlier, terms such as *battery, mayhem,* and *bloodshed* were not present in many of the assault recognizances that bore descriptions appropriate to such offenses.

8. R. Burn, *The Justice of the Peace, and Parish Officer,* Vol. I, 24th ed. (London: A. Strahan, 1825), 226. See also E. H. East, *A Treatise of the Pleas of the Crown,* Vol. I (London: A. Strahan, 1803), 406.

9. For a discussion of the variety of acts described in assault recognizances, see chapter 5. Appendix A and chapter 2 elaborate on JPs' freedom in writing recognizances.

10. Note that the 105 recognizances to appear to prosecute an assault (type *b* in appendix A, figure A.1) have also been used as accounts of petty violence, except where stated in the quantitative analyses.

11. Of the 7,129 recognizances to appear to answer a charge of assault, 9 percent (636) also bound the defendant to keep the peace (combining types *a* and *c*); 21 percent (1,527) were to be of good behavior (combining types *a* and *d*); and 32 percent

(2,301) simply added the condition that the defendant was not allowed "to depart the court without licence" (type *e*). Of the remaining recognizances, 14 percent (1,002) bound the defendant for a combination of keeping the peace, good behavior, or not departing the court without permission, leaving 24 percent where there was no extra condition other than to appear to answer the assault charge (type *a*). None of these conditions bear any significant relationship to the severity of the offense or its description. While, in theory, recognizances for maintaining good behavior were more serious than those for the peace, in practice there was little distinction between the two; and they seem to have been used rather arbitrarily, at the discretion of each individual JP. See Robert Shoemaker, "Using Quarter Sessions Records as Evidence in the Study of Crime and Criminal Justice" *Archives* XX, no. 90 (1993), 151, and Landau, "Appearance at the Quarter Sessions," 34.

12. On the culture of violence in early modern Europe, see, for example, J. R. Farr, *Hands of Honour: Artisans and Their World in Dijon, 1550–1650* (Ithaca: Cornell University Press, 1988), and J. Pitt-Rivers, "Honour and Social Status," in J. G. Peristiany, ed., *Honor and Shame: The Values of Mediterranean Society* (London: Nicholson, 1965).

13. John Beattie, "Violence and Society in Early Modern England," in A. Doob and E. Greenspan, eds., *Perspectives in Criminal Law* (Aurora, Ontario: Canada Law Book Inc., 1985), 42.

14. L. Stone, "Interpersonal Violence in English Society, 1300–1980," *Past and Present* 101 (Nov. 1983), 22–33; J. A. Sharpe, "Debate: The History of Violence in England: Some Observations," *Past and Present* 108 (Aug. 1985), 206–15; L. Stone, "A Rejoinder," *Past and Present* 108 (Aug. 1985), 216–24; S. Amussen, "Punishment, Discipline & Power: The Social Meaning of Violence in Early Modern England," *Journal of British Studies* 34 (Jan 1995); idem, "The Gendering of Popular Culture," in T. Harris, ed., *Popular Culture in England, c. 1500–1850* (New York: St. Martin's Press, 1995); idem, "'Being Stirred to Much Unquietness': Violence and Domestic Violence in Early Modern England," *Journal of Women's History* 6, no. 2 (1994); J. S. Cockburn, "Patterns of Violence in English Society: Homicide in Kent, 1500–1985," *Past and Present* 130 (1991), 70–106; M. Gaskill, *Crime and Mentalities in Early Modern England* (Cambridge: Cambridge University Press, 2000), 203–82; and R. Shoemaker, "Male honour and the decline of public violence in eighteenth-century London," *Social History* 26, no. 2 (May 2001), 190–208.

15. Amussen, "Being Stirred," 75.

16. In addition to the examples that follow, see Robert Shoemaker, *The London Mob: Violence and Disorder in Eighteenth-Century England* (London: Hambledon and London, 2004), and Sharon Howard, "Crime, Communities and Authorities in Early Modern Wales: Denbighshire, 1660–1730," Ph.D. thesis, University of Wales, 2003.

17. Steve Hindle, "The Keeping of the Public Peace," in Paul Griffiths, Adam Fox, and Steve Hindle, eds., *The Experience of Authority in Early Modern England* (New York: St. Martin's Press, 1996), 227.

18. Garthine Walker, *Crime, Gender and Social Order in Early Modern England* (Cambridge: Cambridge University Press, 2003).

19. Hindle, 223, and Walker, 221.

20. Beattie, "Violence," 42.

21. See, for example, E. Foyster, *Manhood in Early Modern England: Honour, Sex and Marriage* (London: Longman, 1999); B. Capp, "The Double Standard Revisited: Plebeian Women and Male Sexual Reputation in Early Modern England," *Past and Present* 162 (1999), 70–100; A. Fletcher, "Manhood, the Male Body, Courtship and the Household in Early Modern England" *History* 84, no. 275 (1999), 419–36.

22. This insight is very much in keeping with studies such as Michèle Cohen's "Manliness, effeminacy and the French: gender and the construction of national character in eighteenth-century England," in T. Hitchcock and M. Cohen, eds., *English Masculinities, 1660–1800* (London: Longman, 1999), 44–62.

23. See, for example, A. Clark, *Women's Silence, Men's Violence: Sexual Assault in England,* 1770–1845 (London: Pandora, 1987); M. Chaytor, "Husband(ry): Narratives of Rape in the Seventeenth Century," *Gender and History* 7 (1995), 378–407; M. Hunt, "Wife Beating, Domesticity and Women's Independence in Eighteenth-Century London," *Gender and History* 4, no. 1 (1992), 10–33; S. Amussen, "Being Stirred to Much Unquietness," 70–89; and E. Foyster, "Male Honour, Social Control and Wife Beating in Late Stuart England," *Transactions of the Royal Historical Society, 6th Series* 6 (1996), 215–24.

24. Peter King explored the judicial attitudes toward women on trial for felonies and mentioned infanticide and murder, but his main focus was upon property crime. P. King, "Gender, crime and justice in late eighteenth- and early nineteenth-century England," in M. L. Arnot and C. Usborne, eds., *Gender and Crime in Modern Europe* (London: UCL Press, 1999), 44–74. John Beattie has also acknowledged women's potential for violence, but his examination of the Surrey Assize records was more interested in the fact that women were more likely to be prosecuted for theft than for assault. J. M. Beattie, "The Criminality of Women in Eighteenth-Century England," *Journal of Social History* viii (1975), 89. On female thieves in the seventeenth century, see Garthine Walker, "Women, theft and the world of stolen goods," in J. Kermonde and G. Walker, eds., *Women, Crime and the Courts in Early Modern England* (London: UCL Press, 1994), 81–105. On defamation, see, for example, Laura Gowing's *Domestic Dangers: Women, Words and Sex in Early Modern London* (Oxford: Clarendon Press, 1996), and "Gender and the Language of Insult in Early Modern London," *History Workshop Journal* 35 (1993), 1–21. Susan Amussen examined women's physical aggression only in the context of witchcraft. S. Amussen, "Punishment, Discipline & Power: The Social Meaning of Violence in Early Modern England," *Journal of British Studies* 34 (Jan 1995), especially pp. 27–31.

25. R. Malcolmson, "Infanticide in the Eighteenth Century," in J. S. Cockburn, ed., *Crime in England, 1550–1800* (Princeton: Princeton University Press, 1977), 187–210; M. Jackson, *New-born Child Murder: Women, Illegitimacy, and the Courts in Eighteenth-Century England* (Manchester: Manchester University Press, 1996); A. May, "'She at first denied it': Infanticide Trials at the Old Bailey," in V. Frith, ed., *Women and History: Voices of Early Modern England* (Concord, Ontario: Irwin Publishing, 1997), 19–49; L. Gowing, "Secret Births and Infanticide in Seventeenth-Century England," *Past and Present* 156 (1997), 87–115.

26. F. Dolan, *Dangerous Familiars: Representations of Domestic Crime in England, 1550–1700* (Ithaca: Cornell University Press, 1994), and J. Wiltenburg, *Disorderly*

Women and Female Power in the Street Literature of Early Modern England and Germany (Charlottesville: University Press of Virginia, 1992).

27. M. Hester, "The Dynamics of Male Domination using the Witch Craze in Sixteenth- and Seventeenth-Century England as a case study," *Women's Studies International Forum* 13 (1990), 11.

28. Shoemaker, *Prosecution and Punishment.*

29. See, for example, Gowing, *Domestic Dangers,* and most recently, T. Meldrum, *Domestic Service and Gender, 1660–1750* (New York: Pearson Education, 2000).

30. M. Hunt, *The Middling Sort: Commerce, Gender and the Family in England, 1680–1780* (Berkeley: University of California Press, 1996), 9.

31. T. Stretton, *Women Waging Law in Elizabethan England* (Cambridge: Cambridge University Press, 1998).

32. D. Hay et al., eds., *Albion's Fatal Tree: Crime and Society in Eighteenth-Century England* (London: Allen Lane, 1975), and E. P. Thompson, *Whigs and Hunters: The Origin of the Black Act* (London: Allen Lane, 1975).

33. L. Radzinowicz, *A History of English Criminal Law and its Administration from 1750.* 4 Vols. (London: Stevens and Sons, 1948–68).

34. D. Hay, "Property, Authority and the Criminal Law," in *Albion's Fatal Tree,* 35.

35. J. M. Beattie, *Crime and the Courts in England, 1660–1800* (Princeton: Princeton University Press, 1986).

36. Unless otherwise stated, "London" has been used to refer to the metropolis rather than only to the City.

37. E. A. Wrigley, "A simple model of London's importance in changing English society and economy, 1650–1750," *Past and Present* 37 (1967), 44.

38. L. Stone, "The Residential Development of the West End of London in the Seventeenth Century," in B. C. Malament, ed., *After the Reformation, essays in honor of J. H. Hexter* (Philapdelphia: University of Pennsylvania Press, 1980), 168, table 1.

39. Wrigley, 46–49.

40. J. M. Beattie, "The Criminality of Women," 97–98.

41. See Shoemaker, *Prosecution and Punishment,* 284–88.

42. N. Landau, "Appearance at the Quarter Sessions," 33.

43. The assizes for Cumberland, Northumberland, and Westmorland are the exception, being held only once a year, until the nineteenth century. J. S. Cockburn, *A History of English Assizes, 1558–1714* (Cambridge: Cambridge University Press, 1972), 19, 45.

44. J. H. Baker, "Criminal Courts and Procedure at Common Law 1550–1800," in *Crime in England,* 30–31.

45. J. A. Sharpe, *Crime in Early Modern England 1550–1750* (London: Longman, 1984), 21–22.

46. Baker, "Criminal Courts and Procedure," 30.

47. The relationship between King's Bench and the Westminster Quarter Sessions is discussed in more detail in appendix A.

48. J. M. Beattie, *Policing and Punishment in the City of London, 1660–1750: Urban Crime and the Limits of Terror* (New York: Oxford University Press, 2001), 12.

49. Ibid., 16. However, pages 20–21 show how, unlike the assizes, the sessions of

the peace for the City and Middlesex County were integrally connected to the Old Bailey sessions of oyer and terminer and jail delivery.

50. W. Holdsworth, *A History of English Law.* Vol. I, 7th ed., A. Goodhart and H. Hanbury, eds. (London: Methuen & Co., 1956), 285.

51. According to John Beattie, the Westminster and Middlesex JPs may have been excluded because of their lower social status. Beattie suggested that, because the meetings of the Old Bailey (like the assizes in the counties) were prominent social occasions, the City magistrates and their families may have been motivated by their distaste for associating with the families of the Westminster and Middlesex Justices whom they felt to be their inferiors. Beattie, *Policing and Punishment,* 13–14.

52. E. A. Reynolds, *Before the Bobbies: The Night Watch and Police Reform in Metropolitan London, 1720–1830* (Stanford: Stanford University Press, 1998), 11.

53. R. Porter, *London: A Social History* (Cambridge: Harvard University Press, 1995), 152.

54. For example, Westminster was governed by twelve life-appointed burgesses, because "neither [the City of] London, nor the Court nor Parliament had ever wished to have to deal with a Lord Mayor of Westminster." G. M. Trevelyan, *Illustrated English Social History, Volume Three: The Eighteenth Century* (London: Longmans, Green and Co., 1942), 42.

55. Stone, 176–77, and Porter, 134.

56. Porter, 96, 140.

57. N. Rogers, *Whigs and Cities: Popular Politics in the Age of Walpole and Pitt* (Oxford: Clarendon Press, 1989), 168.

58. The money wage of a building laborer. L. D. Schwartz, *London in the age of industrialization: Entrepreneurs, labour force and living conditions, 1700–1850* (Cambridge: Cambridge University Press, 1992), 170.

59. The social status of only 415 (6 percent) of the 7,129 prosecutors could be determined, and six of these 415 prosecutors were laborers (for women, their husband's occupation was used, except for the rare occasions where the woman's own occupation was recorded). This is only 1 percent of the 415 total. It seems likely that the real proportion of laborer prosecutors is somewhat higher, however, because most of the 415 complainants' occupations were determined when they bore an aristocratic title, distorting the data in favor of wealthier prosecutors. Untitled prosecutors' status was determined only when they either had entered into a bond to prosecute (which occurred in only 1 percent of all 7,234 assault recognizances) or had been prosecuted themselves and had to enter into recognizance.

60. John Richardson, *The Annals of London: A Year-by-Year Record of a Thousand Years of History* (London: Cassell & Co., 2000), 174.

61. However, Shoemaker calculated that 88 percent of the business of the London Consistory Court came from the metropolis. "The Decline of Public Insult in London 1660–1800," *Past and Present* 169 (November 2000), 99n.

62. Norma Landau cites 6,432 recognizances at Middlesex Quarter Sessions from 1701 to 1705 (less than 1,300 per year), increasing to 2,071 in 1734 but rising still more dramatically to approximately 5,650 a year in the late 1780s (22,593 from 1788 to 1791). "Appearance at the Quarter Sessions," 45, table 1.

Notes to Chapter 2

1. For a concise summary of victims' more passive role in the modern British criminal justice system, see Sandra Walklate, *Victimology: The Victim and the Criminal Justice Process* (London: Unwin Hyman, 1989), 126–28.

2. See appendix A for detailed evidence.

3. MJ/SR2290 R205, 8 May 1717, is a window into the process, as it described Dorothy Hall bringing a warrant to a constable in his bakery and asking him to serve it. In this particular case, the constable refused to serve the warrant and was prosecuted, creating a record of the event for posterity.

4. Beattie, *Policing and Punishment in the City of London, 1660–1750: Urban Crime and the Limits of Terror* (New York: Oxford University Press, 2001), 131, states that "there was no expectation that a constable would investigate crime, discover the perpetrator, formulate and bring the charges . . . [this] was still thought to be the victim's work."

5. See, for example, Douglas Hay, "Prosecution and Power: Malicious Prosecution in the English Courts, 1750–1850," in D. Hay and F. Snyder, eds., *Policing and Prosecution in Britain 1750–1850* (Oxford: Clarendon Press, 1989). Chapter 6 further discusses the corruption of the eighteenth-century criminal justice system.

6. Stephen Greenblatt, *Renaissance Self-Fashioning: From More to Shakespeare* (Chicago: University of Chicago Press, 1980), 2.

7. MSP 1707 Sept/16, The Informacon of Shorland Adams, dated 28 Aug. 1707.

8. MSP 1711 Jy/71, Informacon of James Mortimer of Kingsland Comon in the Parish of St. Mary Islington, dated 2 June 1711.

9. Ibid. They found a halter, a "set of Picklock Keys," and various weapons on the man, resulting in his arrest for horsetheft.

10. *OBP,* 27–29 Apr. 1720 (London, printed for E. Symon by M. Jenour), 4.

11. On the raising of the hue and cry, see E. A. Reynolds, *Before the Bobbies: The Night Watch and Police Reform in Metropolitan London, 1720–1830* (Stanford: Stanford University Press, 1998), 9; R. Shoemaker, "The London 'Mob' in the Early Eighteenth Century," *Journal of British Studies* 26 (July 1987), 287; and J. M. Beattie, *Policing and Punishment,* chapter 3.

12. MSP 1705 Ap/52, The Informacon of Job Fornworth of the Parish of St. James, dated 12 Apr. 1705.

13. MSP 1697 Dec/27–29, ff 27, The Informacon of Elizabeth Webster daughter of Mathew Webster, dated 1 Nov. 1697.

14. MJ/SR2270 R155, 18 June 1716, claimed that because Rebecca Baldwin "Cry'd out Murder," she "was assaulted and beaten for't," and the *OBP,* 15–19 Jan. 1718/9 (London, printed for J. Phillips by M. Jenour), 4–5 recounted a robber saying to his victim, "[D]o you cry out Murder? Damn you, I'll teach you to say murder," and then beating him.

15. DL/C/244 f 264, Hall c. Ruggsby, 15 Jan. 1694/5.

16. DL/C/251 f 438, Clarke c. Barnes, 16 June 1710.

17. MJ/SR2270 R112, 12 May 1716.

18. For recognizances involving prosecutions and counterprosecutions between

different families (presumably representing neighborhood feuds), see MJ/SR1741 R197 (30 Apr.), R220 (3 May), and R222 (4 May) 1689; MJ/SR1841 R31, R32, R33, and R34, 17 July 1694; MJ/SR1855 R42 (21 May) and R37 (18 June) 1695; MJ/SR1969 R150 (27 May), R154 (28 May), and R132 (27 June) 1701; MJ/SR2013 R47 and R49, 8 May 1703; MJ/SR2250 R43 and R44, 14 May 1715; and MJ/SR2353 R24 (24 Aug.) and R23 (29 Aug.) 1720.

19. MJ/SR1873 R122 and R121, 25 Apr. 1696 respectively.

20. MJ/SR1897 R92 and R93, 14 and 10 July 1697 respectively.

21. Robert Shoemaker, 284–85, has noted the greater likelihood of urban disputants to launch a formal prosecution than to come to an informal agreement mediated by a JP.

22. DL/C/259 f 112, Clift c. Lutrell, 21 June 1720.

23. Ibid.

24. Narcissus Lutrell's *A Brief Historical Relation of State Affairs from September 1678 to April 1714* (6 vols., Oxford, 1857) and H. Horowitz, ed., *The Parliamentary Diary of Narcissus Luttrell, 1691–1693* (Oxford: Clarendon Press, 1972) demonstrate Lutrell's involvement in national government. His personal diary reaffirms his movements in elite circles, but it also bears witness to his activities on the bench, referring to dinners with the high Constable and other JPs. See P. Dixon, "Narcissus Lutrell's Private Diary," *Notes and Queries* 207 (1962), 388–92, 411–15, and 452–55.

25. This varied according to the parish. The Webbs recounted "the 'Justices of Covent Garden' . . . sometimes meeting 'by surprise' in one of the taverns of the Strand," while the JPs of St. Margaret's seem to have consistently held their petty sessions "'at the Vestry room' once or twice a month." S. and B. Webb, *English Local Government, Volume 1: The Parish and the County* (London: Frank Cass and Co., 1906, reprinted, 1963), 403, 405.

26. John Beattie describes the City aldermen hearing complaints "in their own residences." However, by the end of our period, JPs' work had become much more formalized. Beattie, *Policing and Punishment,* 92. According to Beattie (110), "[T]he most active, crime-fighting magistrates in the area around Covent Garden to the west of the City thought it necessary to create structures for this work that were in effect courtrooms."

27. In the interrogatory, which was based upon the ministrant's (defendant's) defense, prosecution witnesses were asked, "[D]o you not know . . . that [Clift] was upon the Acc[oun]t of her keeping a disordily house . . . denied a Lycense . . . to sell drink and that her thinking [Lutrell] had a hand in the denying the said Lycense was the Cause of her bringing this suit she having sworn . . . she would be revenged?" DL/C/259, interrogatory 2, f 385, Clift c. Lutrell, 21 June 1720.

28. The alternative forms of prosecution for assault are laid out in appendix A.

29. Tables 2.1 and 2.2 show an overall decrease in the total numbers of assault complainants and defendants before Westminster Quarter Sessions from 1701 to 1705, suggesting that the War of Spanish Succession (1702–13) had a dampening effect on Quarter Sessions' activity.

30. The number of complainants mentioned in more than one recognizance for the same assault is largely balanced out by the number of defendants bound in separate recognizances for assaulting multiple complainants at the same time. One

might have thought that multiple defendants would be more likely to appear in separate recognizances, though they had attacked the same complainant (thus inflating the number of repeat complainants), because they each had to find sureties. Many seem to have used the same sureties and to have been bound on the same recognizance, however. In fact, the total number of recognizances listing more than one defendant is roughly equal to the total number listing multiple complainants (333 and 340 respectively).

31. MJ/SR2295 R51, 21 Aug. 1717 and MJ/SR2310 R30, R31, and R32, 14 June 1718 respectively.

32. MJ/SR2343, R11, R12, and R13, 2 Jan. 1720.

33. MJ/SR1969 R99, 30 June 1701 and MJ/SR2302 R60, 12 May 1704 respectively.

34. Sir Thomas Deveil, *Observations on the practice of a Justice of the Peace: intended for such gentlemen as design to act for Middlex or Westminster* . . . (London, 1747), 13–14.

35. According to Landau (508), indictments for assault filed at Middlesex Quarter Sessions "aimed not at punishing the defendant, but instead at obtaining compensation." Through various formal and informal means, defendants were able to escape many of the punishments the court might exert, by paying the plaintiff directly in return for what was basically a withdrawal of prosecution. N. Landau, "Indictment for Fun and Profit: A Prosecutor's Reward at Eighteenth-Century Quarter Sessions," *Law and History Review* 17, no. 3 (1999), 507–36. Shoemaker (131) has also noted that "it is possible that the number of [Quarter Sessions] indictments which addressed disputes typically heard in civil courts increased during this period" and "the practice of prosecuting civil cases at quarter sessions continued through at least the mid-eighteenth century."

36. MJ/SR2343 R137, 24 Mar. 1720 and MJ/SR1921 R52, 3 Jan. 1698/9 respectively.

37. It is interesting to note that only one of this type of assault recognizance—that brought by shopkeeper Hannah Lee—indicates that the prosecution went on to generate an indictment. MJ/SR2315 R300, 4 Oct. 1718.

38. See MJ/SR1769 R94, 27 Oct. 1690; MJ/SR1902 R16, 23 Nov. 1697; MJ/SR2295 R43, 16 Sept. 1717; MJ/SR2300 R230, 17 Oct. 1717; MJ/SR2300 R99, 14 Dec. 1717; MJ/SR2330 R116, 23 June 1719; MJ/SR2334 R95, 10 Aug. 1719; MJ/SR2339 R49, 11 Nov. 1719. Note that eight of these were brought by women, which further underscores the popularity of recognizances among female prosecutors.

39. WSP 1705 Ap/1, Peticon of Elizabeth White, undated (1705). Petitions were accepted at Quarter Sessions, and, according to a clerk's handbook, the party against whom the petition was presented was given a chance to answer it; if the party did not show up or the evidence against him was convincing, the court could make an Order upon the petition. W. T., *The Office of the Clerk of Assize . . . Together with the Office of the Clerk of the Peace* . . . 2nd Ed. (London: Printed for Henry Twyford, 1682), 178.

40. For further speculation upon the impact of maternal images upon the courts, see chapter 4.

41. N. Z. Davis, *Fiction in the Archives: Pardon Tales and Their Tellers* (Stanford: Stanford University Press, 1987), 16.

42. For detailed evidence on this point, see appendix A. In his investigation of early modern murder cases, Malcolm Gaskill has also emphasized popular agency in legal records. M. Gaskill, *Crime and Mentalities in Early Modern England* (Cambridge: Cambridge University Press, 2000), 203–41.

43. E. Bohun, *The Justice of Peace his Calling and Qualifications* (London: printed for T. Salusbury, 1693), 150. Note also that "[i]n every Warrant . . . where sureties are to be found or required, the Warrant ought to contain the special cause or matter," unless "it be fore some great Crime." W. Shepard, *The Justice of Peace, His Clerks Cabinet* (London: John Steater et al., 1672), 5.

44. We cannot test this theory because none of the manuals explicitly depict JPs using the text of the warrant in drawing up the resulting recognizance, and no warrants have been preserved to be viewed directly.

45. Ibid., 354. See also Nelson, 484. There would not have been any point in reciting a Latin indictment to the defendant, but recognizances had only the names, addresses, and occupations of the principal and sureties in Latin, and the condition—the part that described the offense for which the principal was bound—in English.

46. Words and phrases have been added, above the line of text, in a few recognizances to suggest afterthoughts on the part of the recorder—perhaps prompted by the prosecuting victim. For examples of this type of clerical activity, see J. Hurl-Eamon, "'She being bigg with child is likely to miscarry': Pregnant Victims Prosecuting Assault in Westminster, 1685–1720," *London Journal* 24, no. 2 (1999), 25.

47. MJ/SR2275 R150, 14 July 1716.

48. MJ/SR2275 R169, 20 Aug. 1716.

49. MJ/SR2133 R72, 21 June 1709. Emphasis in original.

50. MJ/SR2275 R59, 7 Sept. 1716.

51. MJ/SR1883 R73, 30 Dec. 1696. For other examples, see MJ/SR1754 R37, 21 Feb. 1689/90; MJ/SR2230 R16, 30 Apr. 1714; and MJ/SR2310 R4, 6 May 1718.

52. MJ/SR2286 unnumbered recognizance to prosecute, 26 Jan. 1716/7.

53. MJ/SR2290 R196, 14 June 1717 and MJ/SR2037 R22, 1 Sept. 1704 respectively.

54. MJ/SR2348 R107, 7 May 1720.

55. *The Compleat Justice* (London, 1656), 19. It should be noted that justicing handbooks encouraged JPs to record fears or threats in recognizances *for the peace* or *good behavior*, and this legal consideration may be behind some of the recognizances where they are mentioned. See, for example, J. Bond, *A Compleat Guide for Justices of the Peace* (London, 1707), 181, which states, "A justice granting the peace . . . must take an Oath of the Party so demanding, that he is in bodily fear &c." However, complainants' fears and defendants' threats are mentioned even in assault recognizances that bind only to appear and do not go on to demand the peace or good behavior. Thus, in some cases at least, fears and threats were recorded simply because the complainants must have impressed the JP with these aspects of the assault.

56. MJ/SR2286 R169, 12 Mar. 1716/7.

57. MJ/SR2290 R37, 29 June 1717 and MJ/SR1860 R19, 21 Aug. 1695 respectively.

58. Michael Dalton, *The Countrey Justice* (London: 1655), 205.

59. The law permitted homicide as self-defense in a quarrel when "the slayer endeavours to decline" to fight, but, "being closely pressed by his antagonist, kills him to avoid his own destruction." Sir William Blackstone, *Commentaries on the Laws of England in Four Books,* Book Four (reprint, Philadelphia: Geo. T. Bisel Co., 1922), 184.

60. C. K. Allen, "The Phlegmatic Englishman in the Common Law," in *Legal Duties and other Essays in Jurisprudence* (Oxford: Clarendon Press, 1931), 81–94.

61. Defendants' narratives tended to emphasize their own passivity. After a dispute of honor arose between Thomas Heath and Samuel Cook, a swordfight resulted in Cook's death. A witness for Heath testified that though Cook grew "Warm, and Angry, and clapt his Hand to his Sword . . . several times," Heath never tried "to draw, or meddle with his sword," adding that there was "no just Provocation given by Mr. Heath at the time of this unhappy incident." *OBP,* 15–17 June 1718 (London). In *OBP,* 27–30 Apr. 1715 (London, printed for Samuel Crouch), 6, a landlord was accused of killing his lodger. The lodger's wife testified that her husband was peaceably packing to leave when the landlord burst in and "threaten'd to fight the deceas'd," but the prisoner's version made the killing an inadvertent result of the lodger's aggression. According to the landlord, "[T]he deceased drew his Sword on him without Provocation." However, fights clearly had occurred in these cases, eliminating the possibility of an acquittal for self-defense. The courts held that any "quarrel" inevitably "arose from some . . . provocation, either in word or deed: and . . . in quarrels both parties may be, and usually are, in some fault" (Blackstone, 187). Thus, both Heath and the landlord were charged with manslaughter and sentenced to be burned in the hand.

62. MJ/SR2334 R138, 20 Aug. 1719.

63. MJ/SR2334 R10, 22 Aug. 1719 and MJ/SR2343 R124, 29 Mar. 1720 respectively.

64. MJ/SR2192 R27, 5 May 1712.

65. S. Howard, "Crime, Communities and Authority in Early Modern Wales: Denbighshire, 1670–1730", Ph.D. thesis, University of Wales, 2003, and R. Paley, ed., *Justice in Eighteenth-Century Hackney: The Justicing Notebook of Henry Norris and the Hackney Petty Sessions Book* (London: London Record Society, 1991).

66. R. Paley, ed., *Justice in Eighteenth-Century Hackney: The Justicing Notebook of Henry Norris and the Hackney Petty Sessions Book* (London: London Record Society, 1991), xxvii.

67. Ibid. and note 59.

68. Shoemaker, 26.

69. Dalton, 187.

70. Ibid. While Dalton is speaking specifically about recognizances to keep the peace, it seems likely that his position could be extended to *all* assaults.

71. For more on trading justices, see appendix A.

72. According to Norma Landau, *The Justices of the Peace, 1679–1760* (Berkeley: University of California Press, 1984), 185, trading justices operated by binding "disputants in recognizances to keep the peace and appear at Quarter Sessions, and then at the disputants' plea releas[ing] those bound from their obligations," and collecting fees for both the implementation and the release of the bond.

73. None of the recognizances were returned *concordantur* (agreed), which would

indicate the defendant's release by the prosecutor from the obligation to appear at Quarter Sessions and which suggest the manipulations of a trading justice. In addition, Robert Shoemaker's analysis of those justices most likely to fit the profile of "trading justices" (because their defendants were least likely to be indicted) identified only two Westminster JPs, John Chamberlayne and James Dewy, who are not overly prominent among the recognizances discussed below. Shoemaker, *Prosecution and Punishment,* table 8.5, 226–27.

74. Douglas Hay, "Dread of the Crown Office: The English Magistracy and the King's Bench 1740–1800," in N. Landau, ed., *Law, Crime and English Society 1660–1840* (Cambridge: Cambridge University Press, 2002), suggests that busier justices with less social cachet—such as those operating in the metropolis—were more vulnerable to the infamy of disciplinary action before King's Bench and may have curbed their activities accordingly, avoiding the more controversial practices. I am grateful to Dr. Hay for allowing me to read this article prior to its publication.

75. For example, in the years 1695, 1705, and 1715, this type of recognizance occurred as follows as a proportion of the total of assault recognizances (to answer) taken in the same year:

1695: 6 of 141 = 4%
1705: 4 of 113 = 4%
1715: 36 of 367 = 10%

The dramatic rise by the end of the period may be due to an increase in trading justices during this period, or it may be because more JPs felt that everyone who came before them had a right to the court's justice, and they thus allowed more formal prosecutions. Shoemaker, *Prosecution and Punishment* (225–27) dealt with the character of the Westminster and Middlesex benches but did not note any dramatic changes in this period.

76. Note that Joseph Keble, *An Assistance to Justices of the Peace for the Easier Performance of their Duty* (London: printed for W. Rawlins et al., 1683), 428, encouraged any JP who had "granted the peace to one that in the Justices judgement . . . require[d] it only out of malice, or for vexation, the Justice may presently in good discretion bind him to the good behaviour that so required the peace." In other words, if JPs were worried that person X was bound to keep the peace toward person Y, when Y really had no genuine cause to fear person X, the JP could then bind person Y to be of good behavior toward X to even the score. Keble makes no mention of assault, but the same principle probably applied for JPs here as well.

77. MJ/SR2255 R164, R160, and R162, 31 Aug. 1715 respectively. For similar examples, see MJ/SR1759 R27 and R26, 7 May 1690; MJ/SR1873 R149 and R148, 13 June 1696; MJ/SR1955 R46 and R47, 8 Aug. 1700; MJ/SR2172 R80 and R79, 26 and 25 Oct. 1711; MJ/SR2343 R98 and R99, 6 Apr. 1720.

78. N. Landau, "Appearance at the Quarter Sessions of Eighteenth-century Middlesex," *London Journal* 23, no. 2 (1998), 34. Robert Shoemaker, "Using Quarter Sessions Records as Evidence in the Study of Crime and Criminal Justice," *Archives* XX, no. 90 (1993), 151, noted that, in theory, keeping good behavior constituted a more serious charge than the peace, but the distinction was not made in practice.

79. Shoemaker, "Using Quarter Sessions," 147.
80. MJ/SR1997 R50 and R48, 25 July 1702 respectively.
81. MJ/SR2325 R150, 3 Feb. 1719.
82. Ibid., R151. Emphasis added.
83. MJ/SR2270 R121 and R122, 18 May 1716 respectively.
84. In addition to the examples presented below, see also MJ/SR2123 R68 and R70, 30 Dec. 1708, and MJ/SR2270 R161 and R160, 21 May 1716.
85. MJ/SR1865 R111 and R110, 8 Aug. 1695 respectively.
86. MJ/SR1969 R136 and R137, 12 May 1701 respectively.
87. MJ/SR2187 R137 and R136, 1 Mar. 1711/2 respectively.
88. MJ/SR1693 R85 and R86, 20 Aug. 1698 respectively.
89. MJ/SR1665 R114 and R116, 23 Feb. 1684/5 respectively.
90. MJ/SR2295 R130, 28 Aug. 1717.
91. Ibid, R129.
92. MJ/SR1964 R45 and R46, 5 Feb. 1700/1 and MJ/SR2057 R95 and R94, 13 Sept. 1705 respectively.
93. MJ/SR1873 R137 and R136, 25 June 1696 respectively. Perhaps the oath is mentioned because the JP was intent upon showing that he could not move either party in a suit he believed to be vexatious, and he wanted their persistence (and thus his innocence) to be clear. It is interesting to note that oaths are mentioned only here and in those recognizances immediately following.
94. MJ/SR1969 R138 and R139, 23 May 1701 and MJ/SR2083 R29 and R30, 30 Dec. 1706 respectively.
95. MJ/SR1798 R239 and R241, 20 May 1692.
96. MJ/SR2245 R200 and R201, 9 Apr. 1715.
97. MJ/SR2260 R153 and R148, 19 and 20 Oct. 1715 respectively.

Notes to Chapter 3

1. Keith Thomas, "The Double Standard," *Journal of the History of Ideas* 20 (1959), 195–216.
2. A. E. Simpson, "Vulnerability and the Age of Female Consent: Legal Innovation and Its Effect on Prosecutions for Rape in Eighteenth-Century London," in G. S. Rousseau and R. Porter, eds., *Sexual Underworlds of the Enlightenment* (Chapel Hill: University of North Carolina Press, 1988), 188, table 1, found that approximately 80 percent of men accused of rape before England's courts in the eighteenth-century were acquitted.
3. See, for example, B. Capp, "Separate Domains? Women and Authority in Early Modern England," in Paul Griffiths et al., eds., *The Experience of Authority in Early Modern England* (London: St. Martin's Press, 1996), 117–45; idem, "The Double Standard Revisited: Plebeian Women and Male Sexual Reputation in Early Modern England," *Past and Present* 162 (1999), 70–98; E. Foyster, *Manhood in Early Modern England: Honour, Sex and Marriage* (London: Longman Ltd, 1999); J. R. Gilllis, *Youth and History: Tradition and Change in European Age Relations, 1770 to the Present* (New York: Academic Press, 1981), 28–31; and L. Roper, *The Holy Household: Women and Morals in Reformation Augsburg* (Oxford: Clarendon Press, 1989), 165–205.
4. See, for example, A. E. Simpson, "The 'Blackmail Myth' and the Prosecution

of Rape and Its Attempt in 18th Century London: The Creation of a Legal Tradition," *The Journal of Criminal Law and Criminology* 77, no. 1 (1986), 101–50, and L. Edelstein, "An Accusation Easily to Be Made? Rape and Malicious Prosecution in Eighteenth-Century England," *The American Journal of Legal History* XLII, no. 4 (October, 1998), 351–90.

5. *OBP,* 9–10 July 1718 (London, printed for J. Phillips by M. Jenour), 7.

6. The alleged rape had occurred May 31, while the trial did not occur until the second week of July.

7. MJ/SR2152 R66, 19 June 1710.

8. MJ/SR2211 R53, 19 May 1713.

9. MJ/SR2315 R245, 4 Oct. 1718.

10. MJ/SR2270 R143, 21 June 1716 and MJ/SR2103 R42, 10 Dec. 1707 respectively.

11. MJ/SR2275 R129, 13 Aug. 1716.

12. Ibid.

13. MJ/SR2310 R44, 18 June 1718.

14. MJ/SR2270 R231, 30 Apr. 1716 and MJ/SR2162 R10, 3 Dec. 1710 respectively.

15. E. Crittall, ed., *The Justicing Notebook of William Hunt, 1744–1749* (Stoke-on-Trent: Wiltshire Record Society, 1982), 41, entry 239, 28 June 1745. For a more in-depth discussion of rape as the theft of the sexual property held by a husband in his wife, see M. Chaytor, "Husband(ry): Narratives of Rape in the Seventeenth Century," *Gender and History* 7 (1995), 378–407, though her methodology has been insightfully critiqued in G. Walker, "Rereading Rape and Sexual Violence in Early Modern England," *Gender and History* 10, no. 1 (1998), 1–25.

16. Crittall, 46, entry 300, 26 Dec. 1745 and 43, entry 262, 4 Sept. 1745 respectively.

17. Ibid., 32, entry 145, 18 Sept. 1744.

18. Simpson, "The 'Blackmail Myth,'" 118.

19. MJ/SR2162 R8, 29 Nov. 1710.

20. St. Margaret's Parish Bastardy Depositions, 16 Oct. 1712, E2574/35.

21. MJ/SR2098 R139, 24 July 1707.

22. Ibid., R140.

23. On the policing of male sodomites, see, for example, A. Bray, *Homosexuality in Renaissance England,* 2nd ed. (New York: Columbia University Press, 1995), 81–114; A. Gilbert, "Buggery and the British Navy, 1700–1861," *Journal of Social History* 10, no. 1 (1976), 72–98; idem, "Sodomy and the Law in Eighteenth- and Early Nineteenth-Century Britain," *Societas* 8, no. 3 (1978), 225–41; R. Norton, *Mother Clap's Molly House: The Gay Subculture in England, 1700–1830* (London: GMP Publishers Ltd., 1992); and R. Trumbach, "Sex, Gender, and Sexual Identity in Modern Culture: Male Sodomy and Female Prostitution in Enlightenment London," *Journal of the History of Sexuality* 2, no. 2 (1991), 186–203.

24. MJ/SR2202 R65, 6 Jan. 1712/3.

25. MJ/SR2032 R72, 11 May 1704.

26. Trumbach, "Sex, Gender and Sexual Identity," 187–88. See Norton, chapters 7 and 8, for contradictory views.

27. Antony Simpson ("The 'Blackmail Myth,'" 123) noted that, unlike those acquitted after claiming to have been falsely charged with heterosexual rape, men

who succeeded in proving that the buggery charge against them was fictitious quite often brought a suit against their former prosecutor for malicious prosecution.

28. See Walker, 6; Stevi Jackson, "The Social Context of Rape; Sexual Scripts and Motivation," *Women's Studies International Quarterly,* 1 (1978), 27–39; and R. Trumbach, *Sex and the Gender Revolution: Volume One: Heterosexuality and the Third Gender in Enlightenment London* (Chicago: University of Chicago Press, 1998), 301.

29. *OBP,* 1–4 May 1717 (London, printed for J. Phillips by M. Jenour), 8; my emphasis.

30. Ibid.

31. Sir William Blackstone, *Commentaries on the Laws of England in Four Books,* Book Four (reprint, Philadelphia: Geo. T. Bisel Co., 1922), 210. The most obvious example of nonprosecution as an indicator of a law's lack of wider social foundation is the fact that almost no husbands prosecuted their wives for assault, though the law afforded them this protection.

32. *OBP,* 10–13 Oct. 1683 (London, s.n.), 2.

33. *OBP,* 28 Feb. 1680/1 (London, printed for T. Davies), 3.

34. Ibid.

35. *Daily Post,* 20 April, 1730, quoted in Ronald Paulson, *Hogarth, His Life, Art and Times,* Vol. I (New Haven: Yale University Press, 1971), 248. See also Simpson, "Vulnerability and the Age of Female Consent," 197, for more examples of rapists maligned by crowds.

36. Alexander Pope, *Epistles to Several Persons (Moral Essays),* ed. F. W. Bateson (1735, reprinted New Haven: Yale University Press, 1951), 83n.

37. *OBP,* 21–23 Apr. 1680 (London, s.n.), 2.

38. Ibid.

39. *The Newgate Calendar* (Ware, Hertfordshire: Wordsworth Editions Ltd., 1997), 70.

40. Of a total of fifteen rape cases recounted in the *OBP* between December 1714 and October 1719 (excluding one where the victim's approximate age is impossible to discern), eight cases (53 percent) had victims younger than fourteen years of age. An additional case described the victim as "an *infant* of 17 years." *OBP,* 12–14 Sept. 1717 (London, printed for J. Phillips by M. Jenour), 6; my emphasis. A typesetter probably inserted the wrong number, and the victim was probably less than fourteen years old, raising the proportion to 60 percent of the fifteen cases.

41. For more on the legal issues surrounding the age of consent, see Antony Simpson, "Vulnerability and the Age of Female Consent," 181–205. Simpson argues that, technically, the age of consent for women could actually have been interpreted as twelve—if rape was prosecuted as a misdemeanor rather than a felony—although this never occurred in practice.

42. Antony Simpson has also noticed the high proportion of young rape prosecutors: "Child molestation must be taken as an important characteristic of rape cases in this century." However, Simpson suggests that this may reflect a true majority of this type of rape, due to a prevalent belief in "defloration" as a cure for venereal disease. Ibid., 192.

43. *OBP,* 11–14 Sept. 1717 (London, printed for J. Phillips by M. Jenour), 6.

44. Ibid.

45. Edelstein, 361.

46. C. Brant, "Speaking of Women: Scandal and the Law in the Mid-Eighteenth Century," in C. Brant and D. Purkiss, eds., *Women, Texts and Histories 1575–1760* (London: Routledge, 1992), 229, and Walker, *Crime, Gender and Social Order in Early Modern England* (Cambridge: Cambridge University Press, 2003), 262.

47. N. Guthrie, "'No Truth or Very Little in the Whole Story'?—A Reassessment of the Mohock Scare of 1712," *Eighteenth-Century Life* 20 (May 1996), 33–56, and D. Statt, "The Case of the Mohocks: Rake Violence in Augustan London," *Social History* 20, no. 2 (1995), 179–99, respectively.

48. Statt, 197, n86.

49. *A proclamation for the Suppressing of Riots, and the Discovery of such as have been guilty of late Barbarities within the Cities of London and Westminster and Parts adjacent,* 17 Mar. 1711/2, in Houghton fMS Eng 1039.

50. *A True List of Names of the Mohocks or Hawkubites who were Apprehended and Taken on Monday Night, Tuesday and this morning* (1711), in Houghton fMS Eng 1039. Guthrie, 38, points out that the list must be fabricated, as none of the names correspond with the men arrested in the legal records.

51. See, for example, Paul Griffiths, *Youth and Authority: Formative Experiences in England, 1560–1640* (New York, Oxford University Press, 1996).

52. *Original Draft Report by a Commission to Enquire into the assaults and injuries on Citizens by the Mohocks since 1 Feb. 1711* (1712), in Houghton fMS Eng 1039.

53. MSP 1712 AP/2, Draft of Warrant for Petty Constables within Westminster Holbourne & Finsbury Divisions to make a return of persons Assaulted by Mohawks, 28 Feb. 1711/2.

54. MSP 1712 AP/9, 3 Apr. 1712.

55. MSP 1712 AP/18, AP/5, and AP/16, 1 Apr. 1712 respectively.

56. *Who Plot Best; The Whigs or the Tories, Being a Brief account of all the Plots that have happen'd within these Thirty years . . .* (London: A. Baldwin, 1712), 14; my emphasis.

57. J. Gay, *An Argument proving from History, Reason and Scripture, that the Present Mohocks and Hawkubites are the Gog and Magog mention'd in the Revelations, and therefore that this vain and transitory world will shortly be brought to its final Dissolution* (1712).

58. *Who Plot Best,* 16.

59. *The Mohocks: A Poem, in Miltonic Verse: Address'd to the Spectator* (London, 1712).

60. J. Swift, *Journal to Stella,* Vol. II, Harold Williams, ed. (Oxford: Clarendon Press, 1948), 511.

61. Neil Guthrie, 33: "the tendency of modern scholars . . . has been to assume that the Mohocks were a figment of the eighteenth-century imagination, with no basis whatsoever in fact."

62. Swift, 511–12. See also 515–16.

63. *The Review,* Vol. VIII, no. 153, 15 Mar. 1712 in W. L. Payne, ed., *The Best of Defoe's Review* (New York: Columbia University Press, 1951), 214–18. For more on

Defoe's alleged connection with the Mohocks, see Guthrie, note 14, referring to a publication "which identifies Defoe as the instigator of a Whig-Presbyterian-Mohock plot, in spite of the *Review*'s pro-Government bias."

64. No. 347, 8 Apr. 1712, in *The Spectator,* Vol. III, ed. D. F. Bond (Oxford: Clarendon Press, 1965), 292–93.

65. Both Statt, 182–83, and Guthrie, 36–37, discuss the close political connection of much of the literature on the Mohocks.

66. *The Gentleman's Library . . . Written by a Gentleman,* 2nd ed. (1722), 128–29; emphasis in original.

67. Swift (509) noted that "the B[isho]p of Salsbry's son is s[ai]d to be of the Gang" and later (516) that "one of those that are taken is a Baronet." Defoe celebrated using the Protestant flail against the Mohocks because it would punish indiscriminately, "though he were my Lord——'s eldest son, or Sir Tho——'s younger brother, or J——ge——'s nephew." *The Review,* Vol. VIII, no. 153, 15 Mar. 1712, 217. Lady Stafford wrote that "the town says Lord Hinchingbrock [*sic*] is among" the Mohocks. Letter of 14 Mar. 1712, in J. J. Cartwright, ed., *The Wentworth Papers, 1705–1709,* (London: Wyman, 1882), 277. The JP's report entitled *Original Draft Report by a Commission to Enquire into the . . . Mohocks* (1712) in Houghton fMS Eng 1039 confirmed Hinchingbrooke's arrest, along with arrests of several other members of the elite male society.

68. See, for example, R. Trumbach, *Sex and the Gender Revolution,* chapter 3, 69–111.

69. On the importance placed upon early rising among the eighteenth-century middling sort, see Margaret R. Hunt, *The Middling Sort: Commerce, Gender and the Family in England, 1680–1780* (Berkeley: University of California Press, 1996), 53–56.

70. *The Mohocks Revel* (1712), verse 8. *Who Plot Best* (14–15) said that the Mohocks actually constituted "a Parcel of Wild young fellows frequenting a Tavern in Fleet Street." John Gay, *The Mohocks: A Tragi-Comical Farce As it was acted near the Watch-house in Covent Garden* (London, 1712), 8, said that "'Tis Wine and a Whore, / That we Mohocks adore, /We'll drink 'till our senses we quench; / When the Liquor is in / We're heighten'd for Sin." *The Spectator,* no. 324, 12 Mar. 1712, 187, reported that Mohocks "take care to drink themselves to a Pitch, that is, beyond the Possibility of attending to any Motions of Reason or Humanity."

71. Among the manuscript papers of Houghton fMS Eng 1039 are records of fines for Richard Buckland, Richard Gifford (both 13 Mar. 1712), and John Williams (14 Mar. 1712) "for being drunk."

72. Order from the Justices of Middlesex and Westminster to the High Constables, undated, Houghton fMS Eng 1039. Defoe's *Review* (Vol. VIII, no. 153, 15 Mar. 1712, 217) noted that the "bullies range our streets in arms by night" and only "in print by day." *The London Gazette,* 17–19 Apr. 1712, listed the times in twelve of the thirteen attacks it recounted, and all had occurred after dark. *The Mohocks Revel,* verse 1, said that the Mohocks "Rule the World by Night, / Tho' others Rule by Day." Swift (509) made sure he "came home early to avoid the Mohaks [*sic*]." In *An Argument from History,* Gay's Mohocks "wander through the streets by night, committing Cruelty," and in his *Trivia, or the art of Walking the streets of London* (1716), 74, the night belonged to the Mohocks. For a broader discussion of night in the context of assault and gender, see chapter 5.

73. *The Town-Rakes: or, The Frolicks of the Mohocks or Hawkubites* (London, 1712) and *A true list of the Names of the Mohocks* respectively.

74. M. Grieco, "The Body, Appearance, and Sexuality," *A History of Women in the West, Volume 3: Renaissance and Enlightenment Paradoxes,* eds. N. Z. Davis and A. Farge (Cambridge: Harvard University Press, 1993), 311–12. Being turned upside-down constituted a severe violation of feminine delicacy, seen in the mortification expressed by Fielding's Sophia after a tumble from a horse, where "the greatest injury . . . was a violent Shock given to her Modesty" in H. Fielding, *Tom Jones* (1749, reprinted New York: Norton Critical edition, 1995), Book XI, chapter II, 371.

75. Gay, *An Argument from History.*

76. *Original Draft Report by a Commission to Enquire into the . . . Mohocks* (1712) in Houghton fMS Eng 1039.

77. MSP 1712 AP/12, 1 Apr. 1712.

78. MSP 1712 AP/27, The Informacon of Mary Ann Kilby Spinster servant to Arthur Painter liveing at the sign of the Castle in the Butcher Row in the Paris of St. Clement Danes, dated 5 Apr. 1712.

79. MSP 1712 AP/28, Informacon of Christian Jones, dated 31 Mar. 1712.

80. *London Gazette,* 17–19 Apr. 1712.

81. Gay, *The Mohocks,* 6.

82. *The Mohocks Revel,* verses 1, 2, and 7.

83. *The Mohocks: A Poem in Miltonic Verse.*

84. *Original Minutes of committal of Diverse Persons concerned in the Mohock disorders* (March 1712) included ten prosecutions for the assault on John Bouch and two for "assaulting John Hamway Esquire, officer of her majesties Justices of the Peace" out of a total of sixteen reported incidents—none of the rest of which were for assaults on constables or watchmen. The *Original Draft Report by a Commission to Enquire into the . . . Mohocks* (1712) had only six of a total of twenty-seven prosecutions, but all six were for the single riot and assault on John Bouch. Records of the Middlesex Quarter Sessions, MJ/SR2188, include Recognizances no. 1–10, dated 14 Mar. 1711, nine of which were also for the riot and assault on John Bouch. One man in the calendar of prisoners, MJ/SR2189, was also charged with the same; the only other possible Mohock was charged with assaulting and wounding a man "& on suspicion of being Mohocks & refusing to find sureties" (entry 25, 4 Apr. 1712).

85. *Who Plot Best,* 14.

86. See chapter 2 for a brief discussion on the legal role of provocation in assault.

87. *The Town-Rakes.*

88. Ibid. and Letter from Lady Wentworth, 14 Mar. 1712, in Cartwright, 277.

89. *The Review,* Vol. VIII, no. 153, 15 Mar. 1712, 215.

90. S. Cohen, *Folk Devils and Moral Panics: The Creation of the Mods & Rockers* (New York: St. Martin's Press, 1972), defines the term on page 9. On historians' use of the concept, see J. Walkowitz, *City of Dreadful Delight: Narratives of Sexual Danger in Late-Victorian London* (Chicago: University of Chicago Press, 1992), and J. Davis, "The London Garotting Panic of 1862: A Moral Panic and the Creation of a Criminal Class in Mid-Victorian England," in V.A.C. Gatrell et al., eds., *Crime and the Law: The Social History of Crime in Western Europe since 1500* (London: Europa Publications Ltd., 1980), 190–213.

91. *The Review,* Vol. VIII, no. 153, 15 Mar. 1712, 215.

92. Letter from Lady Wentworth, 14 Mar. 1712, in Cartwright, 277–78.

93. *The Spectator,* no. 324, 12 Mar. 1712, 188.

94. On dueling, see especially D. Andrews, "The Code of Honour and Its Critics: The Opposition to Duelling in England, 1700–1850," *Social History* 5, no. 3 (1980), 409–34. On middling moral concerns in general, see Hunt, especially chapter 2.

95. This is a proportional increase of 4 percent because prosecutions were increasing in general. A look at all of the recognizances taken from the sessions of 7 April, 1708, up to and including the sessions of 7 January, 1712, shows 62 cases with gentlemen or aristocratic defendants and 278 cases where occupations were listed *other* than gentleman or aristocrat (upper-class men were 18 percent of the total where status or occupation was known). From the sessions of 23 April, 1712 until 5 October, 1715, there were 94 cases involving upper-class men and 325 with defendants of known, nongenteel status or occupation (upper-class men comprising 22 percent of the total).

96. Though MJ/SR 2187 (the April sessions where most of the suspected Mohocks would have been prosecuted) had 18 percent gentlemen of the total defendants in recognizances where a status was listed, the subsequent sessions with higher proportions of genteel defendants are: MJ/SR2207 8 Apr. 1713, 32 percent; MJ/SR2211 2 Jul. 1713, 36 percent; MJ/SR2216 Oct. 1713, 20 percent; MJ/SR2230 24 Jun. 1714, 26 percent; MJ/SR2235 6 Oct. 1714, 24 percent; MJ/SR2240 10 Jan. 1714/5, 32 percent; MJ/SR2245 20 Apr. 1715, 24 percent; MJ/SR2250 8 Jul. 1715, 31 percent.

97. R. Shoemaker, "Using Quarter Sessions Records as Evidence for the Study of Crime and Criminal Justice," *Archives* XX, no. 90 (1993), 151.

98. Guthrie, 33.

99. *OBP,* 17–18 Jan. 1694/5 (London, s.n.), 2.

100. Ibid.

101. Anna. Bryson, *From Courtesy to Civility: Changing Codes of Conduct in Early Modern England* (Oxford: Clarendon Press, 1998), 249.

102. Ibid.

103. J. Hurl-Eamon, "Policing Male Heterosexuality: The Reformation of Manners Societies' Campaign against the Brothels in Westminster, 1690–1720," *The Journal of Social History* 37 (June 2004), 1017–35, describes the arrests of significant numbers of bawdy-house patrons by the members of London's reformation of manners societies.

104. MJ/SR2235 R95, 4 Sept. 1714.

105. MJ/SR2353 R113, 30 Sept. 1720.

106. MJ/SR2348 R98, 27 [month illegible] 1720.

107. MJ/SR2250 R178, 7 June 1715.

Notes to Chapter 4

1. In the eighteenth century "virtuous" motherhood was narrowly defined, and many poorer women fell outside the definition and were denied pride and authority

in their maternity. Even breastfeeding became an avenue for maternal disempowerment when the English government began to equate the obligations of mothering to the pursuit of industrialization and colonization. T. Bowers, *The Politics of Motherhood: British Writing and Culture, 1680–1760* (Cambridge: Cambridge University Press, 1996), and R. Perry, "Colonizing the Breast: Sexuality and Maternity in Eighteenth-Century England," *Journal of the History of Sexuality* 2, no. 2 (1991): 204–34, respectively. Susan Amussen, *An Ordered Society: Gender and Class in Early Modern England* (New York: B. Blackwell, 1988), illustrated the importance placed upon wifely obedience in seventeenth-century England, where maintenance of hierarchy within the family was integrally linked to the stability of the state. Most recently, Laura Gowing has argued that although pregnancy "gave women's desires an urgency that might bring special treatments, as communities vied to provide them with the food and drink they needed for healthy births," it simultaneously disadvantaged these mothers because those same desires "were also representative of the dangers of the female body." Laura Gowing, *Common Bodies: Women, Touch and Power in Seventeenth-Century England* (New Haven: Yale University Press, 2002), 138.

2. Possibly those women did not think of telling the justice that they were pregnant, but it is equally likely that the JPs were often busy and chose to keep the recognizance brief, recording only that a woman was "assaulted and wounded." Unfortunately, there is no discernible pattern to determine why women would or would not have mentioned their pregnancy, and the occurrence of recognizances where pregnancy has been recorded does not vary significantly with the total number per session. Thus the hypothesis that busy justices kept records brief is less plausible. Also no single justice emerged as having a stronger tendency to note pregnancy. Perhaps pregnancy was mentioned in this small number of cases because it was the *focus* of the assault; the assailant may have felt that the woman was carrying an illegitimate child. Again, aside from several cases where the pregnant victim was clearly married (which still does not refute the possibility that her child was considered illegitimate), recognizances do not provide the kind of information necessary to investigate such a possibility.

3. MJ/SR1793 R71, 17 Feb. 1692 and MJ/SR2123 R98, 2 Nov. 1708 respectively; emphasis mine.

4. Perry, 204–34, and K. Wilson, *The Island Race: Englishness, Empire and Gender in the Eighteenth Century* (London: Routledge, 2003), 41–42, 126–28, 178.

5. Along with the examples that follow, see also W. Stubbs and G. Talmash, *The Crown Circuit Companion . . .*, 5th ed. (London, 1783), 110, which includes a sample of an indictment "for assaulting a woman with quick child, so that the child be brought forth dead." Both W. Hawkins, *A Treatise of the Pleas of the Crown . . .*, Vol. I (London, E. Richardson & C. Lintot, 1766), 80, and E. Coke, *Third Part of the Institutes of the Laws of England* (London, 1747), 70, argue that striking a pregnant woman was not murder, but was "a great misprison." Misprisons, according to Blackstone, "are . . . generally understood to be all such high offences as are under the degree of capital, but nearly bordering thereon." W. Blackstone, *Commentaries on the Laws of England,* Book Four (1769, reprinted Philadelphia: Geo. T. Bisel Co., 1922), 119.

6. Giles Jacob, *The Modern Justice . . .* (London, 1720), 302. Note that the Westminster assault recognizances did not refer to any babies born with bruises, so their

mention of the victim's pregnancy was probably not motivated by this particular point of law. Jacob went on to say that the charge of murder was "contra, if the Child be born dead," so the many recognizances recounting miscarriages and the like also did not apply here.

7. R. Burn, *Justice of the Peace and Parish Officer,* Vol. 1 (1755), 129; emphasis mine.

8. Joseph Keble, *An Assistance to Justices of the Peace for the Easier Performance of their Duty* (London: printed for W. Rawlins et al., 1683), 237.

9. MJ/SR1979 R23, 11 Dec. 1701.

10. A. Eccles, *Obstetrics and Gynaecology in Tudor and Stuart England* (Kent, Ohio: Kent State University Press, 1982), 61. For female skepticism of medical theories, see also P. Crawford, "Sexual Knowledge in England, 1500–1750," in Porter and Teach, eds., *Sexual Knowledge,* 82, 92–100. Garthine Walker has also observed the advantages accorded women in self-diagnosis of the early stages of pregnancy, calling it "the discursive potency of pregnancy." G. Walker, *Crime, Gender and Social Order in Early Modern England* (Cambridge: Cambridge University Press, 2003), 62.

11. MJ/SR2118 R39, 4 Sept. 1708. It is possible that Mr. Williams may not have wanted another mouth to feed. Beating as a recognized (though not legal) form of abortion in early modern Europe is discussed in J. M. Riddle, *Eve's Herbs: A History of Contraception and Abortion in the West* (London: Harvard University Press, 1997), 79–80, 126–31, and A. McLaren, *Reproductive Rituals: The Perception of Fertility in England from the Sixteenth Century to the Nineteenth Century* (London: Methuen & Co. Ltd, 1984), 119–22.

12. *English Midwife,* 28–30.

13. L. Lemnius, *The Secret Miracles of Nature . . .* (1658), 11.

14. N. Culpeper, *A directory for Midwives, or, A guide for Women . . .* (1737), 104.

15. Gouge, *Domestical Duties,* Treatise 4, 399.

16. For a discussion of late-seventeenth-century medical theories on prenatal care which sees women as having a certain amount of power through their pregnancy, see Eccles, *Obstetrics and Gynaecology,* 64–66, and R. Porter and L. Hall, *The Facts of Life: The Creation of Sexual Knowledge in Britain, 1650–1950* (New Haven: Yale University Press, 1995), 46–53.

17. J. M. Beattie, "The Criminality of Women in Eighteenth-Century England," *Journal of Social History* 7 (1995), 116n81.

18. Ibid.

19. MJ/SR2098 R138, 28 Jul. 1707.

20. MJ/SR2300 R173, 28 Oct. 1717.

21. Mauriceau recounted how his "cousin's mother, Mrs Dionis . . . whose father being suddenly kill'd with a sword by one of his servants . . . they brought immediately this ill news to his Wife, then eight months gone . . . at which . . . she was . . . surprised with a great trembling, so that she was presently delivered of the said Dionis, who is to this day . . . troubled with a shaking in both hands." Mauriceau, *Diseases of Women,* 64–65. Garthine Walker's research on assault in seventeenth-century Cheshire (60) also uncovered cases in which pregnant women "stressed connections between emotional and physical damage."

22. Mauriceau, *Diseases of Women,* 22.

23. Ibid., 35.

24. John Dunton, *The Nightwalker: or Evening Rambles in Search after Lewd Women . . .*, Vol. II (London, Printed for James Orme, March 1697), 7.

25. MJ/SR2286 R27, 7 Mar. 1717; emphasis mine.

26. MJ/SR2300 R134, 17 Nov. 1717 and MJ/SR1831 R136, 12 Feb. 1693/4 respectively.

27. MJ/SR2286 R88, 18 Jan. 1717.

28. M. Hunt, "Wife Beating, Domesticity and Women's Independence in Eighteenth-Century London," *Gender and History* 4, no. 1 (1992), 18. Also see S. Amussen, "'Being Stirred to Much Unquietness': Violence and Domestic Violence in Early Modern England," *Journal of Women's History* 6, no. 2 (1994), 80.

29. Ibid. See also Hunt (19 and n37) where she describes the JPs' "benign role" in such prosecutions. Hunt and Amussen contend that recognizances were an ineffective tool for wives and that they thus could reveal little about real instances of abuse, and certainly nothing positive about women's positions before the courts.

30. Landau (34) argues that "the proceedings to secure . . . forfeiture" of a recognizance to keep the peace or maintain good behavior "were just too cumbersome."

31. Margaret Hunt looked at "ten cases of spousal abuse that reached the Consistory Court of London in the years 1711 to 1713" (11). Susan Amussen used assize court records of spousal murder, conduct literature offering images of ideal husbandly conduct, and depositions from church court separation cases in her investigation of domestic violence. Elizabeth Foyster examined forty-four Court of Arches divorce cases, 1660–1700, to explore the dangers for male honor inherent in wife beating. E. Foyster, "Male Honour, Social Control and Wife Beating in Late Stuart England," *Transactions of the Royal Historical Society, 6th Series* 6 (1996), 215–24.

32. MJ/SR2334 R26, 7 Aug. 1719.

33. MJ/SR1921 R98, 30 Nov. 1698. This order has also been recorded in an entry of the same date in Justice Dewy's notebook, labeled "Book of Examinacons 1685." Hampshire Record Office, Coventry MSS IM53/1374.

34. From 1685 to 1720 in Westminster there were 1,603 recognizances binding men for assaults on women. Of these, only 20.5 percent described excessive violence (46 "barbarous," 12 "inhuman," 5 "cruel," and 266 "violent"). In contrast, seventy-eight recognizances (50 percent) of all of the assaults upon wives by husbands used such language.

35. MJ/SR2275 R145, 18 July 1716.

36. MJ/SR2339 R81, 22 Oct. 1719.

37. *The Compleat Justice* (London: 1656), 298; emphasis added.

38. *The Compleat Justice* said that husbands were allowed "crave the peace against their wives." However, we should note that violence was much more rarely the topic of these recognizances in practice. In the Westminster Quarter Sessions for this period, there were only three recognizances for violence by wives against husbands. See MJ/SR1873 R102, 14 May 1696 for "assaulting" her husband with the help of another man, MJ/SR2275 R52, 12 Sept. 1716 for "cruelly Beating [her husband] to the endangering of his life," and MJ/SR2330 R50, 25 May 1719 for "assaulting and beating [her husband] in a violent manner."

39. Keble, 412. Keble also said "that a Justice of peace may . . . Command" a hus-

band to be bound over "upon [the JP's] own discretion," if "such a Case [were to] happen . . . in his presence." Thus, wives did not even need to initiate the prosecution; the justices could do it for them in some cases, indicating the heinousness of the offense.

40. For more on JPs adding detail in assault description, see appendix A.

41. Michael Dalton, *The Countrey Justice* (London, 1655), 203, asserted that "to strike at, or offer to strike at a man, although he never hurt, or hit him, this is an assault."

42. Keble, 150; emphasis mine. This right of correction is granted to parents over children, masters over servants, schoolmasters over scholars, jailers over prisoners, and husbands over wives. Note that a number of justicing handbooks (for example, Dalton, 204; W. Nelson, *The Office and Authority of a Justice of the Peace . . .*, 5th ed. (London, 1750), 59; and Jacob, 38, mention this right for every category *except* husbands and wives, making the potential for JPs to frown on husbands' violence of *any* kind more probable, and many handbooks do not address any right of correction at all.

43. MJ/SR2027 R18, 1 Mar. 1704, and MJ/SR2216 R95, 28 Sept. 1713 respectively.

44. MJ/SR2275 R246 14 Aug. 1716 and MJ/SR1718 R134, 9 Jan. 1687/8 respectively.

45. Gouge, *Domestical Duties,* Treatise 4, 409.

46. J. Keane, *Tom Paine: A Political Life* (Boston: Little, Brown, 1995), 6.

47. In practice, by the end of our period, judges would accept preparation of childbed linen or cries for help during labor as evidence of a mother's innocence. McLaren, 129–32; R. Malcolmson, "Infanticide in the Eighteenth Century," in J. S. Cockburn, ed., *Crime in England, 1550–1800* (Princeton: Princeton University Press, 1977), 197; J. M. Beattie, *Crime and the Courts in England,* 1660–1800 (Princeton: Princeton University Press, 1986), 113, 119–20; Allyson May, "'She at first denied it': Infanticide Trials at the Old Bailey," in V. Frith, ed., *Women and History: Voices of Early Modern England* (Concord, Ontario: Irwin Publishing, 1997), 19–23.

48. J. C. Oldham, "On Pleading the Belly: A History of the Jury of Matrons," *Criminal Justice History* 6 (1985), 1–64.

49. Misson, quoted in Radzinowicz, *History of English Criminal Law,* 12n. See also Henry Fielding's *Joseph Andrews* (1742, reprinted with *Shamela* by Oxford University Press, 1980), Book II, Chapter XI, 130, when a man whispered in Fanny Goodwill's ear, after she had been accused of robbery, that "if she had not provided herself a great Belly, he was at her service."

50. Brown, "The Princess of Monaco's Hair: The Revolutionary Tribunal and the Pregnancy Plea," *Journal of Family History* 23, no. 2 (1998), 152.

51. Thirty-three recognizances (38 percent) indicated danger to the child's life (i.e., the possibility of miscarriage or spontaneous abortion), and eighteen recognizances (21 percent) explicitly stressed the danger to the mother's life.

52. Mauriceau, *Diseases of Women,* 131. See also *The English Midwife Enlarged . . . The Whole fitted for the Meanest Capacities* (1682), 238–39.

53. MJ/SR2255 R55, 2 Aug. 1715.

54. Almost all of the thirty-one recognizances brought by servants and apprentices for relatively minor assaults also described the employers' contractual violations. Only two were for assault alone. For the two recognizances that did not simultane-

ously mention contractual violations, see MJ/SR2207 R41, 20 Jan 1712/3 and MJ/SR1960 R129, 14 Oct. 1700 respectively.

55. Though JPs did not officially have the power to order payment of wages, they nevertheless involved themselves in such disputes. Shoemaker, *Prosecution and Punishment,* 90–91.

56. D. Hay, "Master and Servant in England: Using the Law in the Eighteenth and Nineteenth Centuries," in W. Steinmetz, ed., *Private Law and Social Inequality in the Industrial Age: Comparing Legal Cultures in Britain, France, Germany, and the United States* (Oxford: Oxford University Press, 2000), 227–64.

57. Adrian Wilson has represented early modern childbirth as empowering for women in its female unity, but Linda Pollock discovered that often the presence of other women in the lying-in chamber could be a source of conflict rather than consensus, with each participant having her own "experience and knowledge of childbirth and . . . superimposing . . . their point of view on the process." A. Wilson, *The Making of Man Midwifery: Childbirth in England, 1660–1770* (Cambridge: Harvard University Press, 1995); idem, "The Ceremony of Childbirth and Its Interpretation," in V. Fildes, ed., *Women as Mothers in Pre-Industrial England, Essays in Memory of Dorothy McLaren* (New York: Routledge, 1990), 68–107; and L. Pollock, "Childbearing and Female Bonding in Early Modern England," *Social History* 22, no. 3 (1997), 299, respectively. Certainly when the mother was unmarried, the women around her during her pregnancy and lying-in could be far from friends—keeping her under surveillance, authorized to squeeze her breasts if a disguised pregnancy was suspected, and use her labor pains to pry the identity of the baby's father from her. Pollock, "Childbearing and Female Bonding," 286–306, and Gowing, "Secret Births," 87–115. See chapter 5 on the higher number of women accused of assaulting other women.

58. MJ/SR2339 R81, 22 Oct. 1719.

59. See, for example, MJ/SR1836 R84, 8 May 1694; MJ/SR1897 R133, 2 Aug. 1697; MJ/SR1940 R89, 7 Oct. 1699; MJ/SR2098 R89, 12 Sept. 1707; MJ/SR2143 R64, 19 Dec. 1709; MJ/SR2177 R76, 13 July 1711; and MJ/SR2353 R1, 21 Sept. 1720.

60. I am grateful to Robert Shoemaker for this observation.

61. Recognizances MJ/SR1708 R52, 4 June, 1687; MJ/SR1930 R12, 29 June 1699; MJ/SR1940 R89, 7 Oct. 1699; MJ/SR2167 R38, 16 Jan. 1710/1; MJ/SR2108 R34, 26 Feb. 1707/8; and MJ/SR2270 R110, 8 May 1716 state that their husbands' lovers have threatened serious violence against these prosecuting wives.

62. MJ/SR2123 R80, 13 Nov. 1708.

63. MJ/SR2192 R112, 29 May 1712 and MJ/SR2138 R71 5 Aug. 1709 respectively.

64. MJ/SR2250 R203, 16 June 1715.

Notes to Chapter 5

1. Alexandra Shepard, *Meanings of Manhood in Early Modern England* (Oxford: Oxford University Press, 2003), 130.

2. Chapter 4 explores the areas where domestic violence was seen by its victims as violation and was prosecuted.

3. Shani D'Cruze, ed., *Everyday violence in Britain, 1850–1950: Gender and Class* (Harlow: Longman, 2000).

4. Ibid., "Unguarded Passions: Violence, History and the Everyday," 14.

5. M. Feeley and D. Little have discerned a dramatic decline in the number of females accused of felonies at the Old Bailey over the eighteenth century. M. Feeley and D. Little, "The Vanishing Female: The Decline of Women in the Criminal Process, 1687–1912," *Law and Society Review* 25, no. 4 (1991), 719–57.

6. The next section returns to this argument.

7. On the effects of demobilization on property crime, see D. Hay, "War, Dearth and Theft in the Eighteenth Century: The Record of the English Courts," *Past and Present* 95 (May 1982), 117–60.

8. There is no specific legal definition for "violent assault" in the legal literature, and "maiming"—arguably the most serious type of assault (a felony without benefit of clergy)—was mentioned in only six recognizances—not even as often as would seem appropriate, given the description in some other recognizances. It is impossible, therefore, to know for certain why certain assaults were recorded as violent, but it seems safe to assume that a particularly wounded and shaken victim caused the JP to have the assault specified as "violent."

9. Throughout the period twenty-five women and eighty men were bound for "barbarously" assaulting, and five women and nineteen men were bound for "inhumanly" assaulting. Female defendants were thus described these ways in slightly less than one-quarter of the total 129 cases—a lesser proportion than that for assaults as a whole.

10. Henry Fielding, *Tom Jones* (1749, reprinted New York: Norton Critical edition, 1995), Book IV, chapter VIII, 119.

11. James Harvey, *A Collection of Precedents Relating to the Office of a Justice of Peace* (London, 1730), 189–90. See chapter 2 for a similar discussion of assaults where the victims swore that they were "in fear."

12. The raw numbers are as follows: of a total of 859, there were 203 recognizances binding only females for striking, and 656 binding only males.

13. The raw numbers are as follows: of a total of seventy-six, there were ten recognizances binding only females for kicking, and sixty-six binding only males.

14. Garthine Walker, *Crime, Gender and Social Order in Early Modern England* (Cambridge: Cambridge University Press, 2003), 27, observes that "'striking' incorporated a multitude of ways of hitting someone with or without a weapon."

15. On the significance of face slapping in early modern Europe, see J. R. Farr, *Hands of Honour: Artisans and Their World in Dijon, 1550–1650* (Ithaca: Cornell University Press, 1988), 183, and J. Pitt-Rivers, "Honour and Social Status," in J. G. Peristiany, ed., *Honor and Shame: The Values of Mediterranean Society* (London: Nicholson, 1965), 25.

16. Costume historian Alison Settle described "caricatures of Georgian days [where] 'peepers' in Bond Street were shown gazing through quizzing glasses at the female ankle, displayed as a lady stepped into her carriage," in *English Fashion* (London: Collins, 1948), 46.

17. MJ/SR2073 R64, 9 June 1706.
18. MJ/SR2353 R69, 9 Aug. 1720.
19. MJ/SR1964 R82, 24 Jan. 1700/1.
20. Robert Darnton, *The Great Cat Massacre and Other Episodes in French Cultural History* (New York: Vintage Books, 1984), 92–96.
21. MJ/SR1878 R13, 24 Sept. 1696.
22. MJ/SR2103 R131, 13 Dec. 1707.
23. MJ/SR2225 R47, 26 Feb. 1714.
24. MJ/SR2280 R128 31 Oct. 1716.
25. Walker, 27 and 28.
26. MJ/SR2334 R81, 7 July 1719.
27. MJ/SR1826 R124, 15 Dec. 1693.
28. MJ/SR1907 R43, 11 Mar. 1698 and MJ/SR2197 R175, 17 Sept. 1712 respectively.
29. MJ/SR2275 R16, 7 July 1716; my emphasis.
30. "No servant in husbandry, artificer, victualler, or labourer, shall wear sword or dagger," *The Compleat Justice* (London: 1656), 17. Garthine Walker (27) notes that in legal records the use of the word *sword* may actually "have been a 'legal fiction' in many cases that actually referred to a knife."
31. MJ/SR2255 R43, 16 Sept. 1715.
32. MJ/SR2315 R204, 15 July 1718 and MJ/SR2300 R203, 26 Oct. 1717 respectively.
33. MJ/SR1955 R38, 19 Sept. 1700 and MJ/SR2275 R59, 7 Sept. 1716 respectively.
34. MJ/SR2260 R237, 10 Oct. 1715.
35. This does not mean that there was little sexual division of labor. Amanda Vickery argues very effectively that "separate sphere" as an informal ideology is an historical continuity, traceable at least from the Middle Ages and before. A. Vickery, "Golden Age to Separate Spheres? A Review of the Categories and Chronology of English Women's History," *The Historical Journal* 36, no. 2 (1993), 383–414.
36. MJ/SR2152 R15, 2 May 1710. Note that this recognizance did not contain the word *assault*, so it was not included in the quantitative analysis.
37. MJ/SR2255 R54, 16 Aug. 1715 and MJ/SR2353 R139, 11 Sept. 1720 respectively.
38. L. Gowing, *Domestic Dangers: Women, Words, and Sex in Early Modern London* (Oxford: Clarendon Press, 1996), and T. Meldrum, "A Woman's Court in London: Defamation at the Bishop of London's Consistory Court, 1700–1745," *London Journal* 19, no. 1 (1994), 1–20. Both Gowing and Meldrum emphasized women's high level of involvement as prosecutors and perpetrators in defamation suits.
39. MJ/SR2255 R343, 3 Aug. 1715; MJ/SR2300 R203, 29 Oct. 1717; and MJ/SR2325 R15 and R14, 20 Feb. 1719, respectively.
40. MJ/SR2078 ff137, 24 Sept. 1706 and MJ/SR2353 ff138, 14 Sept. 1720 respectively.
41. Statute *6 Geo. I c. 23* made felonious any assault that occurred "with an intent to tear, spoil, cut, burn, or deface . . . the garments or cloaths" of any individual "in the public streets or highways," but it was prompted by very specific types of attacks to serve

the economic interests of a specific group of weavers and thus has probably affected few, if any, of the recognizances here.

42. MJ/SR2280 R179, 15 Oct. 1716.

43. MJ/SR2295 R298, 1 Aug. 1717.

44. MJ/SR2286 unnumbered, 31 Mar. 1717.

45. There are, however, recognizances for torn waistcoats, shirts, and cravats.

46. Farr, 183. Garthine Walker (42 and 90) also acknowledged hair pulling and hat removal as a significant form of insult in seventeenth-century Cheshire.

47. On a more detailed study of the symbolism of wigs (and their absence), including a more detailed explanation of the painting, see Marcia Pointon, *Hanging the Head: Portraiture and Social Formation in Eighteenth-Century England* (London: Yale University Press, 1993), chapter 4.

48. MJ/SR1698 R18, 27 Nov. 1686; MJ/SR1917 R97, 15 Aug. 1698; and MJ/SR2083 R30, 30 Dec. 1706 respectively.

49. In 1735 perukes and periwigs ranged in price from three guineas for a bob peruke to £10 for a short, full-bottomed wig. Janet Arnold, *Perukes & Periwigs* (London: Her Majesty's Stationary Office, 1970), 23.

50. MJ/SR1868 R129, 1 Apr. 1696.

51. Alexandra Shepard (146) noted that beard pulling was a significant part of sixteenth- and seventeenth-century violence.

52. MJ/SR2138 R66, 20 July 1709.

53. MJ/SR2353 R97, 19 Sept. 1720 and MJ/SR2343 R72, 11 Feb. 1719/20 respectively.

54. On ducking scolds, see the debate between D. Underdown, "The Taming of the Scold: The Enforcement of Patriarchal Authority in Early Modern England," in A. J. Fletcher and J. Stevenson, eds., *Order and Disorder in Early Modern England* (Cambridge: Cambridge University Press, 1985), 116–36, and M. Ingram, "'Scolding Women Cucked or Washed': A Crisis in Gender Relations in Early Modern England?," in J. Kermonde and G. Walker, eds., *Women, Crime and the Courts in Early Modern England* (London: UCL Press, 1994), 48–80. Water was also used by the state in the buoyancy test, a notorious method of discovering a witch.

55. MJ/SR2348 R74, 4 May 1720 and G. T. Crook, ed., *The Complete Newgate Calendar* Vol. 2 (London: Navarre Soc. Ltd., 1926), 78, respectively. Taylor was later convicted of housebreaking and was executed in 1691.

56. MJ/SR2300 R87, 7 Nov. 1717 and MJ/SR2250 R115, 7 May 1715 respectively.

57. MJ/SR1860 R117, 12 Sept. 1695.

58. MJ/SR2027 R24, 7 Feb. 1703/4.

59. Farr, 183–84.

60. MJ/SR2348 R106, 5 Jun. 1720 and MJ/SR1665 R18, 23 Mar. 1685 respectively.

61. S. M. Grieco, "The Body, Appearance, and Sexuality," in N. Z. Davis and A. Farge, eds., *A History of Women in the West, Volume 3: Renaissance and Enlightenment Paradoxes* (Cambridge: Harvard University Press, 1993), 51.

62. John Gay, *Trivia, or the Art of Walking the Streets of London* (London, 1716), 27–28.

63. J. M. Beattie, *Crime and the Courts in England, 1660–1800* (New Jersey: Princeton University Press, 1986), 467.

64. L. Radzinowicz, *A History of English Criminal Law and Its Administration from 1750,* Vol. 1 (London: Stevens & Sons Ltd., 1948), 185.

65. MJ/SR1897 R99, 12 July 1697.

66. Slitting noses was also a trademark tactic of the Mohocks in popular literature, discussed in chapter 4.

67. According to a treatise on the Star Chamber by Hudon in the 1630s, "branding in the face and slitting the nose is inflicted upon forgers of false deeds, conspirators to take away the life of innocents, false scandals upon the great judges, and justices of the realm." L. A. Parry, *The History of Torture in England* (London: Sampson Low, Marston & Co., 1933), 9.

68. *Fog's Weekly Journal,* 12 Jun. 1731, quoted in W. Andrews, *Old-Time Punishments* (Hall: William Andrews & Co., 1890), 83.

69. It is not surprising that recognizances bear special description of assaults on noses because the law recognized the severity of nasal injury and accorded such assaults particularly serious penalties: "if any person . . . malitiously . . . slit or cut off the Nose, . . . with intent to disfigure him, that Fact is Felony without Clergy, and the Offender shall suffer the pain of death." W. T., *The Office of the Clerk of Assize . . . Together with the Office of the Clerk of the Peace . . .* 2nd Ed. (London: Printed for Henry Twyford, 1682), 127–28. See also J. Bond, *A Compleat Guide for Justices of the Peace* (London, 1707), 97.

70. MJ/SR1955 R38, 19 Sept. 1700. A "patten" is an iron device with a wooden sole that attached to the owner's shoe to raise him or her out of the mud.

71. *OBP,* 15–16 Jan. 1679/80 (London, s.n.), 1, and MJ/SR 2300 R34, 3 Jan. 1717/18, respectively.

72. MJ/SR2270 R137, 14 June 1716.

73. Though it later appeared that Francis may have simply hidden his wig and trumped up the charge to increase the gravity of his prosecution, this case nevertheless underscores the linkage between slit noses and dishonor. *OBP,* 8–11 Apr. 1719 (London, printed for J. Phillips by M. Jenour), 6–7.

74. J. Epstein, "Spatial Practices/Democratic Vistas," *Social History* 24, no. 3 (October, 1999), 294–310; M. Ogborn, *Spaces of Modernity: London's Geographies, 1680–1780* (London: Guilford Press, 1998), 27–28; M. P. Ryan, *Women in Public: Between Banners and Ballots, 1825–1880* (Baltimore: Johns Hopkins University Press, 1990); R. Shoemaker, "Public Spaces, Private Disputes? Conflict on London's Streets, 1660–1800," in T. Hitchcock and H. Shore, eds., *The Streets of London: From the Great Fire to the Great Stink* (London: Rivers Oram Press, 2003); idem, "Gendered Spaces: Patterns of Mobility and Perceptions of London's Geography, 1660–1750," in J. F. Merritt, ed., *Imagining Early Modern London: Perceptions and Portrayals of the City from Stow to Strype, 1598–1720* (Cambridge: Cambridge University Press, 2001); and J. Walkowitz, *City of Dreadful Delight: Narratives of Sexual Danger in Late-Victorian London* (Chicago: University of Chicago Press, 1992).

75. Walkowitz, 51–52.

76. For example, Blackstone emphasized in the definition of burglary that "the *time*" and "the *place*" must be considered: "The *time* must be by night" because night

provided thieves with anonymity and made their crime more reprehensible, and the place "must be . . . in a *mansion*-house." Thus, homicide was justifiable against "any person [who] attempts a robber or murder of another . . . in the *nighttime.*" Similarly, place was a factor in larceny above the value of twelvepence. If the larceny occurred "in a church or chapel . . . booth or tent . . . market or fair . . . [or] dwelling-house," it was considered a felony without benefit of clergy. Sir William Blackstone, *Commentaries on the Laws of England in Four Books,* Book Four (reprint, Philadelphia: Geo. T. Bisel Co., 1922), 224, 180–81, 240, respectively. Emphasis in original.

77. John Clavell, "A Recantation of an Ill Led Life, 1634," in J. H. P. Pafford, *John Clavell 1601–43: Highwayman, Author, Lawyer, Doctor* (Oxford: Leopard's Head Press, 1993), frontispiece and 29 respectively.

78. *The Genuine History of the Life of Richard Turpin, the Noted Highwayman . . .* (London, 1738), 11.

79. MJ/SR2098 R111, 27 Aug. 1707.

80. Only a total of twenty-four of the recognizances for assaults that occurred in the streets actually named a particular street, and the remaining 45 percent that mention streets outside of Drury Lane and the theatre district did not fall into any discernible pattern.

81. Gay, *Trivia,* 70; emphasis his. Gay also described the "Harlots" standing "Where *Katherine-Street* descends into the *Strand.*"

82. MJ/SR1917 R13, 23 Aug. 1698.

83. MJ/SR2128 R18 and R17, 8 Apr. 1709, respectively.

84. *Compleat Justice,* 339.

85. MSP1707 Jy/81.

86. It is important to note that the many women stopped for nightwalking and similar offenses may have been too poor to find their way into the Westminster recognizances. For a more detailed discussion of the policing of masculinity, see chapter 3 and J. Hurl-Eamon, "Policing Male Heterosexuality: The Reformation of Manners Societies' Campaigns against the Brothels in Westminster, 1690–1720," *The Journal of Social History* 37 (June 2004), 1017–35.

87. MJ/SR2315 R114, 23 Aug. 1718. This is exactly the same wording as the recognizances binding women for nightwalking.

88. MJ/SR2052, 14 Jun. 1715 and MJ/SR2300 R226 12 Oct. 1717 respectively.

89. MSP 1694 Aug/29.

90. MSP 1694, Aug/30.

91. Shoemaker noted that "eighteenth-century houses were frequently public spaces, in which a number of people unrelated, and perhaps even unknown, to each other could be found as lodgers, servants, coworkers and visitors." He went on to say that private space was not limited to the confines of a dwelling house and could encompass an entire court, alley, or yard where passers-by were all known to each other. Shoemaker, "Public Spaces, Private Disputes?" 2.

92. MJ/SR2270 R112, 12 May 1716.

93. MJ/SR2138 R86, 1 Sept. 1709 and MJ/SR1888 R67, R68 and R69, 7 Feb. 1696/7 respectively.

94. MJ/SR1897 R99, 12 July 1697.

95. MJ/SR1873 R96, 12 May 1696 and MJ/SR2343 R135, 26 Jan, 1719/20.
96. MJ/SR2330 R26, 5 June 1719.
97. DL/C/239 f 315, Wickham c. Thompson, 20 Jan. 1679/80.
98. See, for example, DL/C/153 f 358, Bartlett c. Culpepper, 13 May 1710.
99. L. Gowing, *Domestic Dangers: Women, Words, and Sex in Early Modern London* (Oxford: Clarendon Press, 1996), 98.
100. Walker, 34 and 52.
101. MJ/SR2290 R69, 2 June 1717 and MJ/SR2235 R209, 5 Aug. 1714 respectively.
102. MJ/SR2148 R127, 16 Mar. 1710.
103. MJ/SR2255 R13, 13 Sept. 1715.
104. MJ/SR2118 R131, 3 Sept. 1708.
105. Michael Dalton, *The Countrey Justice* (London: 1655), 265.
106. MJ/SR2320 R153, 20 Nov. 1718. Chapter 6 talks about Londoners' knowledge of the rules and restrictions governing bailiffs' and constables' official activities.
107. MJ/SR2325 R108, 11 Feb. 1719.
108. MJ/SR2315 R143, R144 and R145, 23 Sept. 1718 and MJ/SR1670 R14, 15 May 1685 respectively.
109. MJ/SR2032 R87, 30 May 1704.
110. MJ/SR2128 R94, 23 Apr. 1709 and MJ/SR2057 R34, 6 Aug. 1705 respectively.
111. MJ/SR2216 R129, 30 July 1713.
112. See, for example, MJ/SR2108 R75, 31 Jan. 1707/8 and MJ/SR2211 R77, 15 June 1713.
113. Fielding, Book V, Chapter IX, 165.
114. *The Gentleman's Library . . . Written by a Gentleman,* 2nd Ed. (1722), 127 (emphasis his), and *OBP,* 11–13 Apr. 1716 (London, printed for J. Phillips by M. Jenour), 4.
115. Edmund Bohun, *The Justice of Peace His Calling and Qualifications* (London: for T. Salusbury, 1693), 72.
116. MJ/SR1812 R30, 13 Feb. 1692/3 and MJ/SR2295 R146, 7 Aug. 1717 respectively.
117. S. Amussen, "Punishment, Discipline & Power: The Social Meaning of Violence in Early Modern England," *Journal of British Studies* 34 (Jan 1995), 23–27. Amussen looks mainly at homicide cases. Though women were largely absent in these felony trials, they were much more prevalent in the misdemeanor records.
118. MJ/SR2270 R177, 22 Jun. 1716.
119. MJ/SR2144 R50, 19 May 1709 and MJ/SR2118 R36, 31 Jul. 1708 respectively.
120. Alehouse historian Peter Clark notes women's presence in alehouses "regulated by social convention," meaning that women could go with their husbands or in a group of married women (especially to celebrate christenings and churchings). Any other circumstances were "likely to provoke loud comment from neighbours." P. Clarke, *The English Alehouse: A Social History 1200–1830* (London: Longman, 1983), 131. However, Jessica Warner and Frank Ivis argue that women were "accepted as legitimate customers in [London] drinking establishments, whether on their own or as

members of a group of drinkers." J. Warner and F. Ivis, "'Damn you, you informing Bitch': *Vox Populi* and the Unmaking of the Gin Act of 1736," *Journal of Social History* 33, no. 2 (1999), 307.

121. DL/C/255 f 452, Fletcher c. Kitson, 30 Dec. 1715 and DL/C/631 f 286, Cope c. Witty, 14 Nov. 1700 respectively.

122. Sharon Howard, "Crime, Communities and Authority in Early Modern Wales: Denbighshire, 1660–1730," Ph.D. thesis, University of Wales, 2003, reveals significant neighborhood tensions in rural communities as well.

123. There were 257 recognizances where sureties were listed for both the plaintiffs and the defendants. This was either because the prosecutor was also bound to appear or because a plaintiff was later bound by the same defendant for an assault (see chapter 2). Of these recognizances, 154 (59.9 percent) listed at least one surety that was from the same parish as the plaintiff's sureties, 62 (24 percent) listed all three sureties from parishes other than those for the plaintiff, and 41 (15.9 percent) did not name parishes for the sureties or were illegible.

124. DL/C/251 f 438, Clarke c. Barnes, 16 June 1710 and f 442 and DL/C/241 f 253, Jackson c. Villiers, 23 Nov. 1685 respectively.

125. MJ/SR2113 R96, 16 June 1708. The day before, a recognizance had been drawn up binding her neighbors to answer Riggs for "assalting her by Calling her Bawde Whore & such Like approbrious Names & for stricking her Upon the side of her head with a Roaling Pin." MJ/SR2113 R97, 15 June 1708.

126. DL/C/248 f 425, Eardiswick c. Bentley, 15 Aug. 1705.

127. MJ/SR2138 R112, 15 Aug. 1709 and R113, 17 Aug. 1709 respectively. For other interfamilial disputes, see MJ/SR2133 R54, 16 June 1709 and R55, 17 June 1709 respectively; and MJ/SR2334 R38, 7 Sept. 1719.

128. MJ/SR1974 R77, 26 Sept. 1701 and MJ/SR1836 R153, 27 Apr. 1694 respectively.

129. *OBP,* 14 Oct. 1680, (London, printed for T. Davies), 2. It should be noted that the gentleman's anger was fueled by the workmen joking that the clothes would have been ready if he had left them money for drink. On other workplace disputes, see MJ/SR2295 R45, 14 Sept. 1717 and R64, 29 July 1717.

130. MJ/SR2295 R135, 22 July 1717 and MJ/SR1865 R107, 8 Jan. 1695/6 respectively. *OBP,* 6–7 Sept. 1682 (London, s.n.), 2–3, also contains an account of a fight resulting from a card game between a group of artisans at a Hammersmith "Victualling House."

131. MJ/SR2162 R73, 30 Dec. 1710.

132. MJ/SR2108 R75, 31 Jan. 11707/8. For other assault recognizances involving challenges to fight, see MJ/SR2211 R77, 15 Jun. 1713 and MJ/SR2343 R70, 29 Feb. 1719/20. It is interesting to note that in each of these cases the male complainant was not ashamed to answer these challenges to fight with a prosecution rather than a drawn sword.

133. *OBP,* 1–4 May 1717 (London, printed for J. Phillips by M. Jenour), 8; emphasis theirs.

134. MJ/SR2295 R307, 8 Oct. 1717.

135. *OBP,* 24–31 May 1683 (London, printed for L. Curtis), 3.

136. DL/C/244 f 283, Phillips c. Sanderson, 3 Apr. 1695.

137. Gay, 35.

138. PRO, SP 36/50, quoted in E. P. Thompson, "The Moral Economy of the English Crowd in the Eighteenth Century," *Past and Present* 50 (1971), 116. For more on football as a form of protest, see R. Malcolmson, *Popular Recreations in English Society*, 1700–1850 (Cambridge: Cambridge University Press, 1973), 39–40.

139. MJ/SR2260 R141 and R140, 21 Dec. 1715 respectively.

140. Note that one woman, Mary Ellis (a spinster—presumably a relative of Richard's), was bound (R142 for the same date) for being involved in the football match, though not for assault.

Notes to Chapter 6

1. John Brewer, *Sinews of Power: War, Money and the English State, 1688–1783* (London: Unwin Hyman Ltd., 1989).

2. Ian Gilmour, *Riot, Risings and Revolution: Governance and Violence in Eighteenth-Century England* (London: Pimlico, 1993), 9.

3. Ibid., 15–7, and Robert B. Shoemaker, "The London 'Mob' in the Early Eighteenth Century," *Journal of British Studies* 26 (July 1987), 298–99.

4. See, for example, E. P. Thompson, "The Moral Economy of the English Crowd in the Eighteenth Century," *Past and Present* 50 (1971): 76–136; John Stevenson, *Popular Disturbances in England, 1700–1870* (New York: Longman, 1979), 309, 313; and Gilmour, 17.

5. See Paul Kléber Monod, *Jacobitism and the English People, 1688–1788* (Cambridge: Cambridge University Press, 1989), 161–233; Nicholas Rogers, "Popular Protest in Early Hanoverian London," *Past and Present,* no. 79 (1978), 70–100; and idem, "Riot and Popular Jacobitism in Early Hanoverian England," in *Ideology and Conspiracy: Aspects of Jacobitism, 1689–1759,* ed. Evenline Cruickshanks (Edinburgh: John Donald Publishers Ltd., 1982), 70–88, especially pages 76–78.

6. Note that almost immediately after our period, the Excise Bill (1733) and the Gin Act (1736) caused an outbreak of violent confrontations in the capital, and Walpole was assaulted in the heat of opposition to the Excise Bill.

7. MJ/SR2108 R87, 24 Jan. 1707/8.

8. MJ/SR2353 R41, 15 July 1720.

9. *9 Anne c. 16.*

10. For a sense of why contemporaries may have despised certain statesmen, see the anonymously authored pamphlet *A Description of Devils. Containing I. The Devil of a Statesman . . .* (London, printed for J. Millet, [1687?]), 6–7.

11. Brewer, 22.

12. Anon., *The Taxes not Grievous, and therefore not a reason for an Unsafe Peace* (London, 1711), 3–4. On those protesting the tax burden, see, for example, Anon., *Reasons most humbly submitted . . . for the taking off the present duty of Excise upon Beer and Ale . . .* (London, 1695), especially pages 6–7 and 18; James Drake, *An essay concerning the necessity of equal taxes . . .* (London, 1702); and Anon., *A Letter to a Member of Parliament: shewing the justice of a more equal and impartial assessment on land* (London, 1717).

13. MJ/SR1734 R130, 5 Oct. 1688; MJ/SR1693 unnumbered, 13 July 1686; MJ/SR2138 R145, 7 Sept. 1709; MJ/SR2286 R3, 5 Feb. 1716/7 respectively.

14. Note that *A Description of Devils,* page 30, depicted the "Devil of an Overseer" as an officeholder who "makes so many Assessments, [he is] . . . very justly Nick-named Mr. Over-rate."

15. Garthine Walker, *Crime, Gender and Social Order in Early Modern England* (Cambridge: Cambridge University Press, 2003), 254.

16. See, for example, Thomas Forster, *The Layman's Lawyer* . . . (London, 1654); J. P. Gent, *A New Guide for Constables . . . Overseers and Collectors for the Poor* . . . (London, 1692), 127; James Harvey, *A Collection of Precedents, relating to the office of a Justice of the Peace* (London, 1730), 183; Joseph Keble, *An Assistance to Justices of the Peace* (London, 1683), 494.

17. MJ/SR2286 R3, 5 Feb. 1716/7.

18. *Reasons most humbly submitted,* 8.

19. Brewer, 215 and 275n106.

20. John Childs, *The British Army of William III, 1689–1702* (Manchester: Manchester University Press, 1987), 88. On seventeenth-century opposition to a standing army, see Lois Schwoerer, *"No Standing Armies!" The Antiarmy Ideology in Seventeenth-Century England* (Baltimore: Johns Hopkins University Press, 1974).

21. MJ/SR2270 R156, 12 June 1716.

22. MJ/SR2315, unnumbered recognizance to prosecute, 19 July 1718. R 15, 15 July 1718 binds the fishmonger to appear and answer the charges.

23. Ibid., recognizance to prosecute.

24. MJ/SR1679 R52, 12 Nov. 1685 and MJ/SR2353 R67, 20 Aug. 1720.

25. Childs (95) gives the example of "an unwritten policy of quartering troops upon known or suspected Jacobites" in order to punish them.

26. MJ/SR2073 R43, 16 Apr. 1706.

27. See, for example, James II, *By the King, a declaration* . . . 2 Sept. 1688 (London, Printed by Charles Bill, Henry Hills, and Thomas Newcomb, 1688), and William III, *By the Prince of Orange, a declaration* . . . 8 Jan. 1688/9 (London, Printed by Edward Jones, 1688/9). The change is discussed by Childs (93) and Major R. E. Scouller, *The Armies of Queen Anne* (Oxford: Clarendon Press, 1966), 164.

28. MJ/SR2138 R79, 19 Sept. 1709.

29. MJ/SR2098 R24, 5 Aug. 1707 and MJ/SR2103 R16, 25 Oct. 1707. Note that refusal to quarter soldiers was a distinct offense, with specific fines assigned as penalty. Giles Jacob, *The Modern Justice* . . . (London, 1720), 45.

30. MJ/SR2088 R62, 18 Feb. 1706/7. For other refusals to quarter, see MJ/SR2098 R35, 13 Aug. 1707.

31. Childs, 93.

32. See Rogers, *Crowds, Culture and Politics,* 85–121, for popular attitudes toward impressment for England as a whole over the eighteenth century.

33. MJ/SR1868 R58, 26 Feb. 1696.

34. MJ/SR2286 R102, 16 Mar. 1717.

35. Ibid.

36. Ibid.

37. MJ/SR2128 R90, 25 Mar. 1709. Many local government officials could

refuse to cooperate with press gangs. Nicholas Rogers, *Crowds, Culture and Politics,* 93–94, gives examples of JPs and even a mayor who vocally opposed impressment.

38. MJ/SR1831 R 125, 2 Feb. 1694/5 and MJ/SR2047 R34, 10 Feb. 1704/5 respectively.

39. MJ/SR2078 R41, 24 Sept. 1706.

40. MJ/SR2073 R23, 28 May 1706.

41. Rogers, *Crowds, Culture and Politics,* 97–99.

42. MJ/SR2098 R134, 26 Aug. 1707 and MJ/SR2265 R94, 19 Jan. 1715/6 respectively.

43. MJ/SR2295 R269, 6 Aug. 1717.

44. MJ/SR2128 R57, 17 Jan. 1708/9.

45. After *2 & 3 Edw. VI c. 2, s. 3,* there was little or no legislation on desertion until after the Glorious Revolution of 1688. See *1 W & M c. 5 s. 2; 2 W & M, St. 2 c. 8; 4 W & M, c. 13; 13 & 14 Wm III c. 2; 1 Ann St. 2 c. 20;* and *10 Ann c. 13.*

46. George Meriton, *A Guide for Constables, Churchwardens, Overseers of the Poor,* 8th Ed. (London: Printed by Richard and Edward Atkins, 1685), 12.

47. Forty-two women were bound for assaulting on their own or with other women, and an additional seventeen women were bound in recognizances that also mentioned men. Conversely, 313 men were bound for assaulting on their own or with other men, and sixteen were bound for assaulting in mixed groups.

48. MJ/SR2353 R79, 7 Nov. 1720.

49. MJ/SR1917 R21, 2 Sept. 1698 and MJ/SR2353 R84, 19 July 1720 respectively.

50. MJ/SR2325 R3, 22 Jan. 1718/9. Note that Constable Charles Slaughter and his assistants did *not* swear the peace against Francis Tuckwell, the legal formula that would *require* them to claim that they were in danger of their lives. For more on the legal consequences of the words "in danger of life" on an assault recognizance, see chapters 2 and 5.

51. MJ/SR2330 R51, 21 Apr. 1719. As above, Addison swore himself "in danger of his life" without swearing Mackmanus to keep the peace.

52. *A True and Sad Relation of Two Wicked and Bloody Murthers . . .* (London: Printed for J. Clarke, 1680), 1. See also *Great and Bloody News from Turnham Green* (London: Printed for D.M., 1680).

53. T. C. Curtis, "Quarter Sessions Appearances and their Background: A Seventeenth-Century Regional Study," in J. S. Cockburn, ed., *Crime in England, 1550–1800* (Princeton: Princeton University Press, 1977), 142–44, says that most assaults on constables were formally prosecuted rather than informally mediated by JPs.

54. Of the total recognizances for assaults on constables or watchmen, 8.4 percent bear clerical annotations to indicate that the prosecution also generated an indictment, in contrast to 9.5 percent for recognizances as a whole (679 of 7,129 recognizances to answer for an assault), examined in appendix A. Peter King found that assailants who had targeted officials began to be treated more harshly than those who assaulted private individuals only at the end of the eighteenth century. P. King, "Punishing Assault: The Transformation of Attitudes in the English Courts," *Journal of Interdisciplinary History* XXVII, no. 1 (Summer 1996), 43–74.

55. See, for example, Douglas Hay, "Prosecution and Power: Malicious Prosecution in the English Courts, 1750–1850," in D. Hay and F. Snyder, eds., *Policing and Prosecution in Britain, 1750–1850* (Oxford: Clarendon Press, 1989), 343–96; John H. Langbein, "Shaping the Eighteenth-Century Criminal Trial: A View from the Ryder Sources," *The University of Chicago Law Review* 50, no. 1 (1983), 105–14; Ruth Paley, "Thief-Takers in London in the Age of the McDaniel Gang, c. 1745–1754," in *Policing and Prosecution,* 301–42; Sir L. Radzinowicz, *A History of English Criminal Law, Volume Two: The Clash Between Private Initiative and Public Interest in the Enforcement of the Law* (London: Stevens and Sons, 1956), 23.

56. John Paul, *The Compleat Constable* (London: Printed for John Fielding, 1785), 98.

57. Given this assumption, it may be that the number of *genuine* prosecutions that went to indictment was actually proportionately *higher* than the totals for assaults as a whole. The 8.4 percent calculated above would then be doubled to 16.8 percent, more than 7 percent higher than the total for assaults as a whole.

58. DL/C/255 f 386, Hamersley c. Franks, 26 Oct. 1715.

59. Ibid.

60. DL/C/255 f 451, Fletcher c. Kitson, 30 Dec. 1715.

61. Ibid.

62. MJ/SR2286 R169 and R189, 12 Mar. 1717.

63. Ibid., R169.

64. MJ/SR2177 R63, 3 Jul. 1711.

65. *OBP,* 10–11 Oct. 1716 (London, printed for J. Phillips by M. Jenour), 3.

66. MJ/SR1779 R198, 23 Apr. 1691.

67. N. Johnson, *Eighteenth-Century London* (London: HMSO, 1991), 24.

68. E. W., 22, and Paul, 75. See also Meriton, 33.

69. Edmund Bohun, *The Justice of Peace his Calling,* (London: for T. Salusbury, 1693), 149.

70. George, 81–85.

71. R. B. Outhwaite, *Clandestine Marriage in England, 1500–1850* (Rio Grande: Hambleton Press, 1995), 45–57.

72. The "Rules" referred to the areas of several square miles surrounding prisons such as King's Bench and the Fleet, usually inhabited by debtors who had found "friends to stand surety for their debts" and who were thus offered the privilege of living in the Rules. Such residents were virtually exempt from the law, as they were already technically imprisoned, and if they were taken and jailed elsewhere for some other offense, they could obtain a writ of habeas corpus and be removed to King's Bench or the Fleet prison again. See Joanna Innes, "The King's Bench Prison in the Later Eighteenth Century: Law, Authority and Order in a London Debtor's Prison," in J. Brewer and S. Styles, eds., *An Ungovernable People: The English and Their Law in the Seventeenth and Eighteenth Centuries* (London: Hutchinson, 1980), 250–98, quotation from page 256.

73. R. Ingleton, *Arming the British Police: The Great Debate* (London: Frank Cass & Co., 1997), 5–6, depicted the cities' watchmen as "usually armed with a cutlass," and—while some City wards had eighteen or nineteen constables—John Beattie's *Policing and Punishment in the City of London, 1660–1750: Urban Crime and the*

Limits of Terror (New York: Oxford University Press, 2001), 115, gave the example of Cripplegate Without, "in which four constables" served a ward of "close to 2,000 houses."

74. E. W., 13–14.

75. See Beattie, 140–49.

76. MJ/SR2290 R205, 8 May 1717.

77. James Harvey, *A Collection of Precedents Relating to the Office of a Justice of Peace* (London, 1730), 162, gave an example of a warrant "to apprehend the Petty Constable for Breach of Peace" and listed him as a "Taylor." Watchmen could also hold other trades, seen in several recognizances binding watchmen for various dereliction of duty. See, for example, MJ/SR1734 R5, R4 & R2, 5 Oct. 1688 and MJ/SR2138 R101 & R100, 23 July 1709 respectively.

78. Paul, 89.

79. A gentleman was recorded as observing that "the Watch" would "dance all Day long after a Gentleman to get a Pint of Drink of him." *OBP,* 11–14 Jan. 1716/17 (London, printed for J. Phillips by M. Jenour), 3. Similarly, a constable described as a victualer was bound for being drunk in the performance of his office, and another constable was bound for arresting a woman, bringing her into a tavern, and trying "to put his hands up her coats." MJ/SR2103 R7, 21 Nov. 1707 and MJ/SR2062 R100, 30 Oct. 1705 respectively. Beattie (143) said that victualers serving as constables were held with special suspicion, "no doubt because one of the constable's tasks was to ensure that [drinking establishments] were licensed and that they obeyed the laws governing drinking hours." See also M. D. George, *London Life in the Eighteenth Century* (New York: Capricorn Books, 1965), 33–34.

80. W. Nelson, *The Office and Authority of a Justice of the Peace,* 5th Ed. (London, 1750), 176. Beattie (139) in his study of the City of London found that the wards "with a larger and more diverse population [had] more . . . constables . . . among the poorer householders." Though he took care to stress that it was "only a part of the picture," Clive Emsley stated that "the courts show that there were corrupt, ignorant and poor constables during the Tudor and Stuart periods." C. Emsley, *The English Police: A Political and Social History* (London: Longman, 1991), 11. The low-bred nature of London constables was satirized in a seventeenth-century play, which included a song describing the constable as resorting to the tavern, "Drinking many a lusty health," and later arresting "a comely girle" for prostitution, and—"Though it may impaire his health, He sleeps with her for th' good oth' Common-wealth." Henry Glapthorne, *Wit in a Constable: A Comedy written in 1639* (London: Printed by Jo. Okes, for F.C., 1640), Act 5, Scene 1. Though he quoted nonliterary sources that support this image, Emsley (9–10) warned against making too much of the literary ridicule of constables: "Both Dogberry, the headborough in *Much Ado about Nothing,* and Elbow, the simple Constable from *Measure for Measure,* talk in malapropisms, but this is a comic fault allegedly found also in twentieth-century English policemen, and none of the critics of Shakespeare's constables think of condemning twentieth-century policemen as comic and degraded characters for this reason."

81. MJ/SR2295 R57, 21 Aug. 1717.

82. Beattie, 123. The constable in a play enacted in Drury Lane, 1639, vowed to make wrongdoers "stoope Under my staffe of office." Glapthorne, Act 4, Scene 1.

83. MJ/SR2334 R82, 22 Sept. 1719.

84. *OBP,* 14 Oct. 1680 (London, printed for T. Davies), 2.

85. The "marshal's men" referred to here must not be confused with the assistants to the county marshal, who were also known by the same name. The principal function of the latter was to arrest prostitutes and vagrants and to control crowds during public events such as hangings and riots. Beattie, 158–63. The officers of the marshalsea courts, rather than the assistants to the county marshal, are examined in the following pages, because the context in which the term "marshal's men" appears in the assault recognizances suggests that they were the same "marshals men" referred to in *The Ancient Legal Course and Fundamental Constitution of the Pallace Court or Marshalsea* (London: Printed for Robert Crofts, 1663), 52, or the pamphlet by Robert Robins, entitled *A Whip for the Marshalls Court, and their Officers* (London, 1648).

86. J. A. Sharpe, *Crime in Early Modern England, 1550–1750* (London: Longman, 1984), 31. Middlesex shared the City's two sheriffs, who appointed the High Bailiffs, along with "an indefinite number of underlings, called 'foot' bailiffs, [and] 'bound bailiffs,'" who "served both to carry messages and to execute the processes of justice." B. Webb and S. Webb, *English Local Government, Volume 1: The Parish and the County* (London: Franck Cass and Col, 1906, reprinted 1963), 287–89.

87. It is difficult to determine, from the records, which of the four courts a "marshal's man" served, as contemporaries erroneously referred to all of them as either "the Marshalsea court," "the Palace court," or the "Marshall's court" in this time period. D. C. Greene, "The Court of the Marshalsea in Late Tudor and Stuart England," *American Journal of Legal History* XX (1976), 280; Sir William Blackstone, *Commentaries on the Laws of England in Four Books,* Book Three (reprint, Philadelphia: Geo. T. Bisel Co., 1922), 75; and W. Holdsworth, *A History of English Law* Vol. I, 7th Ed., A. Goodhart and H. Hanbury (eds.) (London: Methuen & Co., 1956), 208–9.

88. Along with the sheriff and constables, the bailiffs had to "be in attendance" at Quarter Sessions, "with the obligation of reporting such offences or derelictions of duty as had occurred within their respective jurisdictions," and—because the courts of the verge dealt mostly with debt (discussed below)—marshal's men also resorted to Quarter Sessions to prosecute violence against them. Webb, 296.

89. *Twelve Ingenious Characters: Or, pleasant Descriptions of the Properties of sundry Persons and Things* (London: Printed for S. Norris, 1680), 12.

90. *A True description of the Mint* (London: Printed by A. Baldwin, 1710), 21–22.

91. MJ/SR2330 R76, 11 Apr. 1719. The public whipping of women was banned by *57 Geo 3 c. 75* in 1817, but there is no evidence that it evoked significant popular resentment in this period.

92. Hampshire Record Office, Coventry MSS IM53/1374: entry dated 30 Nov. 1698, in James Dewy's "Book of Examinacons 1685." See also MJ/SR2197 R70, 6 Oct. 1712. Rescues are dealt with in more detail in chapter 7.

93. MJ/SR1868 R207, 13 Apr. 1696 and MJ/SR1960 R29, 29 Oct. 1700.

94. *An Epistle Narrative of the Barbarous Assault and Illegall Arrest of Freder. Turvill, Esq.* (London, 1660), 2.

95. *OBP,* 26–28 May 1680 (London, s.n.), 3.

96. MJ/SR2037 R12, 26 Aug. 1704. See also MJ/SR2260 R214, 7 Oct. 1715, for a description of a marshal's man assaulting a woman.

97. See, for example, MJ/SR1917 R22, 21 Sept. 1680 and MJ/SR2042 R34, 19 Oct. 1704. A bailiff about to be executed for murder described himself as "Guilty of that huffing pride and insolence" typical of those serving in his office. *News from Tybourn: or the Confession and Execution of Three Bayliffs* . . . (London: Printed for D.M., 1675).

98. According to James Sharpe (32), "[C]omplaints of bribery, corruption and extortion against bailiffs were all too widespread and too plausible."

99. Even a defender of the Palace Court was forced to admit to "the petty meane conceit and estimation people generally have had" for the Palace Court, "though its Decrees are as valid and binding as any of the Benches of Law at Westminster." *The Ancient Legal Course,* 48–49. Similarly, Robins—imprisoned on its authority in the mid–seventeenth century—asserted that "that court . . . is of no validity, nor hath any power or Jurisdiction to execute [its] authority . . . upon the ignorant people every day."

100. Douglas Green (275) concluded that "the superior courts at Westminster wanted to limit the Marshalsea's jurisdiction." Robins recounted his indicting two marshal's men for assault because the court they served had no real authority in the seventeenth century. In MJ/SR2295 R128, 28 Aug. 1717, John Felton prosecuted a marshal's man for assault. (Note that Felton's assailant is listed only as a "messenger to the board of green cloth"—one of the four criminal courts of the verge, also known as the Court of the King's Counting House, which allows me to identify him as a marshal's man. I am grateful to conversations with Matthew Szromba for this information. See M. P. Szromba, "The Wicked Man Shall Not Abide in My House: The Courts of the Verge and the English Monarchy, 1660–1760", Ph.D. dissertation, Loyola University, 2004). The officer was also bound "for a contempt in disputing the Constables authority in executing a warrant against him" for that assault.

101. Robins.

102. *Twelve Ingenious Characters,* 10, and *A Description of Devils,* 14, respectively.

103. *An Epistle Narrative,* 4.

104. *News from Tybourn.*

105. MJ/SR2280, R183, 3 Dec. 1716. Succliffe was also charged with barratry which resonates with a case before the Bishop of London's Consistory Court in which a bailiff admitted to calling "Anne Anderson Nasty Comon Bawdy house whore," claiming drunkenness as his defense. DL/C/255 f 186, Anderson c. Blew, 23 Mar. 1714/5.

106. It seems safe to assume that bailiffs were the most obvious, if not the only, officers empowered to arrest those accused of debt in the early eighteenth century, because the studies of imprisonment for debt mention only bailiffs, though they do not explicitly deny constables a role in such arrests. Innes, 255–56; P. Haagen, "Eighteenth-Century English Society and the Debt Law," in S. Cohen and A. Scull, eds., *Social Control and the State: Historical and Comparative Essays* (Oxford: Martin Robertson, 1983), 235–36; and O. R. McGregor, *Social History and Law Reform* (London: Stevens and Sons, 1981), 40.

107. Innes, 255.

108. J. Hoppit, *Risk and Failure in English Business, 1700–1800* (Cambridge: Cambridge University Press, 1987), 33.

109. McGregor, 40.

110. See Innes, 252 and 258–59, and Haagan, 225, who stated that "every creditor had the right to demand the arrest of almost any of his debtors without warning or proof."

111. *The Ancient Legal Course,* 19. In fact, Douglas Greene (275) concluded that by the seventeenth century "the Court of the Verge . . . became a tribunal for the recovery of small claims." See also Blackstone, 75–76.

112. Robins. See also *The Tryal of William Acton.* I. P. H. Duffy, "English Bankrupts, 1571–1861," *The American Journal of Legal History* XXIV (1980), 236, described sympathy for debtors as "common in the literature" of the early eighteenth century. For the more blatant protests against imprisonment for debt that occurred nearer the end of the century, see Innes, 290–98.

113. MJ/SR2270 R 69 and R70, 19 Apr. 1716. See also MJ/SR2325 R144, 1 Apr. 1719 and MJ/SR2295 R155 and R 156, 5 Sept. 1717 for other rescues of debtors.

114. *OBP,* 6 July 1681 (London, I. Guilford), 1–2.

115. *OBP,* 15–16 Jan. 1679/80 (London, s.n.), 3.

116. WSP 1690 Oct/2, 13 Sept. 1690. "The information of William Rawley agt Wm Carman Concerning a Rescue." Note that it was a felony to rescue a person who was arrested, "but if he was not arrested, then the opposing or hindering any Person to apprehend him is a misdemeanour, but no Felony." Nelson, 503–4.

117. Ibid., "The information of David Tymewell, surgian."

Notes to Chapter 7

1. On the nonviolent nature of riots, see John Stevenson, *Popular Disturbances in England, 1700–1870* (New York: Longman, 1979), 313. Robert B. Shoemaker, "The London 'Mob' in the Early Eighteenth Century," *Journal of British Studies* 26 (July 1987), 274, table 1, found the mention of assaults in riots second only in proportion to the mention of disturbance or defamation.

2. See, for example, Nicholas Rogers, *Crowds, Culture and Politics in Georgian Britain* (Oxford: Clarendon Press, 1998), 223.

3. J. Bohstedt, "Gender, Household and Community Politics: Women in English Riots 1790–1810," *Past and Present* 120 (1988), 119–20.

4. See ibid., 88–122, and Shoemaker, "The London 'Mob,'" especially pages 284–86. Bohstedt finds women rioters less violent than men, but he is looking at the end of the eighteenth century, when women are considered less violent in general, judging by the dramatic decline in arrests for violent crime found by M. Feeley and D. Little, "The Vanishing Female: The Decline of Women in the Criminal Process, 1687–1912," *Law and Society Review* 25, no. 4 (1991), 719–57.

5. Sir William Blackstone, *Commentaries on the Laws of England in Four Books,* Book Four (reprint, Philadelphia: Geo. T. Bisel Co., 1922), 146n14; Michael Dalton,

The Countrey Justice (London: 1655), 279; W. Hawkins, *A Treatise of the Pleas of the Crown . . .*, Vol. I (London: E. Richardson & C. Lintot, 1766), c. 65 s 5, 157.

6. Dalton, 282. A similar statement appears in W. Nelson, *The Office and Authority of a Justice of the Peace,* 5th Ed. (London, 1750). However, *1 Hawkins c. 65 s 14,* 159, says that "women are punishable as rioters" and does not specify that they have to be led by a male; and Joseph Keble, *An Assistance to Justices of the Peace for the Easier Performance of their Duty* (London: printed for W. Rawlins, etc. 1683), 647, refers to "sundry women" being convicted of rioting by the Court of Star Chamber, but they were wearing male clothing.

7. Shoemaker, "The London Mob," 298–99, and Ian Gilmour, *Riot, Risings and Revolution: Governance and Violence in Eighteenth-Century England* (London: Pimlico, 1993), 17.

8. MJ/SR2098 R97, 3 Sept. 1707.

9. E. P. Thompson, "'Rough Music': Le charivari anglais," *Annales Economies Sociétés Civilisations* 27 no. 2 (1972): 285–312; Martin Ingram, "Ridings, Rough Music and the 'Reform of Popular Culture' in Early Modern England," *Past and Present* 105 (1984), 79–113.

10. Shoemaker, "The London Mob," 274 (table 1) and 278.

11. MJ/SR2118 R130, 29 Sept. 1708 and MJ/SR2270 R160, 21 May, 1716 respectively. For more examples of assaults and riots "about" the victim's house, see chapter 5.

12. MJ/SR2305 R135, 18 Feb. 1718.

13. MJ/SR2286 R175 and R176, 29 Mar. 1717.

14. MJSR2182 R126, 7 Dec. 1711 and MJ/SR1836 R66, 16 Apr. 1694.

15. MJSR2290 R110, 22 May 1717.

16. MJ/SR2172 R44, 17 Apr. 1711.

17. MJ/SR2052 R19, 17 Apr. 1705.

18. MJ/SR2133 R62, 21 June 1709.

19. MJ/SR2093 R4, 28 Apr. 1707. See also Recognizances 2, 3, and 5, which bound the male rioter-assailants. Sir Richard Buckley is absent in the *Dictionary of National Biography.* The only surviving record of a man by this name is a pamphlet that he authored in 1690, entitled *The Proposal for Sending Back the Nobility and Gentry of Ireland* (London: Printed for Sir Samuel Holford and Sold by R. Baldwin, 1690). According to Buckley, his proposal provoked "a parcel of Rabble" to "rail and roar at" him, and he referred to "continual calumnies and threats" from them "ever since, to do him some mischief." Unfortunately, there is no concrete evidence to indicate the cause of the 1707 riot against him almost two decades later.

20. Ibid., R2.

21. Of the 150 assault recognizances for "raising a mob," 84, or 56 percent, named female defendants. (Recognizances binding both male and female defendants were not included.) There was no special legal category for "raising a mob," and the closest mention of this type of offense is in Keble, s. XLII no. 2, 663: "if any person . . . raised or caused to be raised twelve persons or above," that person is guilty of riot.

22. Jessica Warner and Frank Ivis, "'Damn you, you informing Bitch': *Vox Populi* and the Unmaking of the Gin Act of 1736," *Journal of Social History* 33, no. 2 (1999), 311, state that the "typical scenario" of women's riot activities "was for women to incite

violence without actually participating in it." They cite E. P. Thompson, Malcolm Thomis, and Jennifer Grimmett to substantiate their claim that, by raising the mob rather than being mere participants in a riot, women were able to remain nonviolent. However, while Thompson, Thomis, and Grimmett offer corroborating evidence of women's significant role as mob raisers, they say nothing to substantiate Ivis and Warner's contention that mob raising was nonviolent. Indeed, in discussing mob raising, Thompson, Thomis, and Grimmett give many examples of women who explicitly used violence to incite their fellow rioters. Malcolm I. Thomis and Jennifer Grimmett, *Women in Protest, 1800–1850* (London: Croom Helm, 1982), 37–39; E. P. Thompson, "The Moral Economy of the English Crowd in the Eighteenth Century," *Past and Present* 50 (1971), 115–16; and idem, *Customs in Common,* (New York: New Press, 1993), 312, 334.

23. MJ/SR2295 R122, 15 Aug. 1717.

24. MJ/SR2113 R94, 17 Jun. 1708.

25. MJ/SR2305 R59, 25 Feb. 1718.

26. MJ/SR2300 R36, 7 Dec. 1717.

27. MJ/SR1798 R241, 20 June 1692.

28. MJ/SR2235 R208, 5 Aug. 1714 and MJ/SR2235 R209, 5 Aug. 1714 respectively.

29. MJ/SR1836 R140, 21 June 1694 and MJ/SR1836 R143, 21 June 1694 respectively.

30. MJ/SR2265 R9, 13 Jan. 1715/6.

31. MJ/SR1878 R63, 23 Sept. 1696 and MJ/SR2128 R25, 24 Feb. 1709 respectively.

32. MJ/SR2255 R81, 23 July 1715 and MJ/SR1855 R41, 15 May 1695 respectively.

33. MJ/SR2221 R10, 2 Jan. 1714.

34. See, for example, Paul Kléber Monod, *Jacobitism and the English People, 1688–1788* (Cambridge: Cambridge University Press, 1989), 250.

35. Rogers, *Crowds,* 215–47.

36. There are ten recognizances binding women to answer seditious words charges, and ten binding men. Nicholas Rogers (*Crowds,* 223) found a grand total of 238 prosecutions for seditious words in the metropolis between 1714 and 1716, and while only 15 percent of these charged women, he argues that this was much higher than the percentage of women charged with any more serious, Jacobite-related offense.

37. MJ/SR2108 R142, 30 Mar. 1708.

38. MJ/SR1997 R3 and R44, 30 Sept. 1702. On Henry Campions's Jacobitism, see Monod, 284.

39. MJ/SR1997 R96, 5 Oct. 1702.

40. MJ/SR2310 R70, 17 June 1718.

41. MJ/SR2260 R151, 1 Nov. 1715.

42. MJ/SR2315 R199, and one unnumbered recognizance to prosecute, 11 Aug. 1718.

43. Rogers, *Crowds,* 224–25.

44. J. M. Beattie, *Policing and Punishment in London, 1660–1750: Urban Crime and the Limits of Terror* (New York: Oxford University Press, 2001), 256, 387–90.

45. Monod, 234.

46. Sir William Blackstone, *Commentaries on the Laws of England in Four Books,* Book Four (reprint, Philadelphia: Geo. T. Bisel Co., 1922), 80.

47. Paul Monod asks whether "drunken or angry or antagonistic expressions [can] be interpreted as evidence of political sentiments" and suggests that a toast to King James might sometimes be no more than "a playful jest without serious content" (239).

48. Three of the eleven women (27 percent) in contrast to two of the seventeen men (12 percent) accused of speaking seditious words used violent imagery as part of their sedition.

49. MJ/SR1551 R55, 26 Nov. 1689 and MJ/SR2330 R78, 8 Apr. 1719 respectively.

50. *OBP,* 8, 9, 11 Apr. 1719 (London, printed for J. Phillips by M. Jenour), 4.

51. *OBP,* 12–15 Oct. 1715 (London, printed for S. Crouch), 2, and MJ/SR2295 R13, 3 Aug. 1717, respectively.

52. Roger B. Manning, "The origins of the Doctrine of Sedition," *Albion* 12, no. 2 (1980), 104. Interestingly, only Ann Murkott was bound "for speaking treasonable words," yet she does not appear to fall within the definition.

53. *OBP,* 7–9 Sept. 1715 (London, printed for S. Crouch), 2.

54. MJ/SR2255 R72, 19 Sept. 1715. For assaults accompanied by seditious words, see also MJ/SR2078 R86, 21 Aug. 1706; MJ/SR2265 R82, 21 Feb. 1715/6; MJ/SR2270 R125, 21 May 1716; MJ/SR2270 R152, 12 June 1716; MJ/SR2270 R155, 18 June 1716; MJ/SR2270 R153, 23 June 1716; and MJ/SR2315 R267, 8 Aug. 1718 respectively.

55. MJ/SR1841 R181, 17 July 1694.

56. MJ/SR1873 R99, 14 May 1696.

57. MJ/SR2310 R40, 30 May 1718.

58. MJ/SR2295 R49, 29 Aug. 1717.

59. MJ/SR2315 R87, 15 Aug. 1718.

60. Mughouses were the meeting places for Loyal Societies, which toasted the King at every meeting with a "Mug of true English Ale." George Waldron, *A Speech Made to the Loyal Society at the Mug-House in Long Acre 7 June 1716* (London, 1716), 12.

61. *OBP,* 6–10 Sept. 1716 (London, printed for J. Phillips by M. Jenour), 2; emphasis in original.

62. *OBP,* 10–11 Oct. 1716 (London, printed for J. Phillips by M. Jenour), 2. Note that "patens" are clogs or overshoes worn to keep the wearer out of the mud; they often contained hard wooden or iron soles.

63. Ibid.; emphasis in original. For a similar account, see *OBP,* 6–10 Sept. 1716 (London, printed for J. Phillips by M. Jenour), 3–4.

64. *OBP,* 10–11 Oct. 1716 (London, printed for J. Phillips by M. Jenour), 3.

65. *An Account of the riots, tumults, and other treasonable practices since his Majesty's accession to the throne . . .* (London, 1715), 8, 24.

66. *The Tryal of William Acton, Deputy-keeper and Turnkey* (London: Printed for A. Moor, 1729).

67. Ibid.

68. Paul, 95. See also, Meriton, 31–34; *Exact Constable,* 29; and Sheppard, chapter 2, section 1, no. 18.

69. Nelson, 180.

70. Keble, 223.

71. MJ/SR1822, R97, 28 July 1693 and MJ/SR2018 R128, 30 Sept.1703 respectively.

72. Sir Thomas Deveil, *Observations on the practice of a Justice of the Peace: intended for such gentlemen as design to act for Middlex or Westminster* (London, 1747), 18–19.

73. MJ/SR2083 R67, 28 Nov. 1706.

74. Ibid. and R101 respectively.

75. The upper marshal "was expected to exercise a general if vague supervision over night-time policing by riding around the City several times a week"—but the sheer volume of his task, coupled with the likelihood of his own corruption, meant that such supervision rarely occurred in practice. Beattie, 159.

76. B. Harris, "Women and Politics in Early Tudor England," *The Historical Journal* 23, no. 2 (1990), 260.

77. MJ/SR2118 R76, 28 July 1708. R77 bound John Parish for the same offense.

78. MJ/SR1779 R46, 29 Apr. 1691 and MJ/SR2013 R18, 27 July, 1703 respectively.

79. MJ/SR2013 R18; ibid.

80. MJ/SR1912 R63, 1 May 1698 and MJ/SR2260 R192 (for Joseph) & R193 (for Anne), 21 Nov. 1715, respectively.

81. MJ/SR2221 R25, 23 Oct. 1713. See chapter 5 for the possible significance of removing a man's hat and wig in an assault.

82. MJ/SR1969 R33, 27 May 1701 and MJ/SR2042 R1, 7 Oct. 1704 respectively.

83. On the prevalence of uncontracted marriages in England, see A. Lawrence, *Women in England 1500–1760: A Social History* (London: Weidenfeld and Nicholson, 1994), 50–51, and Outhwaite, 45, who cited R. L. Brown's estimates on the number of Fleet marriages. (In our period, there were 2,251 in 1700; 3,679 in 1710; and 4,021 in 1720).

84. MJ/SR1960 R128, 19 Oct. 1700.

85. MJ/SR1888 R42, 14 Jan 1697.

86. MJ/SR1921 R36, 25 Oct. 1698.

87. MJ/SR2013 R32, 28 June 1703. Note that the recognizance indicates that Hill was successful in rescuing only one of the "wenches."

88. MJ/SR2310 R200, 15 May 1718. This example resonates with that of Jane Cox, who performed a similar rescue by smuggling in "an chisel a mallet & a long Rope" to enable a male prisoner to make his escape. MJ/SR2295 R263, 14 Aug. 1717. A group of "Confederates" of Newgate prisoners, whose gender is not specified, helped the prisoners escape by providing them with "two saw knives [and] two Plough-coulters," which allowed the "dextrous" prisoners "to saw off all their Irons, and make a large breach in the Wall, and sliding down by a Rope, ma[k]e their escapes." *OBP* 26 Feb.–1 Mar. 1679/80 (London, printed by D.M.), 4.

89. MJ/SR1826 R85, 4 Nov. 1693. According to the *OED,* a vizard-mask was

worn to conceal the face, and women who wore such masks were associated with prostitution—to the extent that prostitutes could be called "vizards."

90. Ibid. Such transvestism emerges a few times in the legal records of London over this period. John Ridgway was "taken up in womens apparel" in 1701 and could give "no good account of himself," so he was bound over. MJ/SR1979 R36, 22 Jan 1701. The Old Bailey heard a trial in 1717 of a man "indicted for assaulting and robbing" a woman while he was wearing "a Ridinghood"—a feminine item of dress. *OBP*, 1–4, May, 1717 (London, printed for J. Phillips by M. Jenour), 5–6. See also D. Cressy, *Travesties and Transgressions in Tudor and Stuart England: Tales of Discord and Dissension* (New York: Oxford University Press, 2000), 109–10, and E. P. Thompson, "The Moral Economy of the English Crowd in the Eighteenth Century," *Past and Present* 50 (1971), 115–16.

91. N. Z. Davis, "Women on Top," in *Society and Culture in Early Modern France* (Stanford: Stanford University Press, 1965), 132. The use of the clothing of the opposite sex for disguise was occasionally a tactic for female rescuers as well, and Richard Vincent was accompanied by Hannah Whiston and Sarah Brounchier, both spinsters, who were "drest up in mens cloths" to rescue Mr. St. Legar.

92. MJ/SR1826 R90 & R89, 1 Oct. 1693 respectively. These recognizances are also interesting because the women, as their own sureties, were bound for £150—perhaps because (as their recognizances state) the focus of their rescue, Mr. Gibson St. Legar, was in jail for "concealing and conveying away Esq Leviston after he had killed Mr Charles Howard." In other words, they were caught rescuing the rescuer of a murderer.

93. WSP1690, Oct. 2, 13 Sept. 1690; MJ/SR2013 R32, 28 June 1703; and MJ/SR2286 R43, 19 Apr. 1717.

94. This observation is based on a search of the pre-nineteenth-century publications listed in the English Short Title Catalogue under the keyword *rescue*.

95. Ruth B. Bottigheimer, *Grimms' Bad Girls and Bold Boys: The Moral and Social Vision of the Tales* (New Haven: Yale University Press, 1987), 101, and Shuli Barzilai, "'Say that I had a lovely face': The Grimms' 'Rapunzel,' Tennyson's 'Lady of Shalott,' and Atwood's *Lady Oracle*," *Tulsa Studies in Women's Literature* 19, no. 2 (Fall 2000), 231–54.

96. Robert Darnton, *The Great Cat Massacre and Other Episodes in French Cultural History* (New York: Vintage Books, 1985), 37, 45, 51.

Notes to Chapter 8

1. N. Landau, "Appearance at the Quarter Sessions of Eighteenth-Century Middlesex," *London Journal* 23, no. 2 (1998), 30–52.

2. R. B. Shoemaker, "The London 'Mob' in the Early Eighteenth Century," *Journal of British Studies* 26 (July 1987), 273–304.

3. These points are outlined in more detail in Appendix A.

4. See, for example, James Sharpe, "Such Disagreement betwyx Neighbours: Litigation and Human Relations in Early Modern England," in John Bossy, ed., *Disputes and Settlements: Law and Human Relations in the West* (New York: Cambridge University Press, 1983), 169–70.

Notes to Appendix A

1. For example, mayhem, which was an assault of particular violence "with intent to maim or disfigure" the victim, was a "felony without benefit of clergy." Sir William Blackstone, *Commentaries on the Laws of England in Four Books,* Book Four (reprint, Philadelphia: Geo. T. Bisel Co., 1922), 207. Assaults such as MJ/SR2270 R137, 14 June 1716, where the victim's nose was slit and the alleged offender was bound only to appear at the next sessions and be of good behavior in the interim, legally constituted mayhem. The victim should have been forced to prosecute by indictment from the outset, yet the recognizance suggests that she did not.

2. Shoemaker, *Prosecution and Punishment,* 6–7.

3. Only indictments found to be "true bills" by a grand jury would go on to a trial. Hay discovered that over half of the indictments for assault in late-eighteenth-century Staffordshire were not found to be true bills, suggesting that the reason was that the grand jury dismissed them as either vexatious or more civil than criminal prosecutions. "Prosecution and Power: Malicious Prosecution in the English Courts, 1750–1850," in D. Hay and F. Snyder, eds., *Policing and Prosecution in Britain 1750–1850* (Oxford: Clarendon Press, 1989), 362n.

4. Note that there are no extant recognizances for Westminster between 1680 and 1685; after that date, however, there is a virtually complete set.

5. Without a justice's signature, a recognizance was invalid and was not returned to Quarter Sessions. Assault recognizances needed only one JP's signature, unlike recognizances such as those binding alehouse keepers, which required two justices' signatures, or those to bind over someone who "depraved the sacrament," which required three. W. S[hepard], *A New Survey of the Justice of Peace his Office* (London: J.S., 1659), 16, and idem, *The Office of a Justice of Peace,* 219–20.

6. Sureties were generally bound for at least £20, and the offender for twice that amount, according to Norma Landau, "Appearance at the Quarter Sessions of Eighteenth-Century Middlesex," *London Journal* 23, no. 2 (1998)," 33. Some, though not all, female defendants who were bound on their own recognizances were bound *sup' impr* (on pain of imprisonment) rather than listing a monetary sum. The totals for which sureties were bound were dependent on the laws and principles governing bail, examples of which can be seen in Matthew Bacon, *A New Abridgement of the Law,* Vol. 1, 7th Ed. (London: A. Strahan, 1831), 494–95, and Charles Viner, *A General Abridgement of Law and Equity,* Vol. 3 (Hampshire, 1741), 467. Duke of Schomberg v. Murrey, 12 Mod. 420.Mich.12.W.3. However, JPs had considerable discretionary powers in deciding the amount and reliability of sureties.

7. Recognizances for prosecutors or witnesses to appear in assault cases are fairly rare, probably because they were used only for very serious cases, and thus exist in greater numbers for felonies, as Shoemaker notes. R. Shoemaker, "Using Quarter Sessions Records as Evidence for the Study of Crime and Criminal Justice," *Archives* XX, no. 90 (October 1993), 147.

8. The Westminster recognizances for the peace clearly show that certain JPs would bind a person to keep the peace unto the king and his subjects, while others would specifically name the complainant. In other words, the mention of a specific complainant in recognizances for the peace depended more upon the proclivities of the JP than on any legal consideration.

9. A recognizance for the peace or good behavior was often referred to in the justicing handbooks as a "surety" for the peace or good behavior. In lay terms, an eighteenth-century Londoner might also be said to "swear the peace against" someone when binding him or her to keep the peace.

10. This is recognizances of type (f), those which bound a defendant to answer an assault, who was also prosecuted by indictment for the same offense. There are 679 recognizances that probably went to indictment, because they bear clerical annotations in their margins that mention an indictment. However, not all recognizances that went to indictment may have consistently recorded this fact, and only 88 percent (6,280) in total bear legible clerical annotations. Shoemaker's study of the recognizances as a whole for the county found that "28 per cent of the defendants who were bound over to appear at quarter sessions were also indicted," and Shoemaker added 5 percent to "account for the fact that the clerks did not always record the existence of indictments in the relevant recognizance." *Prosecution and Punishment,* 31.

11. This is substantiated by Shoemaker's findings for the metropolis as a whole, in *Prosecution and Punishment,* table 3.5.

12. John Beattie's data from the London Justice Room Charge Book (Oct. 1729–30) shows 172 (plus an additional 3 involving assaults on officers) of a total of 234 persons accused of assault having "settled" their cases. Though the table deals only with those assaults that went to indictment or were settled, or those in which the charges were dismissed (not giving numbers of assaults that were bound over to allow for a comparative reading), it is still clear that a substantial number of assault cases could be dealt with informally. J. M. Beattie, *Policing and Punishment in the City of London, 1660–1750: Urban Crime and the Limits of Terror* (New York: Oxford University Press, 2001), table 2.2.

13. Prisoners who were not released prior to the next Quarter Sessions might appear in the "Gaol Calendars"—records of those in prison at the time of each Quarter Sessions. However, these calendars served as wrappers for the sessions' rolls and are in very poor condition—much too illegible to provide a reliable indication of the numbers and types of assaults prosecuted in this way. Beattie's work on Lord Mayor Ashurst's charge book found fourteen of thirty-three alleged assailants (42 percent) committed for want of sureties in January–June 1694. Beattie, *Policing and Punishment,* tables 2.1 and 2.2 respectively. Beattie noted (97) that Ashurst's work was "clearly only a fraction" of the assaults in the city of London at this time. Douglas Hay's study of the extant Staffordshire Assize and Quarter Sessions Gaol Calendars (1752–1802) found only 9 of 183 indicted assaults (4.9 percent) that were not bailed and were committed to jail before trial. The proportion rises to 10.5 percent in the period 1806–1817. I am grateful to Dr. Hay for sharing this evidence.

14. "It is probable that women used recognizances more frequently than any other type of legal procedure in the secular courts." R. Shoemaker, *Prosecution and Punishment,* 207.

15. For lists of allowable fees charged by the JP and his clerk, see, for example, W.T., *The Office of the Clerk of Assize . . . Together with the Office of the Clerk of the Peace* . . . 2nd Ed. (London: Printed for Henry Twyford, 1682), 250–51, and J. Bond, *A Compleat Guide for Justices of the Peace* (London, 1707), 93.

16. One hundred eighty-two of the 3,542 recognizances in which the defendant's occupation could be determined were laborers.

17. Peter King, "Decision-Makers and Decision-Making in the English Criminal Law, 1750–1800," *The Historical Journal* 27, no. 1 (1984), 32.

18. The only clues to the disposition of recognizances are in marginal Latin inscriptions, which appear on only 87 percent of all of the assault recognizances. More than half (3,748) read only "*ven & exon*" (*venit et exoneratur*), simply that the defendant had appeared and met the conditions of his binding over. ("*Venit & exoneratur*" means "he/she came & was/is exonerated." I am grateful to Bridget Howlett (of the L.M.A.), Ian Gentles, and Norma Landau for their help with translating my abbreviations.) Another 904 said that the recognizance had been "respited," usually meaning that the recognizance was carried over into another Quarter Sessions because the complainant had a legitimate excuse for not proceeding at that point in time.

19. Susan Amussen dismissed recognizances completely as a source for her study of domestic violence, and Peter King rejected them in favor of indictments for his study of assault, because indictments "record the verdict and the punishment." S. Amussen, "'Being Stirred to Much Unquietness': Violence and Domestic Violence in Early Modern England," *Journal of Women's History* 6, no. 2 (1994), 80, and P. King, "Punishing Assault: The Transformation of Attitudes in the English Courts," *Journal of Interdisciplinary History* XXVII, no. 1 (Summer 1996), 48, respectively. Chapter 4 questions Amussen's interpretation of domestic violence more directly.

20. E. H. East's, *A Treatise of the Pleas of the Crown,* Vol. I (London: A. Strahan, 1803), 406–7, explicitly counted "finding sureties" as one of the punishments for assault, along with fines and imprisonment. Joel Samaha argued that the recognizance was effective in both punishing and preventing crime in Elizabethan Colchester, though he believed that the effectiveness relied on Colchester's compact geography allowing "close supervision in the community." J. B. Samaha, "The Recognizance in Elizabethan Law Enforcement," *American Journal of Legal History* xxv, no. 3 (1981), 197. J. S. Cockburn has been critical of Samaha's findings. See, for example, J. S. Cockburn, "Trial by the Book? Fact and Theory in the Criminal Process 1558–1625," in J. H. Baker, ed., *Legal Records and the Historian* (London: Royal Historical Society, 1978), 63.

21. S. Hindle, "The Keeping of the Public Peace," in Paul Griffiths, Adam Fox, and Steve Hindle, eds., *The Experience of Authority in Early Modern England* (New York: St. Martin's Press, 1996), 235. Note that Hindle dealt only with recognizances to keep the peace, but even sureties guaranteeing only accused assailants' appearance in court might wish to prevent him or her from harming the victim further because they wished to avoid having to act as the defendant's sureties again in the future.

22. N. Landau, "Appearance at the Quarter Sessions," detailed the meticulous enforcement of appearance at Quarter Sessions, where defendants who failed to appear could have their recognizance estreated, and they and their sureties would have to scramble to pay the resulting fines in order to avoid being liable for their very expensive bonds, and if the accused assailants were unable to comply at any stage in the process, they risked imprisonment. Even those who appeared had to pay 2s to the Quarter Sessions Clerk, plus an additional 4d for the town crier. Landau, 35, 47n.

23. Those who were prosecuted by indictments were almost always bound to appear and answer the charge or were imprisoned if they were unable to provide suitable sureties. In addition, prosecutors could go to a lawyer, instead of a clerk, for an

indictment, but this was a more expensive route, and as a result was probably rarely used. I am grateful to Douglas Hay for this information.

24. Though there were many areas where a JP was prohibited from informal mediation, JPs were encouraged to deal with assault cases in this way. Shoemaker, *Prosecution and Punishment,* 24.

25. Norma Landau, *The Justices of the Peace, 1679–1760* (Berkeley: University of California Press, 1984), 184–85. Trading Justices were seen to be most prevalent in London, where they could drum up "a perpetual flow of business." Webb, 324. Norma Landau found that the introduction of stipends for JPs in 1791 dramatically reduced the number of recognizances returned to the Middlesex Quarter Sessions, suggesting that the use of the recognizance as a prosecutorial tool was significantly influenced by the pecuniary needs of the Justices. N. Landau, "The Trading Justice's Trade," in idem, ed., *Law, Crime and English Society 1660–1840* (Cambridge: Cambridge University Press, 2002). I am grateful to Dr. Landau for allowing me to see this article prior to its publication.

26. Shoemaker, "The Decline of Public Insult in London 1660–1800," *Past and Present,* no. 169 (November 2000), 104.

27. Ibid.

28. This group, therefore, is responsible for 4,717 recognizances, or 66 percent of the total.

29. Of the total number of recognizances for assault, 2,265 bore descriptions that could not be classed under one of the 275 categories created for the database without special clarification.

30. On the authority of statutes *5 & 6 Ed. 6 c. 4; 22 & 23 Car. 2 c. 1;* and *5 H. 4 c. 5,* respectively, a person caught drawing a weapon in a church or churchyard "shall forfeit one of his ears," and an assailant who "malitiously cut out the tongue, put out the Eye, slit or cut off the Nose, or disabled any Member of another, with intent to disfigure him, that Fact is Felony without Clergy, and the Offender shall suffer the pain of death." W.T., *The Office of the Clerk of Assize,* 121, 127–28, respectively. See also Bond, 73. For more on these types of assaults, see chapter 5.

31. W. Nelson, *The Office and Authority of a Justice of the Peace,* 5th Ed. (London, 1750), 59. The importance of including "*Vi & Armis*" had continued in practice, though, in fact, the phrase was actually not essential after a statute of 1545. J. H. Baker, "The Refinement of English Criminal Jurisprudence, 1500–1848," in L. Knafla, ed., *Crime and Criminal Justice in Europe and Canada* (Waterloo: Wilfred Laurier University Press, 1979), 23, 40n29. In addition, evidence has been found to indicate that the rules regarding the wording of indictments were not as strictly followed and policed as the handbooks recommended. See Cockburn, "Trial by the Book," 60–79; and Baker, "The Refinement," 17–42.

32. This issue is also discussed in chapter 2.

33. Jacob, 406. See also Bond, 251. A historiographical debate exists as to whether the JPs actually performed such duties, though the argument focuses upon the late-sixteenth-century assizes. John Langbein asserted that the JP had to "prepare himself to assume where necessary the forensic role of prosecutor at trial" (*Prosecuting Crime in the Renaissance: England, Germany, France* [Cambridge: Harvard University Press, 1974], 35). J. S. Cockburn has since disagreed with him, arguing that the

attendance lists from the assizes revealed that a "majority" of justices regularly failed to appear ("Trial by the book," 70).

34. Shoemaker, *Prosecution and Punishment,* 234.

35. For the low rate of recidivism suggested by the assault recognizances, see chapter 2.

36. Landau, *The Justices of the Peace, 1679–1760,* 345–59, and D. Hay, "Dread of the Crown Office," in N. Landau, ed., *Law, Crime and English Society 1660–1840* (Cambridge: Cambridge University Press, 2002).

37. A writ of *certiorari* removed the defendant's indictment from Quarter Sessions to King's Bench, but it did not affect any recognizances made at Quarter Sessions. Writs of *mandamus* removed JPs' personal discretion and subjected them to the dictates of King's Bench, but this writ was almost never used, according to Norma Landau, *The Justices of the Peace, 1679–1760,* 345n. *Habeas corpus* writs served only to check JPs' errors in writing warrants, and only those resulting in imprisonment; and, of course, warrants that resulted in imprisonment were not connected with recognizances.

38. Defendants already bound before a justice for an identical offense could obtain a writ of *supersedeas* to prevent a second JP from forcing them to enter into another recognizance. The writ of *supplicavit,* on the other hand, had very specific instructions on how recognizances should be drawn up, but, according to Earl Jowitt, "[T]his writ was seldom used, for when application had been made to the superior courts, they had usually taken the recognizances there, under the statute of 1623, *21 Jac. I c. 8.*" Earl Jowitt, ed., *The Dictionary of English Law,* Vol. II (London: Sweet & Maxwell Ltd., 1959), 1706.

39. See, for example, Nelson, 93, and Jacob, 354.

40. William Shepard's handbook for clerks gives a series of examples of the Latin section on the sureties and explains that "by these [samples] all other recognizances may be made, for they are after one form." The section that follows only vaguely describes the wording for the various offenses that may appear in a recognizance, significantly stating that a JP could draw up his recognizances "after the same manner [as the samples], *by changing only that which is to be changed.*" Shepard, *The Justice of Peace, His Clerks Cabinet,* 100, 104; emphasis added. William Lambard, *Einrarcha . . .* (London, 1614), 107, included only the Latin portion dealing with the sureties' information and alluded vaguely to "a condition added or endorsed in English" in his examples of the proper forms for recognizances. James Harvey (191) had only an "&c." where the specifics of the offense would appear. See also Nelson, 390; Robert Gardiner, *En[c]hiridion clericale* (London, 1712), 18; Joseph Higgs, *A Guide to Justices: being modern English precedents . . .* (London, 1734), 128, 168; Edward Crocker, *The Young Clerk's Tutor Enlarged,* 14th Ed. (London, 1700), 7–13.

41. For example, Giles Jacob (42) included forms for an indictment and a warrant for assault, but not for a recognizance. Michael Dalton offered forms for recognizances for the peace, for good behavior, to appear (again with "&c" for the offense), or even "for him that hath dangerously hurt one," but none explicitly mentioned assault. M. Dalton, *The Countrey Justice* (London, 1655), 439–44. W. Stubbs and G. Talmash, *The Crown Circuit Companion . . . ,* 5th Ed. (London, 1783), 106–16, laid out forms of indictment for a wide variety of assaults, ranging from "common assault" to "an assault

and beating out an eye," but did not include a similarly systematic treatment of assault recognizances.

Notes to Appendix B

1. L. Gowing, *Domestic Dangers: Women, Words and Sex in Early Modern London* (Oxford: Clarendon Press, 1996), 30–32, provides an overview of the structure of the church courts.

2. W. Hale, ed., *A Series of Precedents and Proceedings in Criminal Causes* . . . (first printed 1847, Edinburgh: Bratton Publishing Ltd., 1973), 50. "Penance," here, meant "the penalty of shaming by public apology." T. Meldrum, "A Woman's Court in London: Defamation at the Bishop of London's Consistory Court, 1700–45," *London Journal* 19, no. 1 (1994), 4.

3. Hale, 50.

4. Ninety-five percent of defamation producents (plaintiffs) who came before the Bishop of London's Consistory Court, 1700–45, were female. T. Meldrum, "A Woman's Court in London: Defamation at the Bishop of London's Consistory Court, 1700–45," *London Journal* 19, no. 1 (1994), 6, table 2.

5. Ecclesiastical law in the diocese of London was administered by the consistory, the lower commissary, and the Archdeacon's courts, but the Consistory Court saw the overwhelming majority of defamation litigation. Gowing, *Domestic Dangers*, 50–51.

6. "By the 1680s the . . . pamphlets published after each session of the court included a substantially complete record of all the cases that had been tried, revealing for the first time in a systematic way the numbers of men and women convicted and acquitted, and the range of punishments imposed on the guilty." J. M. Beattie, *Policing and Punishment in the City of London, 1660–1750: Urban Crime and the Limits of Terror* (New York: Oxford University Press, 2001), 2–3. On their dramatically increased breadth and accuracy at the end of the eighteenth century, see S. Devereaux, "The City and the Sessions Paper: 'Public Justice' in London, 1770–1800," *Journal of British Studies* 35 (October 1996), 466–503.

7. M. Harris, "Trials and Criminal Biographies: A Case Study in Distribution," in R. Myers and M. Harris, eds., *Sale and Distribution of Books from 1700* (Oxford: Oxford Polytechnic Press, 1982), 5 and 28n4. Harris also noted (7) that the contents of the *OBP* were regulated when "the Court of Aldermen agreed that nothing should be published without the assent of the Lord Mayor and the other Justices present." Legal historian John Langbein has since testified to their accuracy. J. Langbein, "The Criminal Trial before the Lawyers," *The University of Chicago Law Review* 45, no. 2 (Winter 1978), 267–72.

8. John Beattie (*Policing and Punishment,* 21) described a situation where a "Devon country gentleman," who also happened to be a JP, employed an agent in London "to buy books and keep him informed of the doings in the capital." He was regularly sent information from the *OBP,* either in the text of a letter or in entire copies. Those outside the direct administration of justice were also interested in the contents of the *OBP,* however, and Langbein ("The Criminal Trial," 269) cited the

example of a reader John Newton who, in 1684, referred to "*the Monthly News from the Old Bailey*" in his 1684 sermon, *The Penitent Recognition of Joseph's Brethren: A Sermon Occasioned by Elizabeth Ridgeway,* iii; emphasis in original. Harris (13) offers the most convincing evidence of their popularity: the publishers annually paid £100 for the rights to publish them—they clearly must have anticipated high profits from the sale of about sixteen issues at around 6 d. per issue. Beattie, *Policing and Punishment* (22) considered the *OBP* to be sufficiently popular to have an impact on public perceptions of crime, referring also to the Ordinary of Newgate's account and other pamphlets as "having shaped the public's sense of crime as a growing social problem."

9. In total, sixty-nine papers have been used for their accounts of violent crime, consisting of 204 cases. The actual number of cases is less than 204 because in some sessions, especially in the earlier years, there could be several publications of the same sessions.

10. Selection criteria consisted of a defamation case which (1) was recorded in the Allegation, Libel and Sentence books; (2) gave more description of the insult than simply "whore"; (3) was not from the parts of the diocese outside the metropolis; and (4) had progressed to the point where depositions had been generated. When the four conditions had been met for five cases in each of the years sampled (1680, 1685, 1690, and so on, including 1720), the sample was considered to be sufficient.

11. The producents would begin their suit with a libel, consisting of a list of points stating their position, and the ministrants would answer each of the points, "usually with a denial." The depositions were the next stage in the process. Gowing, *Domestic Dangers,* 38.

12. Ibid., 38–39.

13. The socioeconomic status of the parties in the defamation cases at the Consistory Court is as difficult to ascertain as that of complainants in recognizances. Tim Meldrum (3 and 7) estimated that to prosecute in the eighteenth-century church courts, one might need as much as £10, and he assumed that the majority—both litigants and witnesses—came from the middling sort.

14. On the likelihood of few cases continuing to the point of sentencing in the sixteenth century, see Gowing, *Domestic Dangers,* 39 and 61.

15. Ibid., 45 and 38 respectively.

16. Laura Gowing (41–48) has written insightfully about the way in which the witnesses making their depositions can be seen as consciously constructing a legal narrative, complicated by recollection, moral judgment, and personal concerns.

Bibliography

Primary Sources (Unpublished)

Manuscripts

HAMPSHIRE RECORD OFFICE
Coventry MSS
1M53/1373–74 Notebooks kept by James Dewy, JP, 1692–1703

HARVARD UNIVERSITY LIBRARY
Houghton fMS Eng 1039 Collection of papers relating to the Mohocks

LONDON METROPOLITAN ARCHIVES
Consistory Court of London
DL/C/143–158 Allegation, Libel and Sentence Books, 1680–1720
DL/C/239–259, 631 Deposition Books, 1680–1720
Middlesex Sessions
MJ/SR2188–2189 Middlesex Sessions Rolls, Mar. 1711/2–Apr. 1712
MSP1690–1715 Middlesex Sessions Papers, 1690–1715
Westminster Sessions
MJ/SR1665–2353 Westminster Sessions Rolls, Apr. 1685–Oct. 1720
WSP1690–1720 Westminster Sessions Papers, 1690–1720

PUBLIC RECORD OFFICE
Adm 106/326 R154 Letter of Anne Maverly to the Navy Board, 15 Jun. 1677

WESTMINSTER PUBLIC LIBRARY
E2574-E2575 St. Margaret's Parish Bastardy Depositions, 1712–1720

Primary Sources (Published)

Periodicals

Old Bailey Proceedings (*OBP*), 1679–1720
The Female Tatler, 15–18, 20–22 July; 10–12, 22–24 Aug., 1709

Berrow's Worcester Journal, 23 Feb.–2 Mar. 1739
The London Gazette, 17–19 Apr. 1712

Books, Pamphlets, Etc.

An Account of the riots, tumults, and other treasonable practices since his Majesty's accession to the throne. . . . London, 1715.

The Ancient Legal Course and Fundamental Constitution of the Pallace Court or Marshalsea. London: Printed for Robert Crofts, 1663.

Bacon, Matthew. *A New Abridgement of the Law.* Vol. 1. 7th Ed. London: A. Strahan, 1831.

Blackstone, Sir W. *Commentaries on the Laws of England in Four Books.* First printed 1765–69. Philadelphia: Geo. T. Bisel Co., 1922.

Bohun, Edmund. *The Justice of Peace his Calling and Qualifications.* London: Printed for T. Salusbury, 1693.

Bond, D. F. *The Spectator.* Vol. III. Oxford: Clarendon Press, 1965.

Bond, J. *A Compleat Guide for Justices of the Peace.* London, 1707.

Buckley, Sir Richard. *The Proposal for Sending Back the Nobility and Gentry of Ireland.* London: Printed for Sir Samuel Holford and Sold by R. Baldwin, 1690.

Burn, R. *The Justice of the Peace, and Parish Officer.* Vol. I. 1755 and 24th Ed. London: A. Strahan, 1825.

Cartwright, J. J., ed. *The Wentworth Papers, 1705–1709.* London: Wyman, 1882.

A Catalogue of Jilts, Cracks, Prostitutes, Night-walkers, Whores, ... London: 1691.

Clavell, J. "A Recantation of an Ill Led Life, 1634." In J. H. P. Pafford, *John Clavell 1601–43: Highwayman, Author, Lawyer, Doctor.* Oxford: Leopard's Head Press, 1993.

Coke, E. *Third Part of the Institutes of the Laws of England.* London, 1747.

The Compleat Justice. London, 1656.

C[onset], H. *The Practice of the Spiritual or Ecclesiastical Courts.* London: Printed for T. Basset, 1685.

Crittall, E., ed. *The Justicing Notebook of William Hunt, 1744–1749.* Stoke-on-Trent: Wiltshire Record Society, 1982.

Crocker, Edward. *The Young Clerk's Tutor Enlarged.* 14th Ed. London, 1700.

Crook, G. T., ed. *The Complete Newgate Calendar.* Vol. 2. London: Navarre Soc. Ltd., 1926.

The Cry of Blood. London: Printed for R. Janeway, 1680.

Culpeper, N. *A directory for Midwives, or, A guide for Women. . . .* 1737.

Dalton, Michael. *The Countrey Justice.* London, 1655.

A Description of Devils. Containing I. The Devil of a statesman. . . . London: Printed for J. Millet [1687?].

Deveil, Sir Thomas. *Observations on the practice of a Justice of the Peace: intended for such gentlemen as design to act for Middlex or Westminster. . . .* London, 1747.

Dixon, P. "Narcissus Lutrell's Private Diary." *Notes and Queries* 207 (1962):388–92, 411–15, and 452–55.

Dunton, John. *The Nightwalker: or Evening Rambles in Search of Lewd Women. . . .* London: Printed for James Orme, 1696.

Drake, James. *An essay concerning the necessity of equal taxes. . . .* London, 1702.

East, E. H. *A Treatise of the Pleas of the Crown.* Vol. I. London: A. Strahan, 1803.

The English Midwife Enlarged. . . . The Whole fitted for the Meanest Capacities. 1682.

An Epistle Narrative of the Barbarous Assault and Illegall Arrest of Freder. Turvill, Esq. London, 1660.

Fielding, Henry. *Joseph Andrews* and *Shamela.* 1742 and 1741 respectively. Reprinted Oxford: Oxford University Press, 1980.

———. *Tom Jones.* 1749. Reprinted New York: Norton Critical edition, 1995.

———. *Amelia.* 1751. Reprinted Middletown, CT: Wesleyan University Press, 1983.

———. *An Enquiry into the Causes of the Late Increase of Robbers.* London: A Millar, 1751.

Forster, Thomas. *The Layman's Lawyer. . . .* London, 1654.

Gardiner, Robert. *En[c]hiridion clericale.* London, 1712.

Gay, J. *An Argument proving from History, Reason and Scripture, that the Present Mohocks and Hawkubites are the Gog and Magog mention'd in the Revelations, and therefore that this vain and transitory world will shortly be brought to its final Dissolution.* 1712.

———. *The Mohocks: A Tragi-Comical Farce As it was acted near the Watch-house in Covent Garden.* London, 1712.

———. *Trivia, or the art of Walking the streets of London.* 1716.

Gent, J. P. *A New Guide for Constables . . . Overseers and Collectors for the Poor. . . .* London, 1692.

The Gentleman's Library. . . . Written by a Gentleman. 2nd Ed. 1722.

The Genuine History of the Life of Richard Turpin, the noted highwayman. . . . London, 1738.

Glapthorne, Henry. *Wit in a Constable: A Comedy written in 1639.* London: Printed by Jo. Okes, for F.C., 1640.

Gouge, W. *Of Domestical Duties.* 1622. Reprinted Amsterdam, 1976.

Great and Bloody News from Turnham Green. London: Printed for D.M., 1680.

Great and Horrible News from the West of England. . . . London, 1679.

Harvey, James. *A Collection of Precedents Relating to the Office of a Justice of Peace. . . .* London, 1730.

Hawkins, W. *A Treatise of the Pleas of the Crown. . . .* Vol. I. London: E. Richardson & C. Lintot, 1766, and Vol. II. 6th Ed. Dublin, 1788.

Hayward, A. *Lives of the most Remarkable Criminals who have been condemned and Executed. . . .* 1735.

Hell upon Earth, or the town in an uproar. London, 1729.

Higgs, Joseph. *A Guide to Justices: being modern English precedents. . . .* London, 1734.

Horowitz, H., ed. *The Parliamentary Diary of Narcissus Luttrell, 1691–1693.* Oxford: Clarendon Press, 1972.

Jacob, Giles. *The Modern Justice.* London, 1720.

———. *A New Law Dictionary. . . .* London: E & R. Nutt, 1729.

James II. *By the King, a declaration. . . .* 2 Sept. 1688. London, Printed by Charles Bill, Henry Hills, and Thomas Newcomb, 1688.

"A Jest, or Master Constable." London: Printed for Francis Grove. In *Roxburghe III,* 208.

Keble, Joseph. *An Assistance to Justices of the Peace.* London, 1683.

Lambard, William. *Einrarcha.* . . . London, 1614.

Lemnius, L. *The Secret Miracles of Nature.* . . . 1658.

A Letter to a Member of Parliament: shewing the justice of a more equal and impartial assessment on land. London, 1717.

Lincolne, E. *The Countesse of Lincolnes Nurserie.* 1628. Reprinted Amsterdam, 1975.

Lutrell, N. *A Brief Historical Relation of State Affairs from September 1678 to April 1714.* 6 Vols. Oxford, 1857.

Makin, B. *An Essay to Revive the Antient Education of Gentlewomen.* . . . 1673.

Mauriceau, F. *The Diseases of Women with Child and in Childbed.* . . . 1683.

Meriton, George. *A Guide for Constables, Churchwardens, Overseers of the Poor.* 8th Ed. London: Printed by Richard and Edward Atkins, 1685.

The Mohocks: A Poem, in Miltonic Verse: Address'd to the Spectator. London, 1712.

The Mohocks Revel. 1712.

Nelson, W. *The Office and Authority of a Justice of the Peace.* 5th Ed. London, 1750.

News from Tybourn: or the Confession and Execution of Three Bayliffs. . . . London: Printed for D.M., 1675.

Osborn, F. *Advice to a Son.* . . . 6th Ed. Oxford, 1658.

Paul, John. *The Compleat Constable.* London: Printed for John Fielding, 1785.

Payne, W. L., ed. *The Best of Defoe's Review.* New York: Columbia University Press, 1951.

Pope, A. *Epistles to Several Persons (Moral Essays),* ed. F. W. Bateson. 1735. Reprinted New Haven: Yale University Press, 1951.

Reasons most humbly submitted . . . for the taking off the present duty of Excise upon Beer and Ale. . . . London, 1695.

Robins, Robert. *A Whip for the Marshalls Court, and their Officers.* London, 1648.

Savile, Sir G. *The Lady's New-years-gift or Advice to a Daughter by the late Lord Marquis of Halifax.* 1688. Reprinted 1927.

Shaw, Joseph. *Parish Law.* London, 1733.

S[hepard], W. *A New Survey of the Justice of Peace his Office.* London: J.S., 1659.

Shepard, W. *The Justice of Peace, His Clerks Cabinet.* London: John Steater et al., 1672.

Sheppard, W. *The Office of a Justice of Peace.* London: Printed for W. Lee et al., 1662.

Steele Sir R., ed. *The Ladies Library, Written by a Lady.* Vol. II. 1714.

Stubbs, W., and G. Talmash. *The Crown Circuit Companion.* . . . 5th Ed. London, 1783.

Swift, J. *Journal to Stella.* Vol. II, edited by Harold Williams. Oxford: Clarendon Press, 1948.

The Taxes not Grievous, and therefore not a reason for an Unsafe Peace. London, 1711.

The Town-Rakes: or, The Frolicks of the Mohocks or Hawkubites. London, 1712.

A True description of the Mint. London: Printed by A. Baldwin, 1710.

A True and Sad Relation of Two Wicked and Bloody Murthers. . . . London: Printed for J. Clarke, 1680.

The Tryal of William Acton, Deputy-keeper and Turnkey. London: Printed for A. Moor, 1729.

Twelve Ingenious Characters: Or, pleasant Descriptions of the Properties of sundry Persons and Things. London: Printed for S. Norris, 1680.

T., W. *The Office of the Clerk of Assize . . . Together with the Office of the Clerk of the Peace. . . .* 2nd Ed. London: Printed for Henry Twyford, 1682.

Viner, Charles. *A General Abridgement of Law and Equity.* Vol. 3. Hampshire, 1741.

Waldron, G. *A Speech Made to the Loyal Society at the Mug-House in Long Acre 7 June 1716.* London, 1716.

W., E. *The Exact Constable.* London: Printed for H. Brome, 1660.

Who Plot Best; The Whigs or the Tories, Being a Brief account of all the Plots that have happen'd within these Thirty years. . . . London: A. Baldwin, 1712.

William III. *By the Prince of Orange, a declaration. . . .* 8 Jan. 1688/9. London: Printed by Edward Jones, 1688/89.

Woodward, J. *A rebuke to the sin of uncleanliness. By a Minister of the Church of England.* London, 1740.

Secondary Sources

Allen, C. K. "The Phlegmatic Englishman in the Common Law." In *Legal Duties and Other Essays in Jurisprudence.* Oxford: Clarendon Press, 1931.

Amussen, S. *An Ordered Society: Gender and Class in Early Modern England.* New York: B. Blackwell, 1988.

———. "'Being Stirred to Much Unquietness': Violence and Domestic Violence in Early Modern England." *Journal of Women's History* 6, no. 2 (1994):70–89.

———. "The Gendering of Popular Culture." In *Popular Culture in England, c. 1500–1850,* edited by T. Harris. New York: St. Martin's Press, 1995.

———. "Punishment, Discipline & Power: The Social Meaning of Violence in Early Modern England." *Journal of British Studies* 34 (Jan. 1995):1–34.

Andrews, D. "The code of honour and its critics: the opposition to duelling in England, 1700–1850." *Social History* 5, no. 3 (1980):409–34.

Andrews, W. *Old-Time Punishments.* Hall: William Andrews & Co., 1890.

Arnold, J. *Perukes & Periwigs.* London: Her Majesty's Stationary Office, 1970.

Baker, J. H. "Criminal Courts and Procedure at Common Law 1550–1800." In *Crime in England, 1550–1800,* edited by J. S. Cockburn. Princeton: Princeton University Press, 1977.

———. "The Refinement of English Criminal Jurisprudence, 1500–1848." In *Crime and Criminal Justice in Europe and Canada,* edited by L. Knafla. Waterloo: Wilfred Laurier University Press, 1979.

Barzilai, S. "'Say that I had a lovely face': The Grimms' 'Rapunzel,' Tennyson's 'Lady of Shalott,' and Atwood's *Lady Oracle.*" *Tulsa Studies in Women's Literature* 19, no. 2 (Fall 2000):231–54.

Beattie, J. M. "The Criminality of Women in Eighteenth-Century England." *Journal of Social History* viii (1975):80–116.

———. "Judicial Records and the Measurement of Crime in Eighteenth-Century England." In *Crime and Criminal Justice in Europe and Canada.*

———. "Violence and Society in Early Modern England." In *Perspectives in Criminal Law,* edited by A. Doob and E. Greenspan. Aurora, Ontario: Canada Law Book Inc., 1985.

———. *Crime and the Courts in England, 1660–1800.* New Jersey: Princeton University Press, 1986.

———. *Policing and Punishment in the City of London, 1660–1750: Urban Crime and the Limits of Terror.* New York: Oxford University Press, 2001.

Bohstedt, J. "Gender, Household and Community Politics: Women in English Riots 1790–1810." *Past and Present* 120 (1988):88–122.

Bottigheimer, Ruth B. *Grimms' Bad Girls and Bold Boys: The Moral and Social Vision of the Tales.* New Haven: Yale University Press, 1987.

Bowers, T. *The Politics of Motherhood: British Writing and Culture, 1680–1760.* Cambridge: Cambridge University Press, 1996.

Brant, C. "Speaking of Women: Scandal and the Law in the Mid-Eighteenth Century." In *Women, Texts and Histories 1575–1760,* edited by C. Brant and D. Purkiss. London: Routledge, 1992.

Bray, A. *Homosexuality in Renaissance* England. 2nd Ed. New York: Columbia University Press, 1995.

Breitenburg, M. "Anxious Masculinity: Sexual Jealousy in Early Modern England." *Feminist Studies* 19, no. 2 (1993):377–98.

Brewer, J., and S. Staves, S., eds. *Early Modern Conceptions of Property.* London: Routledge, 1995.

Brewer, J. *Sinews of Power: War, Money and the English State, 1688–1783.* London: Unwin Hyman Ltd., 1989.

Bristow, E. J. *Vice and Vigilance: Purity Movements in Britain since 1700.* London: Gill and Macmillan, 1977.

Brown, S. "The Princess of Monaco's Hair: The Revolutionary Tribunal and the Pregnancy Plea." *Journal of Family History* 23, no. 2 (1998):136–58.

Bryson, A. *From Courtesy to Civility: Changing Codes of Conduct in Early Modern England.* Oxford: Clarendon Press, 1998.

Capp, B. "Separate Domains? Women and Authority in Early Modern England." In *The Experience of Authority in Early Modern England,* edited by Paul Griffiths et al. London: St. Martin's Press, 1996.

———. "The Double Standard Revisited: Plebeian Women and Male Sexual Reputation in Early Modern England." *Past and Present,* no. 162 (1999):70–100.

Chaytor, M. "Husband(ry): Narratives of Rape in the Seventeenth Century." *Gender and History* 7 (1995):378–407.

Childs, J. *The British Army of William III, 1689–1702.* Manchester: Manchester University Press, 1987.

Clark, A. *Women's Silence, Men's Violence: Sexual Assault in England, 1770–1845.* London: Pandora, 1987.

Clarke, P. *The English Alehouse: A Social History 1200–1830.* London: Longman, 1983.

Cockburn, J. S. *A History of English Assizes, 1558–1714.* Cambridge: Cambridge University Press, 1972.

———. "Trial by the Book? Fact and Theory in the Criminal Process 1558–1625." In *Legal Records and the Historian,* edited by J. H. Baker. London: Royal Historical Society, 1978.

Cohen, M. "Manliness, Effeminacy and the French: Gender and the Construction of National Character in Eighteenth-Century England." In *English Masculinities, 1660–1800,* edited by T. Hitchcock and M. Cohen. London: Longman, 1999.

Cohen, S. *Folk Devils and Moral Panics: The Creation of the Mods & Rockers.* New York: St. Martins Press, 1972.

Colley, L. *Britons: Forging the Nation, 1707–1837.* New Haven: Yale University Press, 1992.

Corfield, P. J. *The Impact of English Towns, 1700–1800.* Oxford: Oxford University Press, 1982.

Crawford, P. "Attitudes to Pregnancy from a Woman's Spiritual Diary, 1687–8." *Local Population Studies* 21 (1978):43–45.

———. "The Construction and Experience of Maternity in Seventeenth-Century England." In *Women as Mothers in Pre-Industrial England, Essays in Memory of Dorothy McLaren,* edited by V. Fildes. New York: Routledge, 1990.

———. "Sexual Knowledge in England, 1500–1750." In *Sexual Knowledge, Sexual Science: The History of Attitudes to Sexuality,* edited by R. Porter and M. Teich. Cambridge: Cambridge University Press, 1994.

Cressy, D. *Travesties and Transgressions in Tudor and Stuart England: Tales of Discord and Dissension.* New York: Oxford University Press, 2000.

Curtis, T. C. "Quarter Sessions Appearances and their Background: A Seventeenth-Century Regional Study." In *Crime in England, 1550–1800,* edited by J. S. Cockburn. Princeton: Princeton University Press, 1977.

Curtis, T. C., and W. A. Speck. "The Societies for the Reformation of Manners: A Case Study in the Theory and Practice of Moral Reform." *Literature and History* 3 (March 1976):45–64.

D'Cruze, S. "Approaching the History of Rape and Sexual Violence: Notes Towards Research." *Women's History Review* 1, no. 3 (1993):377–96.

———, ed. *Everyday Violence in Britain, 1850–1950: Gender and Class.* Harlow: Longman, 2000.

Darnton, R. *The Great Cat Massacre and Other Episodes in French Cultural History.* New York: Vintage Books, 1984.

Davis, J. "The London Garotting Panic of 1862: A Moral Panic and the Creation of a Criminal Class in Mid-Victorian England." In *Crime and the Law: The Social History of Crime in Western Europe since 1500,* edited by V. A. C. Gatrell et al. London: Europa Publications Ltd., 1980.

Davis, N. Z. "Women on Top." In *Society and Culture in Early Modern France.* Stanford: Stanford University Press, 1965.

———. *Fiction in the Archives: Pardon Tales and Their Tellers.* Stanford: Stanford University Press, 1987.

Davison, L. et al., eds. "Introduction: The Reactive State: English Governance and Society, 1689–1750." In *Stilling the Grumbling Hive: The Response to Social and Economic Problems in England, 1689–1750.* New York: St. Martin's Press, 1992.

Devereaux, S. "The City and the Sessions Paper: 'Public Justice' in London, 1770–1800." *Journal of British Studies* 35 (Oct. 1996):466–503.

Dobash, R. P., and R. E. Dobash. "Community Response to Violence against Wives: Charivari, Abstract Justice and Patriarchy." *Social Problems* 28, no. 5 (1981):563–79.

Dolan, F. *Dangerous Familiars: Representations of Domestic Crime in England, 1550–1700.* Ithaca: Cornell University Press, 1994.

Duffy, I. P. H. "English Bankrupts, 1571–1861." *The American Journal of Legal History* XXIV (1980):283–305.

Eccles, A. *Obstetrics and Gynaecology in Tudor and Stuart England.* Kent, OH: Kent State University Press, 1982.

Edelstein, L. "An Accusation Easily to Be Made? Rape and Malicious Prosecution in Eighteenth-Century Enlgand." *The American Journal of Legal History* XLII, no. 4 (Oct. 1998):351–90.

Emsley, C. *The English Police: A Political and Social History.* London: Longman, 1991.

Epstein, J. "Spatial Practices/Democratic Vistas." *Social History* 24, no. 3 (Oct. 1999):294–310.

Erickson, A. L. *Women and Property in Early Modern England.* New York: Routledge, 1993.

Farr, J. R. *Hands of Honour: Artisans and Their World in Dijon, 1550–1650.* Ithaca: Cornell University Press, 1988.

Feeley, M., and D. Little. "The Vanishing Female: The Decline of Women in the Criminal Process, 1687–1912." *Law and Society Review* 25, no. 4 (1991):719–57.

Ferraro, J. M. "The Power to Decide: Battered Wives in Early Modern Venice." *Renaissance Quarterly* 48, no. 3 (1995):492–512.

Finlay, F., and B. Shearer. "Population Growth and Suburban Expansion." In *London 1500–1700: The Making of the Metropolis,* edited by A. Beier and R. Finlay. New York: Longman, 1986.

Fletcher, A. "Manhood, the Male Body, Courtship and the Household in Early Modern England." *History* 84, no. 275 (1999):419–36.

Foyster, E. "Male Honour, Social Control and Wife Beating in Late Stuart England." *Transactions of the Royal Historical Society, 6th Series* 6 (1996):215–24.

———. *Manhood in Early Modern England: Honour, Sex and Marriage.* London: Longman, 1999.

Gaskill, M. *Crime and Mentalities in Early Modern England.* Cambridge: Cambridge University Press, 2000.

George, M. D. *London Life in the Eighteenth Century.* New York: Capricorn Books, 1965.

Gilbert, A. "Buggery and the British Navy, 1700–1861." *Journal of Social History* 10, no. 1 (1976):72–98.

———. "Sodomy and the Law in Eighteenth and Early Nineteenth-Century Britain." *Societas* 8, no. 3 (1978):225–41.

Gillis, J. *Youth and History: Tradition and Change in European Age Relations, 1770 to the Present.* New York: Academic Press, 1981.

———. *For Better, For Worse: British Marriages, 1600 to the present.* New York: Oxford University Press, 1985.

Gilmour, I. *Riot, Risings and Revolution: Governance and Violence in Eighteenth-Century England.* London: Pimlico, 1993.

Gowing, L. "Gender and the Language of Insult in Early Modern London." *History Workshop Journal* 35 (1993):1–21.

———. *Domestic Dangers: Women, Words and Sex in Early Modern London.* Oxford: Clarendon Press, 1996.

———. "Secret Births and Infanticide in Seventeenth-Century England." *Past and Present,* no. 156 (1997):87–115.

———. *Common Bodies: Women, Touch and Power in Seventeenth-Century England.* New Haven: Yale University Press, 2003.

Greenblatt, S. *Renaissance Self-Fashioning: From More to Shakespeare.* Chicago: University of Chicago Press, 1980.

Greene, D. C. "The Court of the Marshalsea in Late Tudor and Stuart England." *American Journal of Legal History* XX, (1976):267–79.

Gregory, J. "*Homo religious:* masculinity and religion in the long eighteenth century." In *English Masculinities, 1660–1800.*

Grieco, S. M. "The Body, Appearance, and Sexuality." In *A History of Women in the West, Volume 3: Renaissance and Enlightenment Paradoxes,* edited by N. Z. Davis and A. Farge. Cambridge: Harvard University Press, 1993.

Griffiths, P. *Youth and Authority: Formative Experiences in England, 1560–1640.* New York, Oxford University Press, 1996.

Guthrie, N. "'No Truth or Very Little in the Whole Story'?—A Reassessment of the Mohock Scare of 1712." *Eighteenth-Century Life* 20 (May 1996):33–56.

Haagen, P. "Eighteenth-Century English Society and the Debt Law." In *Social Control and the State: Historical and Comparative Essays,* edited by S. Cohen and A. Scull. Oxford: Martin Robertson, 1983.

Hale, W., ed. *A Series of Precedents and Proceedings in Criminal Causes. . . .* First printed 1847. Edinburgh: Bratton Publishing Ltd., 1973

Harris, B. "Women and Politics in Early Tudor England." *The Historical Journal* 23, no. 2 (1990):259–81.

Harris, M. "Trials and Criminal Biographies: A Case Study in Distribution." In *Sale and Distribution of Books from 1700,* edited by R. Myers and M. Harris. Oxford: Oxford Polytechnic Press, 1982.

Harris, T. *London Crowds in the Reign of Charles II: Propaganda and Politics from the Restoration until the Exclusion Crisis.* Cambridge: Cambridge University Press, 1987.

Hay, D. "Property, Authority and the Criminal Law." In *Albion's Fatal Tree: Crime and Society in Eighteenth-Century England,* edited by D. Hay et al. London: Allen Lane, 1975.

———. "War, Death and Theft in the Eighteenth Century: The Record of the English Courts." *Past and Present* 95 (May 1982):117–60.

———. "Prosecution and Power: Malicious Prosecution in the English Courts, 1750–1850." In *Policing and Prosecution in Britain 1750–1850,* edited by D. Hay and F. Snyder. Oxford: Clarendon Press, 1989.

———. "Master and Servant in England: Using the Law in the Eighteenth and Nineteenth Centuries." In *Private Law and Social Inequality in the Industrial Age: Comparing Legal Cultures in Britain, France, Germany, and the United States,* edited by W. Steinmetz. Oxford: Oxford University Press, 2000.

———. "Dread of the Crown Office." In *Law, Crime and English Society 1660–1840,* edited by N. Landau. Cambridge: Cambridge University Press, 2002.

Hay, D., and N. Rogers. *Eighteenth-Century English Society: Shuttles and Swords.* Oxford: Oxford University Press, 1997.

Herrup, C. "The Patriarch at Home: The Trial of the Second Earl of Castlehaven for Rape and Sodomy." *History Workshop Journal* 41 (Spring 1996):1–18.

Hester, M. The Dynamics of Male Domination using the Witch Craze in Sixteenth- and Seventeenth-Century England as a Case Study." *Women's Studies International Forum* 13 (1990):9–19.

Hindle, S. "The Shaming of Margaret Knowsley: Gossip, Gender and the Experience of Authority in Early Modern England." *Continuity and Change* 9, no. 3 (1994):391–419.

———. "The Keeping of the Public Peace." In *The Experience of Authority in Early Modern England,* edited by Paul Griffiths, Adam Fox, and Steve Hindle. New York: St. Martin's Press, 1996.

Hobsbawm, E. J. "The Tramping Artisan." In *Labouring Men: Studies in the History of Labour.* London: Weidenfeld and Nicolson, 1969.

Holdsworth, W. *A History of English Law.* Vol. I, edited by A. Goodhart and H. Hanbury. 7th Ed. London: Methuen & Co., 1956, and Vol. VIII, Boston: Little, Brown & Co., 1926.

Hoppit, J. *Risk and Failure in English Business, 1700–1800.* Cambridge: Cambridge University Press, 1987.

Howard, S. "Crime, Communities and Authority in Early Modern Wales: Denbighshire, 1660–1730." Ph.D. thesis, University of Wales, 2003.

Humfrey, P. "Female Servants and Women's Criminality in Early Eighteenth-Century London." In *Criminal Justice in the Old World and the New: Essays in Honour of J. M. Beattie,* edited by G. T. Smith et al. Toronto: Centre of Criminology, University of Toronto, 1998.

Hunt, M. "Wife Beating, Domesticity and Women's Independence in Eighteenth-Century London" *Gender and History* 4, no. 1 (1992):10–33.

———. *The Middling Sort: Commerce, Gender and the Family in England, 1680–1780.* Berkeley: University of California Press, 1996.

Hurl-Eamon, J. "'She being bigg with child is likely to miscarry': Pregnant Women Prosecuting Assault in London, 1685–1720." *London Journal* 24, no. 2 (1999):18–33.

———. "Domestic Violence Prosecuted: Women Binding over Their Husbands for Assault at Westminster Quarter Sessions, 1685–1720." *Journal of Family History* 26, no. 4 (2001): 435–54.

———. "Policing Male Heterosexuality: The Reformation of Manners Societies' Campaign against the Brothels in Westminster, 1680–1720." *Journal of Social History* 37 (June 2004):1017–35.

———. "The Westminster Impostors: Impersonating Law Enforcement in Early Eighteenth-Century London." *Eighteenth-Century Studies* 38, no. 3 (2005): 463–85.

Ingleton, R. *Arming the British Police: The Great Debate.* London: Frank Cass & Co., 1997.

Ingram, M. "Ridings, Rough Music and the 'Reform of Popular Culture' in Early Modern England." *Past and Present* 105 (1984):79–113.

———. *Church Courts, Sex and Marriage in England, 1570–1640.* Cambridge: Cambridge University Press, 1987.

———. "'Scolding Women Cucked or Washed': A Crisis in Gender Relations in Early Modern England?" In *Women, Crime and the Courts in Early Modern England,* edited by J. Kermonde and G. Walker. London: UCL Press, 1994.

Innes, J. "The King's Bench Prison in the Later Eighteenth Century: Law, Authority and Order in a London Debtor's Prison." In *An Ungovernable People: The English and their Law in the Seventeenth and Eighteenth Centuries,* edited by J. Brewer and S. Styles. London: Hutchinson, 1980.

Inwood, S. *A History of London.* New York: Carroll & Graff Publishers, Inc., 1998.

Isaacs, T. "The Anglican Hierarchy and the Reformation of Manners, 1688–1738." *Journal of Ecclesiastical History* XXXIII, no. 3 (1982):391–411.

Jackson, M. *New-Born Child Murder: Women, Illegitimacy, and the Courts in Eighteenth-Century England.* Manchester: Manchester University Press, 1996

Jackson, S. "The Social Context of Rape; Sexual Scripts and Motivation." *Women's Studies International Quarterly* 1 (1978):27–39.

Johnson, N. *Eighteenth-Century London.* London: HMSO, 1991.

Jowitt, E., ed. *The Dictionary of English Law.* Vol. II. London: Sweet & Maxwell Ltd., 1959.

Karras, R. M. "The Regulation of Brothels in Later Medieval England." *Signs* 14, no. 2 (1989):399–433.

Keane, J. *Tom Paine: A Political Life.* Boston: Little, Brown, 1995.

Kent, D. A. "'Gone for a Soldier': Family Breakdown and the Demography of Desertion in a London Parish, 2750–1791." *Local Population Studies* 45 (1990):27–42.

King, P. "Decision-Makers and Decision-Making in the English Criminal Law, 1750–1800." *The Historical Journal* 27, no. 1 (1984):43–74.

———. "Punishing Assault: The Transformation of Attitudes in the English Courts." *Journal of Interdisciplinary History* XXVII, no. 1 (Summer 1996):43–74.

———. "Gender, Crime and Justice in Late Eighteenth- and Early Nineteenth-Century England." In *Gender and Crime in Modern Europe,* edited by M. L. Arnot and C. Usborne. London: UCL Press, 1999.

Lamoine, G., ed. *Charges to the Grand Jury, 1689–1803.* Camden Fourth Series, Vol. 43. London: Royal Historical Society, 1992.

Landau, N. *The Justices of the Peace, 1679–1760.* Berkeley: University of California Press, 1984.

———. "Appearance at the Quarter Sessions of Eighteenth-Century Middlesex." *London Journal* 23, no. 2 (1998):30–52.

———. "Indictment for Fun and Profit: A Prosecutor's Reward at Eighteenth-Century Quarter Sessions" *Law and History Review* 17, no. 3 (1999):507–36.

———. "The Trading Justice's Trade." In *Law, Crime and English Society 1660–1840.*

Langbein, J. H. *Prosecuting Crime in the Renaissance: England, Germany, France.* Cambridge: Harvard University Press, 1974.

———. "The Criminal Trial before the Lawyers." *The University of Chicago Law Review* 45, no. 2 (Winter 1978):263–316.

———. "Shaping the Eighteenth-Century Criminal Trial: A View from the Ryder Sources." *The University of Chicago Law Review* 50, no. 1 (1983):1–135.

Lawrence, A. *Women in England 1500–1760: A Social History.* London: Weidenfeld and Nicholson, 1994.

Leneman, L. "'A Tyrant and Tormentor': Violence against Wives in Eighteenth- and Early Nineteenth-Century Scotland." *Continuity and Change* 12, no. 1 (1997):31–54.

Litten, J. "The Funeral Trade in Hanoverian England 1714–1760." In *The Changing Face of Death: Historical Accounts of Death and Disposal,* edited by P. Jupp and G. Howarth. London: Macmillan Press, 1997.

Malcolmson, R. *Popular Recreations in English Society, 1700–1850.* Cambridge: Cambridge University Press, 1973.

———. "Infanticide in the Eighteenth Century." In *Crime in England.*

Manning, R. B. "The origins of the Doctrine of Sedition." *Albion* 12, no. 2 (1980):99–121.

Martenson, R. "The Transformation of Eve: Women's Bodies, Medicine and Culture in Early Modern England." In *Sexual Knowledge, Sexual Science.*

May, A. "'She at first denied it': Infanticide Trials at the Old Bailey." In *Women and History: Voices of Early Modern England,* edited by V. Frith. Concord, Ontario: Irwin Publishing, 1997.

McGregor, O. R. *Social History and Law Reform.* London: Stevens and Sons, 1981.

McLaren, A. *Reproductive Rituals: The Perception of Fertility in England from the Sixteenth Century to the Nineteenth Century.* London: Methuen & Co. Ltd, 1984.

Meldrum, T. "A Woman's Court in London: Defamation at the Bishop of London's Consistory Court, 1700–45." *London Journal* 19, no. 1 (1994):1–20.

———. *Domestic Service and Gender, 1660–1750.* New York: Pearson Education, 2000.

Monod, P. K. *Jacobitism and the English People, 1688–1788.* Cambridge: Cambridge University Press, 1989.

Morgan, G. and P. Rushton. "The magistrate, the community and the maintenance of an orderly society in eighteenth-century England." *Historical Research* 76, no. 191 (February 2003): 54–77.

Mueller, J. C. "Fallen Men: Representations of Male Impotence in Britain." *Studies in Eighteenth-Century Culture* 28 (1999):85–102.

Norton, R. *Mother Clap's Molly House: The Gay Subculture in England, 1700–1830.* London: GMP Publishers Ltd., 1992.

Ogborn, M. *Spaces of Modernity: London's Geographies, 1680–1780.* London: Guilford Press, 1998.

Oldham, J. C. "On Pleading the Belly: A History of the Jury of Matrons." *Criminal Justice History* 6 (1985):1–64.

Outhwaite, R. B. *Clandestine Marriage in England, 1500–1850.* Rio Grande: Hambleton Press, 1995.

Paley, R., ed. *Justice in Eighteenth-Century Hackney: The Justicing Notebook of Henry Norris and the Hackney Petty Sessions Book.* London: London Record Society, 1991.

———. "Thief-Takers in London in the Age of the McDaniel Gang, c. 1745–1754." In *Policing and Prosecution in Britain 1750–1850.*

Parry, L. A. *The History of Torture in England.* London: Sampson Low, Marston & Co., 1933.

Paulson, R. *Hogarth, His Life, Art and Times,* Vol. I. New Haven: Yale University Press, 1971.

Perry, R. "Colonizing the Breast: Sexuality and Maternity in Eighteenth-Century England." *Journal of the History of Sexuality* 2, no. 2 (1991):204–34.

Phillips, R. "Women, Neighbourhood and Family in the Late Eighteenth Century." *French Historical Studies* 18, no. 1 (1993):1–12.

Pitt-Rivers, J. "Honour and Social Status." In *Honor and Shame: The Values of Mediterranean Society,* edited by J. G. Peristiany. London: Nicholson, 1965.

Pointon, M. *Hanging the Head: Portraiture and Social Formation in Eighteenth-Century England.* London: Yale University Press, 1993.

———. *Strategies for Showing: Women, Possession, and Representation in English Visual Culture, 1665–1800.* Oxford: Oxford University Press, 1997.

Pollock, L. "Childbearing and Female Bonding in Early Modern England." *Social History* 22, no. 3 (1997):286–306.

Porter, R. "Rape: Does It Have a Historical Meaning?" In *Rape,* edited by R. Porter and S. Tomaselli. Oxford: Basil Blackwell Ltd, 1986.

———. *London: A Social History.* Cambridge: Harvard University Press, 1995.

Porter, R., and L. Hall. *The Facts of Life: The Creation of Sexual Knowledge in Britain, 1650–1950.* New Haven: Yale University Press, 1995.

Radzinowicz, L. *A History of English Criminal Law and its Administration from 1750.* 4 Vols. London: Stevens and Sons, 1948–68.

Reiss, A. J., Jr., and J. A. Roth, eds. *Understanding and Preventing Violence.* Washington, DC: National Academy Press, 1993.

Reynolds, E. A. *Before the Bobbies: The Night Watch and Police Reform in Metropolitan London, 1720–1830.* Stanford: Stanford University Press, 1998.

Richardson, J. *The Annals of London: A Year-by-Year Record of a Thousand Years of History.* London: Cassell & Co., 2000.

Riddle, J. M. *Eve's Herbs: A History of Contraception and Abortion in the West.* London: Harvard University Press, 1997.

Roach, J. *Social Reform in England, 1780–1880.* London: B. T. Batsford Ltd., 1978.

Rogers, N. "Popular Protest in Early Hanoverian London." *Past and Present,* no. 79 (1978):70–100.

———. "Riot and Popular Jacobitism in Early Hanoverian England." In *Ideology and Conspiracy: Aspects of Jacobitism, 1689–1759,* edited by Evenline Cruickshanks. Edinburgh: John Donald Publishers Ltd., 1982.

———. *Whigs and Cities: Popular Politics in the Age of Walpole and Pitt.* Oxford: Clarendon Press, 1989.

———. *Crowds, Culture and Politics in Georgian Britain.* Oxford: Clarendon Press, 1998.

Roper, L. *The Holy Household: Women and Morals in Reformation Augsburg.* Oxford: Clarendon Press, 1989.

Rudé, G. *Hanoverian London, 1714–1808.* London: Secker & Warburg, 1971.

Rushton, P. "The Matter in Variance: Adolescents and Domestic Conflict in the Pre-Industrial Economy of Northeast England, 1600–1800." *Journal of Social History* 25, no. 1 (1991):89–107.

Ryan, M. P. *Women in Public: Between Banners and Ballots, 1825–1880.* Baltimore: Johns Hopkins University Press, 1990.

Samaha, J. B. "The Recognizance in Elizabethan Law Enforcement." *American Journal of Legal History* xxv, no. 3 (1981):189–204.

Schwartz, L. D. *London in the Age of Industrialization: Entrepreneurs, Labour Force and Living Conditions, 1700–1850.* Cambridge: Cambridge University Press, 1992.

Schwoerer, L. *"No Standing Armies!" The Antiarmy Ideology in Seventeenth-Century England.* Baltimore: Johns Hopkins University Press, 1974.

Scott, G. R. *The History of Torture throughout the Ages.* London: Luxor Press, 1959.

Scouller, Major R. E. *The Armies of Queen Anne.* Oxford: Clarendon Press, 1966.

Settle, A. *English Fashion.* London: Collins, 1948.

Sharpe, J. A. "Such Disagreement betwyx Neighbours: Litigation and Human Relations in Early Modern England." In *Disputes and Settlements: Law and Human Relations in the West,* edited by John Bossy. New York: Cambridge University Press, 1983.

———. *Crime in Early Modern England 1550–1750.* London: Longman, 1984.

———. "Debate: The History of Violence in England: Some Observations." *Past and Present* 108 (Aug. 1985):206–15.

Shepard, A. *Meanings of Manhood in Early Modern England.* Oxford: Oxford University Press, 2003.

Shoemaker, R. B. "The London 'Mob' in the Early Eighteenth Century." *Journal of British Studies* 26 (July 1987):273–304.

———. *Prosecution and Punishment: Petty Crime and the Law in London and Rural Middlesex, c. 1660–1725.* Cambridge: Cambridge University Press, 1991.

———. "Using Quarter Sessions Records as Evidence for the Study of Crime and Criminal Justice." *Archives* XX, no. 90 (Oct. 1993):145–57.

———. "The Decline of Public Insult in London 1660–1800." *Past and Present,* no. 169 (Nov. 2000):97–131.

———. "Gendered Spaces: Patterns of Mobility and Perceptions of London's Geography, 1660–1750." In *Imagining Early Modern London: Perceptions and Portrayals of the City from Stow to Strype, 1598–1720,* edited by J. F. Merritt. Cambridge: Cambridge University Press, 2001.

———. "Male Honour and the Decline of Public Violence in Eighteenth-Century London." *Social History* 26, no. 2 (May 2001):190–208.

———. "Public Spaces, Private Disputes? Conflict on London's Streets, 1660–1800." In *The Streets of London 1660–1780,* edited by T. Hitchcock and H. Shore. London: Rivers Oram Press, 2003.

———. "Reforming the City: The Reformation of Manners Campaign in London, 1690–1738." In *Stilling the Grumbling Hive.*

———. *The London Mob: Violence and Disorder in Eighteenth-Century England.* London: Hambledon and London, 2004.

Simpson, A. E. "The 'Blackmail Myth' and the Prosecution of Rape and Its Attempt in 18th Century London: The Creation of a Legal Tradition." *The Journal of Criminal Law and Criminology* 77, no. 1 (1986):101–50.

———. "Vulnerability and the Age of Female Consent: Legal Innovation and Its Effect on Prosecutions for Rape in Eighteenth-Century London." In *Sexual Underworlds of the Enlightenment,* edited by G. S. Rousseau and R. Porter. Chapel Hill: University of North Carolina Press, 1988.

Statt, D. "The Case of the Mohocks: Rake Violence in Augustan London." *Social History* 20, no. 2 (1995):179–99.

Staves, S. *Married Women's Separate Property in England, 1660–1833.* Cambridge: Harvard University Press, 1990.

Stevenson, J. *Popular Disturbances in England, 1700–1870.* New York: Longman, 1979.

Stone, L. "The Residential Development of the West End of London in the Seventeenth Century." In *After the Reformation, essays in honor of J. H. Hexter,* edited by B. C. Malament. Philadelphia: University of Pennsylvania Press, 1980.

———. "Interpersonal Violence in English Society, 1300–1980." *Past and Present* 101 (Nov. 1983):22–33.

———. "A Rejoinder." *Past and Present* 108 (Aug. 1985):216–24.

Stretton, T. *Women Waging Law in Elizabethan England.* Cambridge: Cambridge University Press, 1998.

Tadmor, N. "The Concept of the Household-Family in Eighteenth-Century England." *Past and Present* 151 (1996):11–40.

Teague, F. *Bathusa Makin, Woman of Learning.* Lewisburg: Bucknell University Press, 1998.

Thomis, Malcolm I., and Jennifer Grimmett. *Women in Protest, 1800–1850.* London: Croom Helm, 1982.

Thompson, E. P. "The Moral Economy of the English Crowd in the Eighteenth Century." *Past and Present* 50 (1971):76–136.

———. "'Rough Music': Le Charivari Anglais." *Annales Economies Sociétés Civilisations* 27, no. 2 (1972):285–312.

———. *Whigs and Hunters: The Origin of the Black Act.* London: Allen Lane, 1975.

———. *Customs in Common.* New York: New Press, 1993.

Travitsky, B. "The New Mother of the English Renaissance: Her Writings on Motherhood." In *The Lost Tradition: Mothers and Daughters in Literature,* edited by C. N. Davidson and E. M. Broner. New York: F. Ungar Publishing Co., 1980.

Trevelyan, G. M. *Illustrated English Social History, Volume Three: The Eighteenth Century.* London: Longmans, Green and Co., 1942.

Trumbach, R. "Sex, Gender, and Sexual Identity in Modern Culture: Male Sodomy and Female Prostitution in Enlightenment London." *Journal of the History of Sexuality* 2, no. 2 (1991):186–203.

———. *Sex and the Gender Revolution: Volume One: Heterosexuality and the Third Gender in Enlightenment London.* Chicago: University of Chicago Press, 1998.

Underdown, D. "The Taming of the Scold; The Enforcement of Patriarchal Authority in Early Modern England." In *Order and Disorder in Early Modern England,* edited by A. J. Fletcher and J. Stevenson. Cambridge: Cambridge University Press, 1985.

Vickery, A. "Golden Age to Separate Spheres? A Review of the Categories and Chronology of English Women's History." *The Historical Journal* 36, no. 2 (1993):383–414.

Walker, G. "Women, Theft and the World of Stolen Goods." In *Women, Crime and the Courts in Early Modern England,* edited by J. Kermonde and G. Walker. London: UCL Press, 1994.

———. "Domestic Relations in Early Modern England." *History Workshop Journal* 41 (1996):280–85.

———. "Rereading Rape and Sexual Violence in Early Modern England." *Gender and History* 10, no. 1 (1998):1–25.

———. *Crime, Gender and Social Order in Early Modern England.* Cambridge: Cambridge University Press, 2003.

Walklate, S. *Victimology: The Victim and the Criminal Justice Process.* London: Unwin Hyman, 1989.

Walkowitz, J. *City of Dreadful Delight: Narratives of Sexual Danger in Late-Victorian London.* Chicago: University of Chicago Press, 1992.

Warner, J., and F. Ivis. "'Damn you, you informing Bitch': *Vox Populi* and the Unmaking of the Gin Act of 1736." *Journal of Social History* 33, no. 2 (1999):299–330.

Webb, B., and Webb, S. *English Local Government, Volume 1: The Parish and the County.* First printed 1906, London: Frank Cass and Co., 1963.

Wilson, A. "The Ceremony of Childbirth and Its Interpretation." In *Women as Mothers in Pre-Industrial England.*

———. *The Making of Man Midwifery: Childbirth in England, 1660–1770.* Cambridge: Harvard University Press, 1995.

Wilson, K. *The Island Race: Englishness, Empire and Gender in the Eighteenth Century.* London: Routledge, 2003.

Wiltenburg, J. *Disorderly Women and Female Power in the Street Literature of Early Modern England and Germany.* Charlottesville: University Press of Virginia, 1992.

Wrightson, K. *English Society, 1580–1680.* London: Hutchinson, 1982.

Wrigley, E. A. "A Simple Model of London's Importance in Changing English Society and Economy, 1650–1750." *Past and Present* 37 (1967):44–70.

INDEX

HISTORY OF CRIME AND CRIMINAL JUSTICE
David R. Johnson and Jeffrey S. Adler, Series Editors

The series explores the history of crime and criminality, violence, criminal justice, and legal systems without restrictions as to chronological scope, geographical focus, or methodological approach.

Pursuing Johns: Criminal Law Reform, Defending Character, and New York City's Committee of Fourteen, 1920–1930
Thomas C. Mackey

Social Control in Europe: Vol. 1, 1500–1800
Edited by Herman Roodenburg and Pieter Spierenburg

Social Control in Europe: Vol. 2, 1800–2000
Edited by Clive Emsley, Eric Johnson, and Pieter Spierenburg

Policing the City: Crime and Legal Authority in London, 1780–1840
Andrew T. Harris

Written in Blood: Fatal Attraction in Enlightenment Amsterdam
Pieter Spierenburg

Crime, Justice, History
Eric H. Monkkonen

The Rule of Justice: The People of Chicago versus Zephyr Davis
Elizabeth Dale

Five Centuries of Violence in Finland and the Baltic Area
Heikki Ylikangas, Petri Karonen, and Martti Lehti

Prostitution and the State in Italy, 1860–1915, 2nd Edition
Mary Gibson

Homicide, North and South: Being a Comparative View of Crime against the Person in Several Parts of the United States
H. V. Redfield

Rethinking Southern Violence: Homicides in Post–Civil War Louisiana, 1866–1884
Gilles Vandal

Violent Death in the City: Suicide, Accident, and Murder in Nineteenth-Century Philadelphia, 2nd Edition
Roger Lane

Controlling Vice: Regulating Brothel Prostitution in St. Paul, 1865–1883
Joel Best

Cops and Bobbies: Police Authority in New York and London, 1830–1870, 2nd Edition
Wilbur R. Miller

Race, Labor, and Punishment in the New South
Martha A. Myers

Men and Violence: Gender, Honor, and Rituals in Modern Europe and America
Edited by Pieter Spierenburg

Murder in America: A History
Roger Lane

www.ingramcontent.com/pod-product-compliance
Lightning Source LLC
LaVergne TN
LVHW091052080826
845145LV00002B/715

* 9 7 8 0 8 1 4 2 5 7 2 9 6 *